OUR MUTUAL FRIEND

By

CHARLES DICKENS

Philadelphia

Porter & Coates

OUR MUTUAL FRIEND.

In Four Books.

BOOK THE FIRST. THE CUP AND THE LIP.

CHAPTER I.

ON THE LOOK-OUT.

In these times of ours, though concerning the exact year there is no need to be precise, a boat of dirty and disreputable appearance, with two figures in it, floated on the Thames, between Southwark Bridge which is of iron, and London Bridge which is of stone, as an autumn evening was closing in.

The figures in this boat were those of a strong man with ragged grizzled hair and a sun-browned face, and a dark girl of nineteen or twenty, sufficiently like him to be recognisable as his daughter. The girl rowed, pulling a pair of sculls very easily; the man, with the rudder-lines slack in his hands, and his hands loose in his waistband, kept an eager look-out. He had no net, hook, or line, and he could not be a fisherman; his boat had no cushion for a sitter, no paint, no inscription, no appliance beyond a rusty boat-hook and a coil of rope, and he could not be a waterman; his boat was too crazy and too small to take in a cargo for delivery, and he could not be a lighterman or river-carrier; there was no clue to what he looked for, but he looked for something, with a most intent and searching gaze. The tide, which had turned an hour before, was running down, and his eyes watched every little race and eddy in its broad sweep, as the boat made slight headway against it, or drove stern foremost before it, according as he directed his daughter by a movement of his head. She watched his face as earnestly as he watched the river. But, in the intensity of her look there was a touch of dread or horror.

Allied to the bottom of the river rather than the surface, by reason of the slime and ooze with which it was covered, and its sodden state, this boat and the two figures in it obviously were doing something that they often did, and were seeking what they often sought. Half savage as the man showed, with no covering on his matted head, with his brown arms bare to between the elbow and the shoulder, with the loose knot of a looser kerchief lying low on his bare breast in a wilderness of beard and whisker, with such dress as he wore seeming to be made out of the mud that begrimed his boat, still there was business-like usage in his steady gaze. So with every lithe action of the girl, with every turn of her wrist, perhaps most of all with her look of dread or horror; they were things of usage.

"Keep her out, Lizzie. Tide runs strong here. Keep her well afore the sweep of it."

Trusting to the girl's skill and making no use of the rudder, he eyed the coming tide with an absorbed attention. So the girl eyed him. But, it happened now, that a slant of light from the setting sun glanced into the bottom of the boat, and, touching a rotten stain there which bore some resemblance to the outline of a muffled human form, coloured it as though with diluted blood. This caught the girl's eye, and she shivered.

"What ails you?" said the man, immediately aware of it, though so intent on the advancing waters; "I see nothing afloat."

The red light was gone, the shudder was gone, and his gaze, which had come back to the boat for a moment, travelled away again. Wheresoever the strong tide met with an impediment, his gaze paused for an instant. At every mooring chain and rope, at every stationary boat or barge that split the current into a broad-arrow-head, at the offsets from the piers of Southwark Bridge, at the paddles of the river steamboats as they beat the filthy water, at the floating logs of timber lashed together lying off certain wharves, his shining eyes darted a hungry look. After a darkening hour or so, suddenly the rudder-lines tightened in his hold, and he steered hard towards the Surrey shore.

Always watching his face, the girl instantly answered to the action in her sculling; presently the boat swung round, quivered as from a sudden jerk, and the upper half of the man was stretched out over the stern.

The girl pulled the hood of a cloak she wore, over her head and over her face, and, looking backward so that the front folds of this hood were turned down the river, kept the boat in that direction going before the tide. Until now, the boat had barely held her own, and had hovered about one spot; but now, the banks changed swiftly, and the deepening shadows and the kindling lights of London Bridge were passed, and the tiers of shipping lay on either hand.

It was not until now that the upper half of the man came back into the boat. His arms were wet and dirty, and he washed them over the side. In his right hand he held something, and he washed that in the river too. It was money. He chinked it once, and he blew upon it once, and he spat upon it once,—"for luck," he hoarsely said—before he put it in his pocket.

"Lizzie!"

The girl turned her face towards him with a start, and rowed in silence. Her face was very pale. He was a hook-nosed man, and with that and his bright eyes and his ruffled head, bore a certain likeness to a roused bird of prey.

"Take that thing off your face."

She put it back.

"Here! and give me hold of the sculls. I'll take the rest of the spell."

"No, no, father! No! I can't indeed. Father!—I cannot sit so near it!"

He was moving towards her to change places, but her terrified expostulation stopped him and he resumed his seat.

"What hurt can it do you?"

"None, none. But I cannot bear it."

"It's my belief you hate the sight of the very river."

"I—I do not like it, father."

"As if it wasn't your living! As if it wasn't meat and drink to you!"

At these latter words the girl shivered again, and for a moment paused in her rowing, seeming to turn deadly faint. It escaped his attention, for he was glancing over the stern at something the boat had in tow.

"How can you be so thankless to your best friend, Lizzie? The very fire that warmed you when you were a baby, was picked out of the river alongside the coal barges. The very basket that you slept in, the tide washed ashore. The very rockers that I put it upon to make a cradle of it, I cut out of a piece of wood that drifted from some ship or another."

Lizzie took her right hand from the scull it held, and touched her lips with it, and for a moment held it out lovingly towards him; then, without speaking, she resumed her rowing, as another boat of similar appearance, though in rather better trim, came out from a dark place and dropped softly alongside.

"In luck again, Gaffer?" said a man with a squinting leer, who sculled her, and who was alone. "I know'd you was in luck again, by your wake as you come down."

"Ah!" replied the other, drily. "So you're out, are you?"

"Yes, pardner."

There was now a tender yellow moonlight on the river, and the new comer, keeping half his boat's length astern of the other boat, looked hard at its track.

"I says to myself," he went on, "directly you hove in view, Yonder's Gaffer, and in luck again, by George if he ain't! Scull it is, pardner—don't fret yourself—I didn't touch him." This was in answer to a quick impatient movement on the part of Gaffer: the speaker at the same time unshipping his scull on that side, and laying his hand on the gunwale of Gaffer's boat and holding to it.

"He's had touches enough not to want no more, as well as I make him out, Gaffer! Been a knocking about with a pretty many tides, ain't he, pardner? Such is my out-of-luck ways, you see! He must have passed me when he went up last time, for I was on the look-out below bridge here. I a'most think you're like the wulturs, pardner, and scent 'em out."

He spoke in a dropped voice, and with more than one glance at Lizzie, who had pulled on her hood again. Both men then looked with a weird unholy interest at the wake of Gaffer's boat.

"Easy does it, betwixt us. Shall I take him aboard, pardner?"

"No," said the other. In so surly a tone that the man, after a blank stare, acknowledged it with the retort:

"—Arn't been eating nothing as has disagreed with you, have you, pardner?"

"Why, yes, I have," said Gaffer. "I have been swallowing too much of that word, Pardner. I am no pardner of yours."

"Since when was you no pardner of mine, Gaffer Hexam, Esquire?"

"Since you was accused of robbing a man. Accused of robbing a live man!" said Gaffer, with great indignation.

"And what if I had been accused of robbing a dead man, Gaffer?"

"You COULDN'T do it."

"Couldn't you, Gaffer?"

"No. Has a dead man any use for money? Is it possible for a dead man to have money? What world does a dead man belong to? T'other world. What world does money belong to? This world. How can money be a corpse's? Can a corpse own it, want it, spend it, claim it, miss it? Don't try to go confounding the rights and wrongs of things in that way. But it's worthy of the sneaking spirit that robs a live man."

"I'll tell you what it is——."

"No you won't. *I*'ll tell you what it is. You've got off with a short time of it or putting your hand in the pocket of a sailor, a live sailor. Make the most of it and think yourself lucky, but don't think after that to come over *me* with your pardners. We have worked together in time past, but we work together no more in time present nor yet future. Let go. Cast off!"

"Gaffer! If you think to get rid of me this way——."

"If I don't get rid of you this way, I'll try another, and chop you over the fingers with the stretcher, or take a pick at your head with the boat-hook. Cast off! Pull you, Lizzie. Pull home, since you won't let your father pull."

Lizzie shot ahead, and the other boat fell astern. Lizzie's father, composing himself into the easy attitude of one who had asserted the high moralities and taken an unassailable position, slowly lighted a pipe, and smoked, and took a survey of what he had in tow. What he had in tow, lunged itself at him sometimes in an awful manner when the boat was checked, and sometimes seemed to try to wrench itself away, though for the most part it followed submissively. A neophyte might have fancied that the ripples passing over it were dreadfully like faint changes of expression on a sightless face; but Gaffer was no neophyte and had no fancies.

CHAPTER II.

THE MAN FROM SOMEWHERE.

Mr. and Mrs. Veneering were bran-new people in a bran-new house in a bran-new quarter of London. Everything about the Veneerings was spick and span new. All their furniture was new, all their friends were new, all their servants were new, their plate was new, their carriage was new, their harness was new, their horses were new, their pictures were new, they themselves were new, they were as newly married as was lawfully compatible with their having a bran-new baby, and if they had set up a great-grandfather, he would have come home in matting from the Pantechnicon, without a scratch upon him, French polished to the crown of his head.

For, in the Veneering establishment, from the hall-chairs with the new coat of arms, to the grand pianoforte with the new action, and up-stairs again to the new fire-escape, all things were in a state of high varnish and polish. And what was observable in the furniture, was observable in the Veneerings—the surface smelt a little too much of the workshop and was a trifle sticky.

There was an innocent piece of dinner-furniture that went upon easy castors and was kept over a livery stable-yard in Duke Street, Saint James's, when not in use, to whom the Veneerings were a source of blind confusion. The name of this article was Twemlow. Being first cousin to Lord Snigsworth, he was in frequent requisition, and at many houses might be said to represent the dining-table in its normal state. Mr. and Mrs. Veneering, for example, arranging a dinner, habitually started with Twemlow, and then put leaves in him, or added guests to him. Sometimes, the table consisted of Twemlow and half-a-dozen leaves; sometimes, of Twemlow and a dozen leaves; sometimes, Twemlow was pulled out to his utmost extent of twenty leaves. Mr. and Mrs. Veneering on occasions of ceremony faced each other in the centre of the board, and thus the parallel still held; for, it always happened that the more Twemlow was pulled out, the further he found himself from the centre, and the nearer to the sideboard at one end of the room, or the window-curtains at the other.

But, it was not this which steeped the feeble soul of Twemlow in confusion. This he was used to, and could take soundings of. The abyss to which he could find no bottom, and from which started forth the engrossing and ever-swelling difficulty of his life, was the insoluble question whether he was Veneering's oldest friend, or newest friend. To the excogitation of this problem, the harmless gentleman had devoted many anxious hours, both in his lodgings over the livery stable-yard, and in the cold gloom, favourable to meditation, of St. James's Square. Thus. Twemlow had first known Veneering at his club, where Veneering then knew nobody but the man who made them known to one another, who seemed to be the most intimate friend he had in the world, and whom he had known two days--the bond of union between their souls, the nefarious conduct of the committee respecting the cookery of a fillet of veal, having been accidentally cemented at that date. Immediately upon this, Twemlow received an invitation to dine with Veneering, and dined: the man being of the party. Immediately upon that, Twemlow received an invitation to dine with the man, and dined: Veneering being of the party. At the man's were a Member, an Engineer, a Payer-off of the National Debt, a Poem on Shakespeare, a Grievance, and a Public Office, who all seemed to be utter strangers to Veneering. And yet immediately after that, Twemlow received an invitation to dine at Veneering's, expressly to meet the Member, the Engineer, the Payer-off of the National Debt, the Poem on Shakespeare, the Grievance, and the Public Office, and, dining, discovered that all of them were the most intimate friends Veneering had in the world, and that the wives of all of them (who were all there) were the objects of Mrs. Veneering's most devoted affection and tender confidence.

Thus it had come about, that Mr. Twemlow had said to himself in his lodgings, with his hand to his forehead: "I must not think of this. This is enough to soften any man's brain,"—and yet was always thinking of it, and could never form a conclusion.

This evening the Veneerings give a banquet. Eleven leaves in the Twemlow; fourteen in company all told. Four pigeon-breasted retainers in plain clothes stand in line in the hall. A fifth retainer, proceeding up the staircase with a mournful air—as who should say, "Here is another wretched creature come to dinner; such is life!"—announces, "Mis-ter Twemlow!"

Mrs. Veneering welcomes her sweet Mr. Twemlow. Mr. Veneering welcomes his dear Twemlow. Mrs. Veneering does not expect that Mr. Twemlow can in nature care much for such insipid things as babies, but so old a friend must please look at baby. "Ah! You will know the friend of your family better, Tootleums," says Mr. Veneering, nodding emotionally at that new article, "when you begin to take notice." He then begs to make his dear Twemlow known to his two friends, Mr. Boots and Mr. Brewer—and clearly has no distinct idea which is which.

But now a fearful circumstance occurs.

"Mis-ter and Mis-sis Podsnap!"

"My dear," says Mr. Veneering to Mrs. Veneering, with an air of much friendly interest, while the door stands open, "the Podsnaps."

A too, too smiling large man, with a fatal freshness on him, appearing with his wife, instantly deserts his wife and darts at Twemlow with:

"How do you do? So glad to know you. Charming house you have here. I hope we are not late. So glad of this opportunity, I am sure!"

When the first shock fell upon him, Twemlow twice skipped back in his neat little shoes and his neat little silk stockings of a bygone fashion, as if impelled to leap over a sofa behind him; but the large man closed with him and proved too strong.

"Let me," says the large man, trying to attract the attention of his wife in the distance, "have the pleasure of presenting Mrs. Podsnap to her host. She will be," in his fatal freshness he seems to find perpetual verdure and eternal youth in the phrase, "she will be so glad of the opportunity, I am sure!"

In the meantime, Mrs. Podsnap, unable to originate a mistake on her own account, because Mrs. Veneering is the only other lady there, does her best in the way of handsomely supporting her husband's, by looking towards Mr. Twemlow with a plaintive countenance and remarking to Mrs. Veneering in a feeling manner, firstly, that she fears he has been rather bilious of late, and, secondly, that the baby is already very like him.

It is questionable whether any man quite relishes being mistaken for any other man; but Mr. Veneering having this very evening set up the shirt-front of the young Antinous (in new worked cambric just come home), is not at all complimented by being supposed to be Twemlow, who is dry and weazen and some thirty years older. Mrs. Veneering equally resents the imputation of being the wife of Twemlow. As to Twemlow, he is so sensible of being a much better bred man than Veneering, that he considers the large man an offensive ass.

In this complicated dilemma, Mr. Veneering approaches the large man with extended hand, and smilingly assures that incorrigible personage that he is delighted to see him: who in his fatal freshness instantly replies:

"Thank you. I am ashamed to say that I cannot at this moment recall where we met, but I am so glad of this opportunity, I am sure!"

Then pouncing upon Twemlow, who holds back with all his feeble might, he is haling him off to present him, as Veneering, to Mrs. Podsnap, when the arrival of more guests unravels the mistake. Whereupon, having re-shaken hands with Veneering as Veneering, he re-shakes hands with Twemlow as Twemlow, and winds it all up to his own perfect satisfaction by saying to the last-named, "Ridiculous opportunity—but so glad of it, I am sure!"

Now, Twemlow having undergone this terrific experience, having likewise noted the fusion of Boots in Brewer and Brewer in Boots, and having further observed that of the remaining seven guests four discreet characters enter with wandering eyes and wholly decline to commit themselves as to which is Veneering, until Veneering has them in his grasp;—Twemlow having profited by these studies, finds his brain wholesomely hardening as he approaches the conclusion that he really is Veneering's oldest friend, when his brain softens again and all is lost, through his eyes encountering Veneering and the large man linked together as twin brothers in the back drawing-room near the conservatory door, and through his ears informing him in the tones of Mrs. Veneering that the same large man is to be baby's godfather.

"Dinner is on the table!"

Thus the melancholy retainer, as who should say, "Come down and be poisoned, ye unhappy children of men!"

Twemlow, having no lady assigned him, goes down in the rear, with his hand to his forehead. Boots and Brewer, thinking him indisposed, whisper, "Man faint. Had no lunch." But he is only stunned by the unvanquishable difficulty of his existence.

Revived by soup, Twemlow discourses mildly of the Court Circular with Boots and Brewer. Is appealed to, at the fish stage of the banquet, by Veneering, on the disputed question whether his cousin Lord Snigsworth is in or out of town? Gives it that his cousin is out of town. "At Snigsworthy Park?" Veneering inquires. "At Snigsworthy," Twemlow rejoins. Boots and Brewer regard this as a man to be cultivated; and Veneering is clear that he is a remunerative article. Meantime the retainer goes round, like a gloomy Analytical Chemist; always seeming to say, after "Chablis, sir?"—"You wouldn't if you knew what it's made of."

The great looking-glass above the sideboard reflects the table and the company. Reflects the new Veneering crest, in gold and eke in silver, frosted and also thawed, a camel of all work. The Herald's College found out a Crusading ancestor for Veneering who bore a camel on his shield (or might have done it if he had thought of it), and a caravan of camels take charge of the fruits and flowers and candles, and kneel down to be loaded with the salt. Reflects Veneering; forty, wavy-haired, dark, tending to corpulence, sly, mysterious, filmy—a kind of sufficiently well-looking veiled-prophet, not prophesying. Reflects Mrs. Veneering; fair, aquiline-nosed and fingered, not so much light hair as she might have, gorgeous in raiment and jewels, enthusiastic, propitiatory, conscious that a corner of her husband's veil is over herself. Reflects Podsnap; prosperously feeding, two little light-coloured wiry wings, one on either side of his else bald head, looking as like his hair-brushes as his hair, dissolving view of red beads on his forehead, large allowance of crumpled shirt-collar up behind. Reflects Mrs. Podsnap; fine woman for Professor Owen, quantity of bone, neck and nostrils like a rocking-horse, hard features, majestic head-dress in which Podsnap has hung golden offerings. Reflects Twemlow; grey, dry, polite, susceptible to east wind, First-Gentleman-in-Europe collar and cravat, cheeks drawn in as if he had made a great effort to retire into himself some years ago, and had got so far and had never got any farther. Reflects mature young lady; raven locks, and complexion that lights up well when well-powdered—as it is—carrying on considerably in the captivation of mature young gentleman; with too much nose in his face, too much ginger in his whiskers, too much torso in his waistcoat, too much sparkle in his studs, his eyes, his buttons, his talk, and his teeth. Reflects charming old Lady Tippins on Veneering's right; with an immense obtuse drab oblong face, like a face in a tablespoon, and a dyed Long Walk up the top of her head, as a convenient public approach to the bunch of false hair behind, pleased to patronise Mrs. Veneering opposite, who is pleased to be patronised. Reflects a certain "Mortimer," another of Veneering's oldest friends; who never was in the house before, and appears not to want to come again, who sits disconsolate on Mrs. Veneering's left, and who was inveigled by Lady Tippins (a friend of his boyhood) to come to these people's and talk, and who won't talk. Reflects Eugene, friend of Mortimer; buried alive in the back of his chair, behind a shoulder—with a powder-epaulette on it—of the mature young lady, and gloomily resorting to the champagne chalice whenever proffered by the Analytical Chemist. Lastly, the looking-glass reflects Boots and Brewer, and two other stuffed Buffers interposed between the rest of the company and possible accidents.

The Veneering dinners are excellent dinners—or new people wouldn't come—and all goes well. Notably, Lady Tippins has made a series of experiments on her digestive functions, so extremely complicated and daring, that if they could be published with their results it might benefit the human race. Having taken in provisions from all parts of the world, this hardy old cruiser has last touched at the North Pole, when, as the ice-plates are being removed, the following words fall from her:

"I assure you, my dear Veneering——"

(Poor Twemlow's hand approaches his forehead, for it would seem now, that Lady Tippins is going to be the oldest friend.)

"I assure you, my dear Veneering, that it is the oddest affair! Like the advertising people, I don't ask you to trust me, without offering a respectable reference. Mortimer there, is my reference, and knows all about it."

Mortimer raises his drooping eyelids, and slightly opens his mouth. But a faint smile, expressive of "What's the use!" passes over his face, and he drops his eyelids and shuts his mouth.

"Now, Mortimer," says Lady Tippins, rapping the sticks of her closed green fan upon the knuckles of her left hand—which is particularly rich in knuckles, "I insist upon your telling all that is to be told about the man from Jamaica."

"Give you my honour I never heard of any man from Jamaica, except the man who was a brother," replies Mortimer.

"Tobago, then."

"Nor yet from Tobago."

"Except," Eugene strikes in: so unexpectedly that the mature young lady, who has forgotten all about him, with a start takes the epaulette out of his way: "except our friend who long lived on rice-pudding and isinglass, till at length to his something or other, his physician said something else, and a leg of mutton somehow ended in daygo."

A reviving impression goes round the table that Eugene is coming out. An unfulfilled impression, for he goes in again.

"Now, my dear Mrs. Veneering," quoth Lady Tippins, "I appeal to you whether this is not the basest conduct ever known in this world? I carry my lovers about, two or three at a time, on condition that they are very obedient and devoted; and here is my old lover-in-chief, the head of all my slaves, throwing off his allegiance before company! And here is another of my lovers, a rough Cymon at present, certainly, but of whom I had most hopeful expectations as to his turning out well in course of time, pretending that he can't remember his nursery rhymes! On purpose to annoy me, for he knows how I dote upon them!"

A grisly little fiction concerning her lovers is Lady Tippins's point. She is always attended by a lover or two, and she keeps a little list of her lovers, and she is always booking a new lover, or striking out an old lover, or putting a lover in her black list, or promoting a lover to her blue list, or adding up her lovers, or otherwise posting her book. Mrs. Veneering is charmed by the humour, and so is Veneering. Perhaps it is enhanced by a certain yellow play in Lady Tippins's throat, like the legs of scratching poultry.

"I banish the false wretch from this moment, and I strike him out of my Cupidon (my name for my Ledger, my dear) this very night. But I am resolved to have the account of the man from Somewhere, and I beg you to elicit it for me, my love," to Mrs. Veneering, "as I have lost my own influence. Oh, you perjured man!" This to Mortimer, with a rattle of her fan.

"We are all very much interested in the man from Somewhere," Veneering observes.

Then the four Buffers, taking heart of grace all four at once, say:

"Deeply interested!"
"Quite excited!"
"Dramatic!"
"Man from Nowhere, perhaps!"

And then Mrs. Veneering—for Lady Tippins's winning wiles are contagious—folds her hands in the manner of a supplicating child, turns to her left neighbour, and says, "Tease! Pay! Man from Tumwhere!" At which the four Buffers, again mysteriously moved all four at once, exclaim, "You can't resist!"

"Upon my life," says Mortimer, languidly, "I find it immensely embarrassing to have the eyes of Europe upon me to this extent, and my only consolation is that you will all of you execrate Lady Tippins in your secret hearts when you find, as you inevitably will, the man from Somewhere a bore. Sorry to destroy romance by fixing him with a local habitation, but he comes from the place, the name of which escapes me, but will suggest itself to everybody else here, where they make the wine."

Eugene suggests "Day and Martin's."

"No, not that place," returns the unmoved Mortimer, "that's where they make the Port. My man comes from the country where they make the Cape Wine. But look here, old fellow; it's not at all statistical and it's rather odd."

It is always noticeable at the table of the Veneerings, that no man troubles himself much about the Veneerings themselves, and that any one who has anything to tell, generally tells it to anybody else in preference.

"The man," Mortimer goes on, addressing Eugene, "whose name is Harmon, was only son of a tremendous old rascal who made his money by Dust."

"Red velveteens and a bell?" the gloomy Eugene inquires.

"And a ladder and basket if you like. By which means, or by others, he grew rich as a Dust Contractor, and lived in a hollow in a hilly country entirely composed of Dust. On his own small estate the growling old vagabond threw up his own mountain range, like an old volcano, and its geological formation was Dust. Coal-dust, vegetable-dust, bone-dust, crockery dust, rough dust, and sifted dust—all manner of Dust."

A passing remembrance of Mrs. Veneering, here induces Mortimer to address his next half-dozen words to her; after which he wanders away again, tries Twemlow and finds he doesn't answer, ultimately takes up with the Buffers, who receive him enthusiastically.

"The moral being—I believe that's the right expression—of this exemplary person, derived its highest gratification from anathematising his nearest relations and turning them out of doors. Having begun (as was natural) by rendering these attentions to the wife of his bosom, he next found himself at leisure to bestow a similar recognition on the claims of his daughter. He chose a husband for her, entirely to his own satisfaction and not in the least to hers, and proceeded to settle upon her, as her marriage portion, I don't know how much Dust, but something immense. At this stage of the affair the poor girl respectfully intimated that she was secretly engaged to that popular character whom the novelists and versifiers call Another, and that such a marriage would make Dust of her heart and Dust of her life—in short, would set her up, on a very extensive scale, in her father's business. Immediately, the venerable parent—on a cold winter's night, it is said—anathematised and turned her out."

Here, the Analytical Chemist (who has evidently formed a very low opinion of Mortimer's story) concedes a little claret to the Buffers; who, again mysteriously moved all four at once, screw it slowly into themselves with a peculiar twist of enjoyment, as they cry in chorus, "Pray go on."

"The pecuniary resources of Another were, as they usually are, of a very limited nature. I believe I am not using too strong an expression when I say that Another was hard up. However, he married the young lady, and they lived in a humble dwelling, probably possessing a porch ornamented with honeysuckle and woodbine twining, until she died. I must refer you to the Registrar of the District in which the humble dwelling was situated, for the certified cause of death; but early sorrow and anxiety may have had to do with it, though they may not appear in the ruled pages and printed forms. Indisputably this was the case with Another, for he was so cut up by the loss of his young wife that if he outlived her a year it was as much as he did."

There is that in the indolent Mortimer, which seems to hint that if good society might on any account allow itself to be impressible, he, one of good society, might have the weakness to be impressed by what he here relates. It is hidden with great pains, but it is in him. The gloomy Eugene, too, is not without some kindred touch; for, when that appalling Lady Tippins declares that if Another had survived, he should have gone down at the head of her list of lovers—and also when the mature young lady shrugs her epaulettes, and laughs at some private and confidential comment from the mature young gentleman—his gloom deepens to that degree that he trifles quite ferociously with his dessert-knife.

Mortimer proceeds.

"We must now return, as the novelists say, and as we all wish they wouldn't, to the man from Somewhere. Being a boy of fourteen, cheaply educating at Brussels when his sister's expulsion befell, it was some little time before he heard of it —probably from herself, for the mother was dead; but that I don't know. Instantly, he absconded, and came over here. He must have been a boy of spirit and resource, to get here on a stopped allowance of five sous a week; but he did it somehow, and he burst in on his father, and pleaded his sister's cause. Venerable parent promptly resorts to anathematisation, and turns him out. Shocked and terrified boy takes flight, seeks his fortune, gets aboard ship, ultimately turns up on dry land among the Cape wine: small proprietor, farmer, grower—whatever you like to call it."

At this juncture, shuffling is heard in the hall, and tapping is heard at the dining-room door. Analytical Chemist goes to the door, confers angrily with unseen tapper, appears to become mollified by descrying reason in the tapping, and goes out.

"So he was discovered, only the other day, after having been expatriated about fourteen years."

A Buffer, suddenly astounding the other three, by detaching himself, and asserting individuality, inquires: "How discovered, and why?"

"Ah! To be sure. Thank you for reminding me. Venerable parent dies."

Same Buffer, emboldened by success, says: "When?"

"The other day. Ten or twelve months ago."

Same Buffer inquires with smartness, "What of?" But herein perishes a melancholy example; being regarded by the three other Buffers with a stony stare, and attracting no further attention from any mortal.

"Venerable parent," Mortimer repeats with a passing remembrance that there is a Veneering at table, and for the first time addressing him—"dies."

The gratified Veneering repeats, gravely, "dies;" and folds his arms, and composes his brow to hear it out in a judicial manner, when he finds himself again deserted in the bleak world.

"His will is found," says Mortimer, catching Mrs. Podsnap's rocking-horse's eye. "It is dated very soon after the son's flight. It leaves the lowest of the range of dust-mountains, with some sort of a dwelling-house at its foot, to an old servant who is sole executor, and all the rest of the property—which is very considerable—to the son. He directs himself to be buried with certain eccentric ceremonies and precautions against his coming to life, with which I need not bore you, and that's all—except—" and this ends the story.

The Analytical Chemist returning, everybody looks at him. Not because anybody wants to see him, but because of that subtle influence in nature which impels humanity to embrace the slightest opportunity of looking at anything, rather than the person who addresses it.

"—Except that the son's inheritance is made conditional on his marrying a girl, who at the date of the will, was a child of four or five years old, and who is now a marriageable young woman. Advertisement and inquiry discovered the son in the man from Somewhere, and at the present moment, he is on his way home from there—no doubt, in a state of great astonishment—to succeed to a very large fortune, and to take a wife."

Mrs. Podsnap inquires whether the young person is a young person of personal charms? Mortimer is unable to report.

Mr. Podsnap inquires what would become of the very large fortune, in the event of the marriage condition not being fulfilled? Mortimer replies, that by special testamentary clause it would then go to the old servant above mentioned, passing over and excluding the son; also, that if the son had not been living, the same old servant would have been sole residuary legatee.

Mrs. Veneering has just succeeded in waking Lady Tippins from a snore, by dexterously shunting a train of plates and dishes at her knuckles across the table: when everybody but Mortimer himself becomes aware that the Analytical Chemist is, in a ghostly manner, offering him a folded paper. Curiosity detains Mrs. Veneering a few moments.

Mortimer, in spite of all the arts of the chemist, placidly refreshes himself with a glass of Madeira, and remains unconscious of the document which engrosses the general attention, until Lady Tippins (who has a habit of waking totally insensible), having remembered where she is, and recovered a perception of surrounding objects, says: "Falser man than Don Juan; why don't you take the note from the Commendatore?" Upon which, the chemist advances it under the nose of Mortimer, who looks round at him, and says:

"What's this?"

Analytical Chemist bends and whispers.

"*Who?*" says Mortimer.

Analytical Chemist again bends and whispers.

Mortimer stares at him, and unfolds the paper. Reads it, reads it twice, turns it over to look at the blank outside, reads it a third time.

"This arrives in an extraordinarily opportune manner," says Mortimer then, looking with an altered face round the table: "this is the conclusion of the story of the identical man."

"Already married?" one guesses.

"Declines to marry?" another guesses.

"Codicil among the dust?" another guesses.

"Why, no," says Mortimer; "remarkable thing, you are all wrong. The story is completer and rather more exciting than I supposed. Man's drowned!"

CHAPTER III.

ANOTHER MAN.

As the disappearing skirts of the ladies ascended the Veneering staircase, Mortimer following them forth from the dining-room, turned into a library of bran-new books, in bran-new bindings liberally gilded, and requested to see the messenger who had brought the paper. He was a boy of about fifteen. Mortimer looked at the boy, and the boy looked at the bran-new pilgrims on the wall, going to Canterbury in more gold frame than procession, and more carving than country.

"Whose writing is this?"

"Mine, sir."

"Who told you to write it?"

"My father, Jesse Hexam."

"Is it he who found the body?"

"Yes, sir."

"What is your father?"

The boy hesitated, looked reproachfully at the pilgrims as if they had involved him in a little difficulty, then said, folding a plait in the right leg of his trousers, "He gets his living along-shore."

"Is it far?"

"Is which far?" asked the boy, upon his guard, and again upon the road to Canterbury.

"To your father's?"

"It's a goodish stretch, sir. I come up in a cab, and the cab's waiting to be paid. We could go back in it before you paid it, if you liked. I went first to your office, according to the direction of the papers found in the pockets, and there I see nobody but a chap of about my age who sent me on here."

There was a curious mixture in the boy, of uncompleted savagery, and uncompleted civilisation. His voice was hoarse and coarse, and his face was coarse, and his stunted figure was coarse; but he was cleaner than other boys of his type; and his writing, though large and round, was good; and he glanced at the backs of the books, with an awakened curiosity that went below the binding. No one who can read, ever looks at a book, even unopened on a shelf, like one who cannot.

"Were any means taken, do you know, boy, to ascertain if it was possible to restore life?" Mortimer inquired, as he sought for his hat.

"You wouldn't ask, sir, if you knew his state. Pharaoh's multitude, that were drowned in the Red Sea, ain't more beyond restoring to life. If Lazarus was only half as far gone, that was the greatest of all the miracles."

"Halloa!" cried Mortimer, turning round with his hat upon his head, "you seem to be at home in the Red Sea, my young friend?"

"Read of it with teacher at the school," said the boy.

"And Lazarus?"

"Yes, and him too. But don't you tell my father! We should have no peace in our place, if that got touched upon. It's my sister's contriving."

"You seem to have a good sister."

"She ain't half bad," said the boy; "but if she knows her letters it's the most she does—and them I learned her."

The gloomy Eugene, with his hands in his pockets, had strolled in and assisted at the latter part of the dialogue; when the boy spoke these words slightingly of his sister, he took him roughly enough by the chin and turned up his face to look at it.

"Well, I am sure, sir!" said the boy, resisting; "I hope you'll know me again."

Eugene vouchsafed no answer; but made the proposal to Mortimer, "I'll go with you, if you like?" So, they all three went away together in the vehicle that had brought the boy; the two friends (once boys together at a public school) inside, smoking cigars; the messenger on the box beside the driver.

"Let me see," said Mortimer, as they went along; "I have been, Eugene, upon the honourable roll of solicitors of the High Court of Chancery, and attorneys at Common Law, five years; and—except gratuitously taking instructions, on an average once a fortnight, for the will of Lady Tippins who has nothing to leave—I have had no scrap of business but this romantic business."

"And I," said Eugene, "have been 'called' seven years, and have had no business at all, and never shall have any. And if I had, I shouldn't know how to do it."

"I am far from being clear as to the last particular," returned Mortimer, with great composure, "that I have much advantage over you."

"I hate," said Eugene, putting his legs up on the opposite seat, "I hate my profession."

"Shall I incommode you if I put mine up too?" returned Mortimer. "Thank you. I hate mine."

"It was forced upon me," said the gloomy Eugene, "because it was understood that we wanted a barrister in the family. We have got a precious one."

"It was forced upon me," said Mortimer, "because it was .nderstood that we wanted a solicitor in the family. And we have got a precious one."

"There are four of us, with our names painted on a door-post in right of one black hole called a set of chambers," said Eugene; "and each of us has the fourth of a clerk—Cassim Baba, in the robber's cave—and Cassim is the only respectable member of the party."

"I am one by myself, one," said Mortimer, "high up an awful staircase commanding a burial-ground, and I have a whole clerk to myself, and he has nothing to do but look at the burial-ground, and what he will turn out when arrived at maturity, I cannot conceive. Whether, in that shabby rook's nest, he is always plotting wisdom, or plotting murder; whether he will grow up, after so much solitary brooding, to enlighten his fellow-creatures, or to poison them; is the only speck of interest that presents itself to my professional view. Will you give me a light? Thank you."

"Then idiots talk," said Eugene, leaning back, folding his arms, smoking with his eyes shut, and speaking slightly through his nose, "of Energy. If there is a word in the dictionary under any letter from A to Z that I abominate, it is energy. It is such a conventional superstition, such parrot gabble! What the deuce! Am I to rush out into the street, collar the first man of a wealthy appearance that I meet, shake him, and say, 'Go to law upon the spot, you dog, and retain me, or I'll be the death of you?' Yet that would be energy."

"Precisely my view of the case, Eugene. But show me a good opportunity, show me something really worth being energetic about, and *I'll* show you energy."

"And so will I," said Eugene.

And it is likely enough that ten thousand other young men, within the limits of the London Post-office town-delivery, made the same hopeful remark in the course of the same evening.

The wheels rolled on, and rolled down by the Monument, and by the Tower, and by the Docks; down by Ratcliffe, and by Rotherhithe; down by where accumulated scum of humanity seemed to be washed from higher grounds, like so much moral sewage, and to be pausing until its own weight forced it over the bank and sunk it in the river. In and out among vessels that seemed to have got ashore, and houses that seemed to have got afloat—among bowsprits staring into windows, and windows staring into ships—the wheels rolled on, until they stopped at a dark corner, river-washed and otherwise not washed at all, where the boy alighted and opened the door.

"You must walk the rest, sir; it's not many yards." He spoke in the singular number, to the express exclusion of Eugene.

"This is a confoundedly out-of-the-way place," said Mortimer, slipping over the stones and refuse on the shore, as the boy turned the corner sharp.

"Here's my father's, sir; where the light is."

The low building had the look of having once been a mill. There was a rotten wart of wood upon its forehead that seemed to indicate where the sails had been, but the whole was very indistinctly seen in the obscurity of the night. The boy lifted the latch of the door, and they passed at once into a low circular room, where a man stood before a red fire, looking down into it, and a girl sat engaged in needlework. The fire was in a rusty brazier, not fitted to the hearth; and a common lamp, shaped like a hyacinth-root, smoked and flared in the neck of a stone bottle on the table. There was a wooden bunk or berth in a corner, and in another corner a wooden stair leading above—so clumsy and steep that it was little better than a ladder. Two or three old sculls and oars stood against the wall, and against another part of the wall was a small dresser, making a spare show of the commonest articles of crockery and cooking-vessels. The roof of the room was not plastered, but was formed of the flooring of the room above. This, being very old, knotted, seamed, and beamed, gave a lowering aspect to the chamber; and roof, and walls, and floor, alike abounding in old smears of flour, red-lead (or some such stain which it had probably acquired in warehousing), and damp, alike had a look of decomposition.

"The gentleman, father."

The figure at the red fire turned, raised its ruffled head, and looked like a bird of prey.

"You're Mortimer Lightwood, Esquire; are you, sir?"

"Mortimer Lightwood is my name. What you found," said Mortimer, glancing rather shrinkingly towards the bunk; "is it here?"

"'Taint not to say here, but it's close by. I do everything reg'lar. I've giv' notice of the circumstarnce to the police, and the police have took possession of it. No time ain't been lost, on any hand. The police have put it into print already, and here's what the print says of it."

Taking up the bottle with the lamp in it, he held it near a paper on the wall, with the police heading, BODY FOUND. The two friends read the handbill as it stuck against the wall, and Gaffer read them as he held the light.

"Only papers on the unfortunate man, I see," said Lightwood, glancing from the description of what was found, to the finder.

"Only papers."

Here the girl arose with her work in her hand, and went out at the door.

"No money," pursued Mortimer; "but threepence in one of the skirt-pockets."

"Three. Penny. Pieces," said Gaffer Hexam, in as many sentences.

"The trousers pockets empty, and turned inside out."

Gaffer Hexam nodded. "But that's common. Whether it's the wash of the tide or no, I can't say. Now, here," moving the light to another similar placard, "*his* pockets was found empty, and turned inside out. And here," moving the light to another, "*her* pocket was found empty, and turned inside out. And so was this one's. And so was that one's. I can't read, nor I don't want to it, for I know 'em by their places on the wall. This one was a sailor, with two anchors and a flag and G. F. T. on his arm. Look and see if he warn't."

"Quite right."

"This one was the young woman in grey boots, and her linen marked with a cross. Look and see if she warn't."

"Quite right."

"This is him as had a nasty cut over the eye. This is them two young sisters what tied themselves together with a handkecher. This is the drunken old chap, in a pair of list slippers and a nightcap, wot had offered—it afterwards come out—to make a hole in the water for a quartern of rum stood aforehand, and kept to his word for the first and last time in his life. They pretty well papers the room, you see; but I know 'em all. I'm scholar enough!"

He waved the light over the whole, as if to typify the light of his scholarly intelligence, and then put it down on the table and stood behind it looking intently at his visitors. He had the special peculiarity of some birds of prey, that when he knitted his brow, his ruffled crest stood highest.

"You did not find all these yourself; did you?" asked Eugene.

To which the bird of prey slowly rejoined, "And what might *your* name be, now?"

"This is my friend," Mortimer Lightwood interposed; "Mr. Eugene Wrayburn."

"Mr. Eugene Wrayburn, is it? And what might Mr. Eugene Wrayburn have asked of me?"

"I asked you, simply, if you found all these yourself?"

"I answer you, simply, most on 'em."

"Do you suppose there has been much violence and robbery, beforehand, among these cases?"

"I don't suppose at all about it," returned Gaffer. "I ain't one of the supposing sort. If you'd got your living to haul out of the river every day of your life, you mightn't be much given to supposing. Am I to show the way?"

As he opened the door, in pursuance of a nod from Lightwood, an extremely pale and disturbed face appeared in the doorway—the face of a man much agitated.

"A body missing?" asked Gaffer Hexam, stopping short; "or a body found? Which?"

"I am lost!" replied the man, in a hurried and an eager manner.

"Lost?"

"I—I—am a stranger, and don't know the way. I—I—want to find the place where I can see what is described here. It is possible I may know it." He was panting, and could hardly speak; but, he showed a copy of the newly-printed bill that was still wet upon the wall. Perhaps its newness, or perhaps the accuracy of his observation of its general look, guided Gaffer to a ready conclusion.

"This gentleman, Mr. Lightwood, is on that business."

"Mr. Lightwood?"

During a pause, Mortimer and the stranger confronted each other. Neither knew the other.

"I think, sir," said Mortimer, breaking the awkward silence with his airy self-possession, "that you did me the honour to mention my name?"

"I repeated it after this man."

"You said you were a stranger in London?"

"An utter stranger."

"Are you seeking a Mr. Harmon?"

"No."

"Then I believe I can assure you that you are on a fruitless errand, and will not find what you fear to find. Will you come with us?"

A little winding through some muddy alleys that might have been deposited by the last ill-savoured tide, brought them to the wicket-gate and bright lamp of a Police Station; where they found the Night-Inspector, with a pen and ink, and ruler, posting up his books in a whitewashed office, as studiously as if he were in a monastery on the top of a mountain, and no howling fury of a drunken woman were banging herself against a cell-door in the back-yard at his elbow. With the same air of a recluse much given to study, he desisted from his books to bestow a distrustful nod of recognition upon Gaffer, plainly importing, "Ah! we know all about *you*, and you'll overdo it some day;" and to inform Mr. Mortimer Lightwood and friends, that he would attend them immediately. Then, he finished ruling the work he had in hand (it might have been illuminating a missal, he was so calm), in a very neat and methodical manner, showing not the slightest consciousness of the woman who was banging herself with increased violence, and shrieking most terrifically for some other woman's liver.

"A bull's-eye," said the Night-Inspector, taking up his keys. Which a deferential satellite produced. "Now, gentlemen."

With one of his keys, he opened a cool grot at the end of the yard, and they all went in. They quickly came out again, no one speaking but Eugene; who remarked to Mortimer, in a whisper, "Not *much* worse than Lady Tippins."

So back to the whitewashed library of the monastery—with that liver still in shrieking requisition, as it had been loudly, while they looked at the silent sight they came to see—and there through the merits of the case as summed up by the Abbot. No clue to how body came into river. Very often was no clue. Too late to know for certain, whether injuries received before or after death; one excellent surgical opinion said, before; other excellent surgical opinion said, after. Steward of ship in which gentleman came home passenger, had been round to view, and could swear to identity. Likewise could swear to clothes. And then, you see, you had the papers, too. How was it he had totally disappeared on leaving ship, till found in river? Well! Probably had been upon some little game. Probably thought it a harmless game, wasn't up to things, and it turned out a fatal game. Inquest to-morrow, and no doubt open verdict.

"It appears to have knocked your friend over—knocked him completely off his legs," Mr. Inspector remarked, when he had finished his summing up. "It has given him a bad turn to be sure!" This was said in a very low voice, and with a searching look (not the first he had cast) at the stranger.

Mr. Lightwood explained that it was no friend of his.

"Indeed?" said Mr. Inspector, with an attentive ear; "where did you pick him up?"

Mr. Lightwood explained further.

Mr. Inspector had delivered his summing up, and had added these words, with his elbows leaning on his desk, and the fingers and thumb of his right hand, fitting themselves to the fingers and thumb of his left. Mr. Inspector moved nothing but his eyes, as he now added, raising his voice:

"Turned you faint, sir! Seems you're not accustomed to this kind of work?"

The stranger, who was leaning against the chimney-piece with drooping head, looked round and answered,

"No. It's a horrible sight!"

"You expected to identify, I am told, sir?"

"Yes."

"*Have* you identified?"

"No. It's a horrible sight. O! a horrible, horrible sight!"

"Who did you think it might have been?" asked Mr. Inspector. "Give us a description, sir. Perhaps we can help you."

"No, no," said the stranger; "it would be quite useless. Good night."

Mr. Inspector had not moved, and had given no order; but, the satellite slipped his back against the wicket, and laid his left arm along the top of it, and with his right hand turned the bull's-eye he had taken from his chief—in quite a casual manner—towards the stranger.

"You missed a friend, you know; or you missed a foe, you know; or you wouldn't have come here, you know. Well, then; ain't it reasonable to ask, who was it?" Thus, Mr. Inspector.

"You must excuse my telling you. No class of man can understand better than you, that families may not choose to publish their disagreements and misfortunes, except on the last necessity. I do not dispute that you discharge your duty in asking me the question; you will not dispute my right to withhold the answer. Good night."

Again he turned towards the wicket, where the satellite, with his eye upon his chief, remained a dumb statue.

"At least," said Mr. Inspector, "you will not object to leave me your card, sir?"

"I should not object, if I had one; but I have not." He reddened and was much confused as he gave the answer.

"At least," said Mr. Inspector, with no change of voice or manner, "you will not object to write down your name and address?"

"Not at all."

Mr. Inspector dipped a pen in his inkstand, and deftly laid it on a piece of paper close beside him; then resumed his former attitude. The stranger stepped up to the desk, and wrote in a rather tremulous hand—Mr. Inspector taking sidelong note of every hair of his head when it was bent down for the purpose—"Mr. Julius Handford, Exchequer Coffee House, Palace Yard, Westminster."

"Staying there, I presume, sir?"

"Staying there."

"Consequently, from the country?"

"Eh? Yes—from the country."

"Good-night, sir."

The satellite removed his arm and opened the wicket, and Mr. Julius Handford went out.

"Reserve!" said Mr. Inspector. "Take care of this piece of paper, keep him in view without giving offence, ascertain that he *is* staying there, and find out anything you can about him."

The satellite was gone; and Mr. Inspector becoming once again the quiet Abbot of that Monastery, dipped his pen in his ink and resumed his books. The two friends who had watched him, more amused by the professional manner than suspicious of Mr. Julius Handford, inquired before taking their departure too whether he believed there was anything that really looked bad here?

The Abbot replied with reticence, "couldn't say. If a murder, anybody might have done it. Burglary or pocket-picking wanted 'prenticeship. Not so murder. We were all of us up to that. Had seen scores of people come to identify, and never saw one person struck in that particular way. Might, however, have been Stomach and not Mind. If so, rum stomach. But to be sure there were rum everythings. Pity there was not a word of truth in that superstition about bodies bleeding when touched by the hand of the right person; you never got a sign out of bodies. You got row enough out of such as her—she was good for all night now" (referring here to the banging demands of the liver), "but you got nothing out of bodies if it was ever so."

There being nothing more to be done until the inquest was held next day, the friends went away together, and Gaffer Hexam and his son went their separate way. But, arriving at the last corner, Gaffer bade his boy go home while he turned into a red-curtained tavern, that stood dropsically bulging over the causeway, "for a half-a-pint."

The boy lifted the latch he had lifted before, and found his sister again seated before the fire at her work. Who raised her head upon his coming in and asking:

"Where did you go, Liz?"

"I went out in the dark."

"There was no necessity for that. It was all right enough."

"One of the gentlemen, the one who didn't speak while I was there, looked hard at me. And I was afraid he might know what my face meant. But there! Don't mind me, Charley! I was all in a tremble of another sort when you owned to father you could write a little."

"Ah! But I made believe I wrote so badly, as that it was odds if any one could read it. And when I wrote slowest and smeared out with my finger most, father was best pleased, as he stood looking over me."

The girl put aside her work, and drawing her seat close to his seat by the fire, laid her arm gently on his shoulder.

"You'll make the most of your time, Charley; won't you?"

"Won't I? Come! I like that. Don't I?"

"Yes, Charley, yes. You work hard at your learning, I know. And I work a little, Charley, and plan and contrive a little (wake out of my sleep contriving sometimes), how to get together a shilling now, and a shilling then, that shall make father believe you are beginning to earn a stray living along-shore."

"You are father's favourite, and can make him believe anything."

"I wish I could, Charley! For if I could make him believe that learning was a good thing, and that we might lead better lives, I should be a'most content to die."

"Don't talk stuff about dying, Liz."

She placed her hands in one another on his shoulder, and laying her rich brown cheek against them as she looked down at the fire, went on thoughtfully:

"Of an evening, Charley, when you are at the school, and father's——"

"At the Six Jolly Fellowship-Porters," the boy struck in, with a backward nod of his head towards the public-house.

"Yes. Then as I sit a-looking at the fire, I seem to see in the burning coal—like where that glow is now——"

"That's gas, that is," said the boy, "coming out of a bit of a forest that's been under the mud that was under the water in the days of Noah's Ark. Look here! When I take the poker—so—and give it a dig——"

"Don't disturb it, Charley, or it'll be all in a blaze. It's that dull glow near it, coming and going, that I mean. When I look at it of an evening, it comes like pictures to me, Charley."

"Show us a picture," said the boy. "Tell us where to look."

"Ah! It wants my eyes, Charley."

"Cut away then, and tell us what your eyes make of it."

"Why, there are you and me, Charley, when you were quite a baby that never knew a mother——"

"Don't go saying I never knew a mother," interposed the boy, "for I knew a little sister that was sister and mother both."

The girl laughed delightedly, and her eyes filled with pleasant tears, as he put both his arms round her waist and so held her.

"There are you and me, Charley, when father was away at work and locked us out, for fear we should set ourselves afire or fall out of window, sitting on the door-sill, sitting on other door-steps, sitting on the bank of the river, wandering about to get through the time. You are rather heavy to carry, Charley, and I'm often obliged to rest. Sometimes we are sleepy and fall asleep together in a corner, sometimes we are very hungry, sometimes we are a little frightened, but what is oftenest hard upon us is the cold. You remember, Charley?"

"I remember," said the boy, pressing her to him twice or thrice, "that I snuggled under a little shawl, and it was warm there."

"Sometimes it rains, and we creep under a boat or the like of that; sometimes it's dark, and we get among the gaslights, sitting watching the people as they go along the streets. At last, up comes father and takes us home. And home seems such a shelter after out of doors! And father pulls my shoes off, and dries my feet at the fire, and has me to sit by him while he smokes his pipe long after you are abed, and I notice that father's is a large hand but never a heavy one when it touches me, and that father's is a rough voice but never an angry one when it speaks to me. So, I grow up, and little by little father trusts me, and makes me his companion, and, let him be put out as he may, never once strikes me."

The listening boy gave a grunt here, as much as to say, "But he strikes *me* though!"

"Those are some of the pictures of what is past, Charley."

PODSNAPPERY.

THE PERSON OF THE HOUSE AND THE BAD CHILD.

"Cut away again," said the boy, "and give us a fortune-telling one; a future one."

"Well! There am I, continuing with father, and holding to father, because father loves me, and I love father. I can't so much as read a book, because, if I had learned, father would have thought I was deserting him, and I should have lost my influence. I have not the influence I want to have, I cannot stop some dreadful things I try to stop, but I go on in the hope and trust that the time will come. In the meanwhile I know that I am in some things a stay to father, and that if I was not faithful to him he would—in revenge-like, or in disappointment, or both—go wild and bad."

"Give us a touch of the fortune-telling pictures about me."

"I was passing on to them, Charley," said the girl, who had not changed her attitude since she began, and who now mournfully shook her head; "the others were all leading up. There are you——"

"Where am I, Liz?"

"Still in the hollow down by the flare."

"There seems to be the deuce-and-all in the hollow down by the flare," said the boy, glancing from her eyes to the brazier, which had a grisly skeleton look on its long thin legs.

"There are you, Charley, working your way, in secret from father, at the school; and you get prizes; and you go on better and better; and you come to be a—what was it you called it when you told me about that?"

"Ha, ha! Fortune-telling not know the name!" cried the boy, seeming to be rather relieved by this default on the part of the hollow down by the flare. "Pupil-teacher."

"You come to be a pupil-teacher, and you still go on better and better, and you rise to be a master full of learning and respect. But the secret has come to father's knowledge long before, and it has divided you from father, and from me."

"No it hasn't!"

"Yes it has, Charley. I see, as plain as plain can be, that your way is not ours, and that even if father could be got to forgive your taking it (which he never could be), that way of yours would be darkened by our way. But I see too, Charley——"

"Still as plain as plain can be, Liz?" asked the boy playfully.

"Ah! Still. That it is a great work to have cut your way from father's life, and to have made a new and good beginning. So there am I, Charley, left alone with father, keeping him as straight as I can, watching for more influence than I have, and hoping that through some fortunate chance, or when he is ill, or when—I don't know what—I may turn him to wish to do better things."

"You said you couldn't read a book, Lizzie. Your library of books is the hollow down by the flare, I think."

"I should be very glad to be able to read real books. I feel my want of learning very much, Charley. But I should feel it much more, if I didn't know it to be a tie between me and father.—Hark! Father's tread!"

It being now past midnight, the bird of prey went straight to roost. At mid-day following he re-appeared at the Six Jolly Fellowship-Porters, in the character, not new to him, of a witness before a Coroner's Jury.

Mr. Mortimer Lightwood, besides sustaining the character of one of the witnesses, doubled the part with that of the eminent solicitor who watched the proceedings on behalf of the representatives of the deceased, as was duly recorded in the newspapers. Mr. Inspector watched the proceedings too, and kept his watching closely to himself. Mr. Julius Handford having given his right address, and being reported in solvent circumstances as to his bill, though nothing more was known of him at his hotel except that his way of life was very retired, had no summons to appear, and was merely present in the shades of Mr. Inspector's mind.

The case was made interesting to the public, by Mr. Mortimer Lightwood's evidence touching the circumstances under which the deceased, Mr. John Harmon, had returned to England; exclusive private proprietorship in which circumstances was set up at dinner-tables for several days, by Veneering, Twemlow, Podsnap, and all the Buffers: who all related them irreconcilably with one another, and contradicted themselves. It was also made interesting by the testimony of Job Potterson, the ship's steward, and one Mr. Jacob Kibble, a fellow-passenger, that the deceased Mr. John Harmon did bring over, in a hand-valise with which he did disembark, the sum realised by the forced sale of his little landed property, and that the sum exceeded, in ready money, seven hundred pounds. It was further made interesting, by the remarkable experiences of Jesse Hexam in having rescued from the Thames so many dead bodies, and for whose behoof a rapturous admirer subscribing himself "A Friend to Burial" (perhaps an undertaker), sent eighteen postage stamps, and five "Now Sir"'s to the editor of the Times.

Upon the evidence adduced before them, the Jury found, That the body of Mr. John Harmon had been discovered floating in the Thames, in an advanced state of decay, and much injured; and that the said Mr. John Harmon had come by his death under highly suspicious circumstances, though by whose act or in what precise manner there was no evidence before this Jury to show. And they appended to their verdict, a recommendation to the Home Office (which Mr. Inspector appeared to think highly sensible), to offer a reward for the solution of the mystery. Within eight-and-forty hours, a reward of One Hundred Pounds was proclaimed, together with a free pardon to any person or persons not the actual perpetrator or perpetrators, and so forth in due form.

This Proclamation rendered Mr. Inspector additionally studious, and caused him to stand meditating on river-stairs and causeways, and to go lurking about in boats, putting this and that together. But, according to the success with which you put this and that together, you get a woman and a fish apart, or a Mermaid in combination. And Mr. Inspector could turn out nothing better than a Mermaid, which no Judge and Jury would believe in.

Thus, like the tides on which it had been borne to the knowledge of men, the Harmon Murder—as it came to be popularly called—went up and down, and ebbed and flowed, now in the town, now in the country, now among palaces, now among hovels, now among lords and ladies and gentlefolks, now among labourers and hammerers and ballast-heavers, until at last, after a long interval of slack water, it got out to sea and drifted away.

CHAPTER IV.

THE R. WILFER FAMILY.

REGINALD WILFER is a name with rather a grand sound, suggesting on first acquaintance brasses in country churches, scrolls in stained-glass windows, and generally the De Wilfers who came over with the Conqueror. For, it is a remarkable fact in genealogy that no De Any ones ever came over with Anybody else.

But, the Reginald Wilfer family were of such common-place extraction and pursuits that their forefathers had for generations modestly subsisted on the Docks, the Excise Office, and the Custom House, and the existing R. Wilfer was a poor clerk. So poor a clerk, through having a limited salary and an unlimited family, that he had never yet attained the modest object of his ambition: which was, to wear a complete new suit of clothes, hat and boots included, at one time. His black hat was brown before he could afford a coat, his pantaloons were white at the seams and knees before he could buy a pair of boots, his boots had worn out before he could treat himself to new pantaloons, and by the time he worked round to the hat again, that shining modern article roofed-in an ancient ruin of various periods.

If the conventional Cherub could ever grow up and be clothed, he might be photographed as a portrait of Wilfer. His chubby, smooth, innocent appearance was a reason for his being always treated with condescension when he was not put down. A stranger entering his own poor house at about ten o'clock P.M. might have been surprised to find him sitting up to supper. So boyish was he in his curves and proportions, that his old schoolmaster meeting him in Cheapside, might have been unable to withstand the temptation of caning him on the spot. In short, he was the conventional cherub, after the supposititious shoot just mentioned, rather grey, with signs of care on his expression, and in decidedly insolvent circumstances.

He was shy, and unwilling to own to the name of Reginald, as being too aspiring and self-assertive a name. In his signature he used only the initial R., and imparted what it really stood for, to none but chosen friends, under the seal of confidence. Out of this, the facetious habit had arisen in the neighbourhood surrounding Mincing Lane of making Christian names for him of adjectives and participles beginning with R. Some of these were more or less appropriate: as Rusty, Retiring, Ruddy, Round, Ripe, Ridiculous, Ruminative; others derived their point from their want of application: as Raging, Rattling, Roaring, Raffish. But, his popular name was Rumty, which in a moment of inspiration had been bestowed upon him by a gentleman of convivial habits connected with the drug market, as the beginning of a social chorus, his leading part in the execution of which had led this gentleman to the Temple of Fame, and of which the whole expressive burden ran:

> "Rumty iddity, row dow dow.
> Sing toodlely, teedlely, bow wow wow."

Thus he was constantly addressed, even in minor notes on business, as "Dear Rumty;" in answer to which, he sedately signed himself, "Yours truly, R. Wilfer."

He was clerk in the drug-house of Chicksey, Veneering, and Stobbles. Chicksey and Stobbles, his former masters, had both become absorbed in Veneering, once their traveller or commission agent: who had signalised his accession to supreme power by bringing into the business a quantity of plate-glass window and French-polished mahogany partition, and a gleaming and enormous door-plate.

R. Wilfer locked up his desk one evening, and putting his bunch of keys in his pocket much as if it were his peg-top, made for home. His home was in the Holloway region north of London, and then divided from it by fields and trees. Between Battle Bridge and that part of the Holloway district in which he dwelt, was a tract of suburban Sahara, where tiles and bricks were burnt, bones were boiled, carpets were beat, rubbish was shot, dogs were fought, and dust was heaped by contractors. Skirting the border of this desert, by the way he took, when the light of its kiln-fires made lurid smears on the fog, R. Wilfer sighed and shook his head.

"Ah me!" said he, "what might have been is not what is!"

With which commentary on human life, indicating an experience of it not exclusively his own, he made the best of his way to the end of his journey.

Mrs. Wilfer was, of course, a tall woman and an angular. Her lord being cherubic, she was necessarily majestic, according to the principle which matrimonially unites contrasts. She was much given to tying up her head in a pocket-handkerchief, knotted under the chin. This head-gear, in conjunction with a pair of gloves worn within doors, she seemed to consider as at once a kind of armour against misfortune (invariably assuming it when in low spirits or difficulties), and as a species of full dress. It was therefore with some sinking of the spirit that her husband beheld her thus heroically attired, putting down her candle in the little hall, and coming down the doorsteps through the little front court to open the gate for him.

Something had gone wrong with the house-door, for R. Wilfer stopped on the steps, staring at it, and cried:

"Hal—loa?"

"Yes," said Mrs. Wilfer, "the man came himself with a pair of pincers, and took it off, and took it away. He said that as he had no expectation of ever being paid for it, and as he had an order for another LADIES' SCHOOL door-plate, it was better (burnished up) for the interests of all parties."

"Perhaps it was, my dear; what do you think?"

"You are master here, R. W.," returned his wife. "It is as you think; not as I do. Perhaps it might have been better if the man had taken the door too."

"My dear, we couldn't have done without the door."

"Couldn't we?"

"Why, my dear! Could we?"

"It is as you think, R. W.; not as I do." With those submissive words, the dutiful wife preceded him down a few stairs to a little basement front room, half kitchen, half parlour, where a girl of about nineteen, with an exceedingly pretty figure and face, but with an impatient and petulant expression both in her face and in her shoulders (which in her sex and at her age are very expressive of discontent), sat playing draughts with a younger girl, who was the youngest of the House of Wilfer. Not to encumber this page by telling off the Wilfers in detail and casting them up in the gross, it is enough for the present that the rest were what is called "out in the world," in various ways, and that they were Many. So many, that when one of his dutiful children called in to see him, R. Wilfer generally seemed to say to himself, after a little mental arithmetic, "Oh! here's another of 'em!" before adding aloud, "How de do, John," or Susan, as the case might be.

"Well, Piggywiggies," said R. W., "how de do to-night? What I was thinking of, my dear," to Mrs. Wilfer already seated in a corner with folded gloves, "was, that as we have let our first floor so well, and as we have now no place in which you could teach pupils, even if pupils——"

"The milkman said he knew of two young ladies of the highest respectability who were in search of a suitable establishment, and he took a card," interposed Mrs. Wilfer, with severe monotony, as if she were reading an Act of Parliament aloud. "Tell your father whether it was last Monday, Bella."

"But we never heard any more of it, ma," said Bella, the elder girl.

"In addition to which, my dear," her husband urged, "if you have no place to put two young persons into——"

"Pardon me," Mrs. Wilfer again interposed; "they were not young persons. Two young ladies of the highest respectability. Tell your father, Bella, whether the milkman said so."

"My dear, it is the same thing."

"No it is not," said Mrs. Wilfer, with the same impressive monotony. "Pardon me!"

"I mean, my dear, it is the same thing as to space. As to space. If you have no space in which to put two youthful fellow-creatures, however eminently respectable, which I do not doubt, where are those youthful fellow-creatures to be accommodated? I carry it no further than that. And solely looking at it," said her husband, making the stipulation at once in a conciliatory, complimentary, and argumentative tone—"as I am sure you will agree, my love—from a fellow-creature point of view, my dear."

"I have nothing more to say," returned Mrs. Wilfer, with a meek renunciatory action of her gloves. "It is as you think, R. W.; not as I do."

Here, the huffing of Miss Bella and the loss of three of her men at a swoop, aggravated by the coronation of an opponent, led to that young lady's jerking the draught-board and pieces off the table, which her sister went down on her knees to pick up.

"Poor Bella!" said Mrs. Wilfer.

"And poor Lavinia, perhaps, my dear?" suggested R. W.

"Pardon me," said Mrs. Wilfer, "no!"

It was one of the worthy woman's specialities that she had an amazing power of gratifying her splenetic or worldly-minded humours by extolling her own family: which she thus proceeded, in the present case, to do.

"No, R. W. Lavinia has not known the trial that Bella has known. The trial that your daughter Bella has undergone, is, perhaps, without a parallel, and has been borne, I will say, Nobly. When you see your daughter Bella in her black dress, which she alone of all the family wears, and when you remember the circumstances which have led to her wearing it, and when you know how those circumstances have been sustained, then, R. W., lay your head upon your pillow and say, 'Poor Lavinia!'"

Here, Miss Lavinia, from her kneeling situation under the table, put in that she didn't want to be "poored by pa," or anybody else.

"I am sure you do not, my dear," returned her mother, "for you have a fine brave spirit. And your sister Cecilia has a fine brave spirit of another kind, a spirit of pure devotion, a beau-ti-ful spirit! The self-sacrifice of Cecilia reveals a pure and womanly character, very seldom equalled, never surpassed. I have now in my pocket a letter from your sister Cecilia, received this morning—received three months after her marriage, poor child!—in which she tells me that her husband must unexpectedly shelter under their roof his reduced aunt. 'But I will be true to him, mamma,' she touchingly writes, 'I will not leave him, I must not forget that he is my husband. Let his aunt come!' If this is not pathetic, if this is not woman's devotion——!" The good lady waved her gloves in a sense of the impossibility of saying more, and tied the pocket-handkerchief over her head in a tighter knot under her chin.

Bella, who was now seated on the rug to warm herself, with her brown eyes on the fire and a handful of her brown curls in her mouth, laughed at this, and then pouted and half cried.

"I am sure," said she, "though you have no feeling for me, pa, I am one of the most unfortunate girls that ever lived. You know how poor we are" (it is probable he did, having some reason to know it!), "and what a glimpse of wealth I had, and how it melted away, and how I am here in this ridiculous mourning—which I hate!—a kind of a widow who never was married. And yet you don't feel for me.—Yes you do, yes you do."

This abrupt change was occasioned by her father's face. She stopped to pull him down from his chair in an attitude highly favourable to strangulation, and to give him a kiss and a pat or two on the cheek.

"But you ought to feel for me, you know, pa."

"My dear, I do."

"Yes, and I say you ought to. If they had only left me alone and told me nothing about it, it would have mattered much less. But that nasty Mr. Lightwood feels it his duty, as he says, to write and tell me what is in reserve for me, and then I am obliged to get rid of George Sampson."

Here Lavinia, rising to the surface with the last draughtman rescued, interposed, "You never cared for George Sampson, Bella."

"And did I say I did, miss?" Then, pouting again, with the curls in her mouth: "George Sampson was very fond of me, and admired me very much, and put up with everything I did to him."

"You were rude enough to him," Lavinia again interposed.

"And did I say I wasn't, miss? I am not setting up to be sentimental about George Sampson. I only say George Sampson was better than nothing."

"You didn't show him that you thought even that," Lavinia again interposed.

"You are a chit and a little idiot," returned Bella, "or you wouldn't make such a dolly speech. What did you expect me to do? Wait till you are a woman, and don't talk about what you don't understand. You only show your ignorance!" Then whimpering again, and at intervals biting the curls, and stopping to look how much was bitten off, "It's a shame! There never was such a hard case! I shouldn't care so much if it wasn't so ridiculous. It was ridiculous enough to have a stranger coming over to marry me, whether he liked it or not. It was ridiculous enough to know what an embarrassing meeting it would be, and how we never could pretend to have an inclination of our own, either of us. It was ridiculous enough to know I shouldn't like him—how *could* I like him, left to him in a will, like a dozen of spoons, with everything cut and dried beforehand, like orange chips. Talk of orange flowers indeed! I declare again it's a shame! Those ridiculous points would have been smoothed away by the money, for I love money, and want money—want it dreadfully. I hate to be poor, and we are degradingly poor, offensively poor, miserably poor, beastly poor. But here I am, left with all the ridiculous parts of the situation remaining, and added to them all, this ridiculous dress! And if the truth was known, when the Harmon murder was all over the town, and people were speculating on its being suicide, I dare say those impudent wretches at the clubs and places made jokes about the miserable creature's having preferred a watery grave to me. It's likely enough they took such liberties; I shouldn't wonder! I declare it's a very hard case indeed, and I am a most unfortunate girl. The idea of being a kind of widow, and never having been married! And the idea of being as poor as ever after all, and going into black, besides, for a man I never saw, and should have hated—as far as *he* was concerned—if I had seen!"

The young lady's lamentations were choked at this point by a knuckle, knocking at the half-open door of the room. The knuckle had knocked two or three times already, but had not been heard.

"Who is it?" said Mrs. Wilfer, in her Act-of-Parliament manner. "Enter!"

A gentleman coming in, Miss Bella, with a short and sharp exclamation, scrambled off the hearth-rug and massed the bitten curls together in their right place on her neck.

"The servant girl had her key in the door as I came up, and directed me to this room, telling me I was expected. I am afraid I should have asked her to announce me."

"Pardon me," returned Mrs. Wilfer. "Not at all. Two of my daughters. R. W., this is the gentleman who has taken your first-floor. He was so good as to make an appointment for to-night, when you would be at home."

A dark gentleman. Thirty at the utmost. An expressive, one might say handsome, face. A very bad manner. In the last degree constrained, reserved, diffident, troubled. His eyes were on Miss Bella for an instant, and then looked at the ground as he addressed the master of the house.

"Seeing that I am quite satisfied, Mr. Wilfer, with the rooms, and with their situation, and with their price, I suppose a memorandum between us of two or three lines, and a payment down, will bind the bargain? I wish to send in furniture without delay."

Two or three times during this short address, the cherub addressed had made chubby motions towards a chair. The gentleman now took it, laying a hesitating hand on a corner of the table, and with another hesitating hand lifting the crown of his hat to his lips, and drawing it before his mouth.

"The gentleman, R. W.," said Mrs. Wilfer, "proposes to take your apartments by the quarter. A quarter's notice on either side."

"Shall I mention, sir," insinuated the landlord, expecting it to be received as a matter of course, "the form of a reference?"

"I think," returned the gentleman, after a pause, "that a reference is not necessary; neither, to say the truth, is it convenient, for I am a stranger in London. I require no reference from you, and perhaps, therefore, you will require none from me. That will be fair on both sides. Indeed, I show the greater confidence of the two, for I will pay in advance whatever you please, and I am going to trust my furniture here. Whereas, if you were in embarrassed circumstances—this is merely supposititious——"

Conscience causing R. Wilfer to colour, Mrs. Wilfer, from a corner (she always got into stately corners) came to the rescue with a deep-toned "Per-fectly."

"—Why then I—might lose it."

"Well!" observed R. Wilfer, cheerfully, "money and goods are certainly the best of references."

"Do you think they *are* the best, pa?" asked Miss Bella, in a low voice, and without looking over her shoulder as she warmed her foot on the fender.

"Among the best, my dear."

"I should have thought, myself, it was so easy to add the usual kind of one," said Bella, with a toss of her curls.

The gentleman listened to her, with a face of marked attention, though he neither looked up nor changed his attitude. He sat, still and silent, until his future landlord accepted his proposals, and brought writing materials to complete the business. He sat, still and silent, while the landlord wrote.

When the agreement was ready in duplicate (the landlord having worked at it like some cherubic scribe, in what is conventionally called a doubtful, which means a not at all doubtful, Old Master), it was signed by the contracting parties, Bella looking on as scornful witness. The contracting parties were R. Wilfer, and John Rokesmith, Esquire.

When it came to Bella's turn to sign her name, Mr. Rokesmith, who was standing, as he had sat, with a hesitating hand upon the table, looked at her stealthily, but narrowly. He looked at the pretty figure bending down over the paper and saying, "Where am I to go, pa? Here, in this corner?" He looked at the beautiful brown hair, shading the coquettish face; he looked at the free dash of the signature, which was a bold one for a woman's; and then they looked at one another.

"Much obliged to you, Miss Wilfer."

"Obliged?"

"I have given you so much trouble."

"Signing my name? Yes, certainly. But I am your landlord's daughter, sir."

As there was nothing more to do but pay eight sovereigns in earnest of the bargain, pocket the agreement, appoint a time for the arrival of his furniture and himself, and go, Mr. Rokesmith did that as awkwardly as it might be done, and was escorted by his landlord to the outer air. When R. Wilfer returned, candlestick in hand, to the bosom of his family, he found the bosom agitated.

"Pa," said Bella, "we have got a Murderer for a tenant."

"Pa," said Lavinia, "we have got a Robber."

"To see him unable for his life to look anybody in the face," said Bella. "There never was such an exhibition."

"My dears," said their father, "he is a diffident gentleman, and I should say particularly so in the society of girls of your age."

"Nonsense, our age!" cried Bella, impatiently. "What's that got to do with him?"

"Besides, we are not of the same age:—which age?" demanded Lavinia.

"Never *you* mind, Lavvy," retorted Bella; "you wait till you are of an age to ask such questions. Pa, mark my words! Between Mr. Rokesmith and me, there is a natural antipathy and a deep distrust; and something will come of it!"

"My dear, and girls," said the cherub-patriarch, "between Mr. Rokesmith and me, there is a matter of eight sovereigns, and something for supper shall come of it, if you'll agree upon the article."

This was a neat and happy turn to give the subject, treats being rare in the Wilfer household, where a monotonous appearance of Dutch-cheese at ten o'clock in the evening had been rather frequently commented on by the dimpled shoulders of Miss Bella. Indeed, the modest Dutchman himself seemed conscious of his want of variety, and generally came before the family in a state of apologetic perspiration. After some discussion on the relative merits of veal-cutlet, sweetbread, and lobster, a decision was pronounced in favour of veal-cutlet. Mrs. Wilfer then solemnly divested herself of her handkerchief and gloves, as a preliminary sacrifice to preparing the frying-pan, and R. W. himself went out to purchase the viand. He soon returned, bearing the same in a fresh cabbage-leaf, where it coyly embraced a rasher of ham. Melodious sounds were not long in rising from the frying-pan on the fire, or in seeming, as the firelight danced in the mellow halls of a couple of full bottles on the table, to play appropriate dance-music.

The cloth was laid by Lavvy. Bella, as the acknowledged ornament of the family, employed both her hands in giving her hair an additional wave while sitting in the easiest chair, and occasionally threw in a direction touching the supper: as, "Very brown, ma;" or, to her sister, "Put the saltcellar straight, miss, and don't be a dowdy little puss."

Meantime her father, chinking Mr. Rokesmith's gold as he sat expectant between his knife and fork, remarked that six of those sovereigns came just in time for their landlord, and stood them in a littte pile on the white tablecloth to look at.

"I hate our landlord!" said Bella.

But observing a fall in her father's face, she went and sat down by him at the table, and began touching up his hair with the handle of a fork. It was one of the girl's spoilt ways to be always arranging the family's hair—perhaps because her own was so pretty, and occupied so much of her attention.

"You deserve to have a house of your own; don't you, poor pa?"

"I don't deserve it better than another, my dear."

"At any rate I, for one, want it more than another," said Bella, holding him by the chin, as she stuck his flaxen hair on end, "and I grudge this money going to the Monster that swallows up so much, when we all want—Everything. And if you say (as you want to say; I know you want to say so, pa) 'that's neither reasonable nor honest, Bella,' then I answer, 'Maybe not, pa—very likely—but it's one of the consequences of being poor, and of thoroughly hating and detesting to be poor, and that's my case.' Now, you look lovely, pa; why don't you always wear your hair like that? And here's the cutlet! If it isn't very brown, ma, I can't eat it, and must have a bit put back to be done expressly."

However, as it was brown, even to Bella's taste, the young lady graciously partook of it without reconsignment to the frying-pan, and also, in due course, of the contents of the two bottles: whereof one held Scotch ale and the other rum. The latter perfume, with the fostering aid of boiling water and lemon-peel, diffused itself throughout the room, and became so highly concentrated around the warm fireside, that the wind passing over the house roof must have rushed off charged with a delicious whiff of it, after buzzing like a great bee at that particular chimney-pot.

"Pa," said Bella, sipping the fragrant mixture and warming her favourite ankle; "when old Mr. Harmon made such a fool of me (not to mention himself as he is dead), what do you suppose he did it for?"

"Impossible to say, my dear. As I have told you times out of number since his will was brought to light, I doubt if I ever exchanged a hundred words with the old gentleman. If it was his whim to surprise us, his whim succeeded. For he certainly did it."

"And I was stamping my foot and screaming, when he first took notice of me; was I?" said Bella, contemplating the ankle before mentioned.

"You were stamping your little foot, my dear, and screaming with your little voice, and laying into me with your little bonnet, which you had snatched off for the purpose," returned her father, as if the remembrance gave a relish to the rum; "you were doing this one Sunday morning when I took you out, because I didn't go the exact way you wanted, when the old gentleman, sitting on a seat near, said, 'That's a nice girl; that's a *very* nice girl; promising girl!' And so you were, my dear."

"And then he asked my name, did he, pa?"

"Then he asked your name, my dear, and mine; and on other Sunday mornings, when we walked his way, we saw him again, and—and really that's all."

As that was all the rum and water, too, or, in other words, as R. W. delicately signified that his glass was empty by throwing back his head and standing the glass upside down on his nose and upper lip, it might have been charitable in Mrs. Wilfer to suggest replenishment. But that heroine briefly suggesting "Bedtime" instead, the bottles were put away, and the family retired; she cherubically escorted, like some severe saint in a painting, or merely human matron allegorically treated.

"And by this time to-morrow," said Lavinia when the two girls were alone in their room, "we shall have Mr. Rokesmith here, and shall be expecting to have our throats cut."

"You needn't stand between me and the candle for all that," retorted Bella. "This is another of the consequences of being poor! The idea of a girl with a really fine head of hair, having to do it by one flat candle and a few inches of looking-glass!"

"You caught George Sampson with it, Bella, bad as your means of dressing it are."

"You low little thing. Caught George Sampson with it! Don't talk about catching people, miss, till your own time for catching—as you call it—comes."

"Perhaps it has come," muttered Lavvy, with a toss of her head.

"What did you say?" asked Bella, very sharply. "What did you say, miss?"

Lavvy declining equally to repeat or to explain, Bella gradually lapsed over her hair-dressing into a soliloquy on the miseries of being poor, as exemplified in having nothing to put on, nothing to go out in, nothing to dress by, only a nasty box to dress at instead of a commodious dressing-table, and being obliged to take in suspicious lodgers. On the last grievance as her climax she laid great stress—and might have laid greater, had she known that if Mr. Julius Handford had a twin brother upon earth, Mr. John Rokesmith was the man.

CHAPTER V.

BOFFIN'S BOWER.

OVER against a London house, a corner house not far from Cavendish Square, a man with a wooden leg had sat for some years, with his remaining foot in a basket in cold weather, picking up a living on this wise:—Every morning at eight o'clock, he stumped to the corner, carrying a chair, a clothes-horse, a pair of trestles, a board, a basket, and an umbrella, all strapped together. Separating these, the board and trestles became a counter, the basket supplied the few small lots of fruit and sweets that he offered for sale upon it and became a foot-warmer, the unfolded clothes-horse displayed a choice collection of halfpenny ballads and became a screen, and the stool planted within it became his post for the rest of the day. All weathers saw the man at the post. This is to be accepted in a double sense, for he contrived a back to his wooden stool by placing it against the lamp-post. When the weather was wet, he put up his umbrella over his stock-in trade, not over himself; when the weather was dry, he furled that faded article, tied it round with a piece of yarn, and laid it cross-wise under the trestles: where it looked like an unwholesomely-forced lettuce that had lost in colour and crispness what it had gained in size.

He had established his right to the corner by imperceptible prescription. He had never varied his ground an inch, but had in the beginning diffidently taken the corner upon which the side of the house gave. A howling corner in the winter time, a dusty corner in the summer time, an undesirable corner at the best of times. Shelterless fragments of straw and paper got up revolving storms there, when the main street was at peace; and the water-cart, as if it were drunk or short-sighted, came blundering and jolting round it, making it muddy when all else was clean.

On the front of his sale-board hung a little placard, like a kettle-holder, bearing the inscription in his own small text:

Errands gone
On with fi
Delity By
Ladies and Gentlemen
I remain
Your humble Serv t.
Silas Wegg.

He had not only settled it with himself in the course of time, that he was errand-goer by appointment to the house at the corner (though he received such commissions not half-a-dozen times in a year, and then only as some servant's deputy), but also that he was one of the house's retainers and owed vassalage to it and was bound to leal and loyal interest in it. For this reason, he always spoke of it as "Our House," and, though his knowledge of its affairs was mostly speculative and all wrong, claimed to be in its confidence. On similar grounds he never beheld an inmate at any one of its windows but he touched his hat. Yet, he knew so little about the inmates that he gave them names of his own invention: as "Miss Elizabeth," "Master George," "Aunt Jane," "Uncle Parker"—having no authority whatever for any such designations, but particularly the last—to which, as a natural consequence, he stuck with great obstinacy.

Over the house itself, he exercised the same imaginary power as over its inhabitants and their affairs. He had never been in it, the length of a piece of fat black water-pipe which trailed itself over the area door into a damp stone passage, and had rather the air of a leech on the house that had "taken" wonderfully; but this was no impediment to his arranging it according to a plan of his own. It was a great dingy house with a quantity of dim side window and blank back premises, and it cost his mind a world of trouble so to lay it out as to account for everything in its external appearance. But, this once done, was quite satisfactory, and he rested persuaded that he knew his way about the house blindfold: from the barred garrets in the high roof, to the two iron extinguishers before the main door—which seemed to request all lively visitors to have the kindness to put themselves out, before entering.

Assuredly, this stall of Silas Wegg's was the hardest little stall of all the sterile little stalls in London. It gave you the face-ache to look at his apples, the stomach-ache to look at his oranges, the tooth-ache to look at his nuts. Of the latter commodity he had always a grim little heap, on which lay a little wooden measure which had no discernible inside, and was considered to represent the penn'orth appointed by Magna Charta. Whether from too much east wind or no—it was an easterly corner—the stall, the stock, and the keeper, were all as dry as the Desert. Wegg was a knotty man, and a close-grained, with a face carved out of very hard material, that had just as much play of expression as a watchman's rattle. When he laughed, certain jerks occurred in it, and the rattle sprung. Sooth to say, he was so wooden a man that he seemed to have taken his wooden leg naturally, and rather suggested to the fanciful observer, that he might be expected—if his development received no untimely check—to be completely set up with a pair of wooden legs in about six months.

Mr. Wegg was an observant person, or, as he himself said, "took a powerful sight of notice." He saluted all his regular passers-by every day, as he sat on his stool backed-up by the lamp-post; and on the adaptable character of these salutes he greatly plumed himself. Thus, to the rector, he addressed a bow, compounded of lay deference, and a slight touch of the shady preliminary meditation at church; to the doctor, a confidential bow, as to a gentleman whose acquaintance with his inside he begged respectfully to acknowledge; before the quality he delighted to abase himself; and for Uncle Parker, who was in the army (at least, so he had settled it), he put his open hand to the side of his hat, in a military manner which that angry-eyed buttoned-up inflammatory-faced old gentleman appeared but imperfectly to appreciate.

The only article in which Silas dealt, that was not hard, was gingerbread. On a certain day, some wretched infant having purchased the damp gingerbread-horse (fearfully out of condition), and the adhesive bird-cage, which had been exposed for the day's sale, he had taken a tin box from under his stool to produce a relay of those dreadful specimens, and was going to look in at the lid, when he said to himself, pausing: "Oh! Here you are again!"

The words referred to a broad, round-shouldered, one-sided old fellow in mourning, coming comically ambling towards the corner, dressed in a pea over coat, and carrying a large stick. He wore thick shoes, and thick leather gaiters, and thick gloves like a hedger's. Both as to his dress and to himself, he was of an overlapping rhinoceros build, with folds in his cheeks, and his forehead, and his eyelids, and his lips, and his ears; but with bright, eager, childishly-inquiring grey eyes, under his ragged eyebrows, and broad-brimmed hat. A very odd-looking old fellow altogether.

"Here you are again," repeated Mr. Wegg, musing. "And what are you now? Are you in the Funns, or where are you? Have you lately come to settle in this neighbourhood, or do you own to another neighbourhood? Are you in independent circumstances, or is it wasting the motions of a bow on you? Come! I'll speculate! I'll invest a bow in you."

Which Mr. Wegg, having replaced his tin box, accordingly did, as he rose to bait his gingerbread-trap for some other devoted infant. The salute was acknowledged with:

"Morning, sir! Morning! Morning!"

("Calls me Sir!" said Mr. Wegg to himself. "*He* won't answer. A bow gone!")

"Morning, morning, morning!"

"Appears to be rather a 'arty old cock, too," said Mr. Wegg, as before. "Good morning to *you*, sir."

"Do you remember me, then?" asked his new acquaintance, stopping in his amble, one-sided, before the stall, and speaking in a pouncing way, though with great good-humour.

"I have noticed you go past our house, sir, several times in the course of the last week or so."

"Our house," repeated the other. "Meaning——?"

"Yes," said Mr. Wegg, nodding, as the other pointed the clumsy forefinger of his right glove at the corner house.

"Oh! Now, what," pursued the old fellow, in an inquisitive manner, carrying his knotted stick in his left arm as if it were a baby, "what do they allow you now?"

"It's job work that I do for our house," returned Silas, drily, and with reticence; "it's not yet brought to an exact allowance."

"Oh! It's not yet brought to an exact allowance? No! It's not yet brought to an exact allowance. Oh!—Morn ng, morning, morning!"

"Appears to be rather a cracked old cock," thought Silas, qualifying his former good opinion, as the other ambled off. But, in a moment he was back again with the question:

"How did you get your wooden leg?"

Mr. Wegg replied (tartly to this personal inquiry), "In an accident."

"Do you like it?"

"Well! I haven't got to keep it warm," Mr. Wegg made answer, in a sort of desperation occasioned by the singularity of the question.

"He hasn't," repeated the other to his knotted stick, as he gave it a hug; "he hasn't got—ha!—ha!—to keep it warm! Did you ever hear of the name of Boffin?"

"No," said Mr. Wegg, who was growing restive under this examination. "I never did hear of the name of Boffin."

"Do you like it?"

"Why, no," retorted Mr. Wegg, again approaching desperation; "I can't say I do."

"Why don't you like it?"

"I don't know why I don't," retorted Mr. Wegg, approaching frenzy, "but I don't at all."

"Now, I'll tell you something that'll make you sorry for that," said the stranger, smiling. "My name's Boffin."

"I can't help it!" returned Mr. Wegg. Implying in his manner the offensive addition, "and if I could, I wouldn't."

"But there's another chance for you," said Mr. Boffin, smiling still. "Do you like the name of Nicodemus? Think it over. Nick, or Noddy."

"It is not, sir," Mr. Wegg rejoined, as he sat down on his stool, with an air of gentle resignation, combined with melancholy candour; "it is not a name as I could wish any one that I had a respect for, to call *me* by; but there may be persons that would not view it with the same objections.—I don't know why," Mr. Wegg added, anticipating another question.

"Noddy Boffin," said that gentleman. "Noddy. That's my name. Noddy—or Nick—Boffin. What's your name?"

"Silas Wegg.—I don't," said Mr. Wegg, bestirring himself to take the same precaution as before, "I don't know why Silas, and I don't know why Wegg."

"Now, Wegg," said Mr. Boffin, hugging his stick closer, "I want to make a sort of offer to you. Do you remember when you first see me?"

The wooden leg looked at him with a meditative eye, and also with a softened air as descrying possibility of profit. "Let me think. I ain't quite sure, and yet I generally take a powerful sight of notice, too. Was it on a Monday morning, when the butcher-boy had been to our house for orders, and bought a ballad of me, which, being unacquainted with the tune, I run it over to him?"

"Right, Wegg, right! But he bought more than one."

"Yes, to be sure, sir; he bought several; and wishing to lay out his money to the best, he took my opinion to guide his choice, and we went over the collection together. To be sure we did. Here was him as it might be, and here was myself as it might be, and there was you, Mr. Boffin, as you identically are, with your self-same stick under your very same arm, and your very same back towards us. To—be—sure!" added Mr. Wegg, looking a little round Mr. Boffin, to take him in the rear, and identify this last extraordinary coincidence, "your wery self-same back!"

"What do you think I was doing, Wegg?"

"I should judge, sir, that you might be glancing your eye down the street."

"No Wegg. I was a listening."

"Was you, indeed?" said Mr. Wegg, dubiously.

"Not in a dishonourable way, Wegg, because you was singing to the butcher; and you wouldn't sing secrets to a butcher in the street, you know."

"It never happened that I did so yet, to the best of my remembrance," said Mr. Wegg, cautiously. "But I might do it. A man can't say what he might wish to do some day or another." (This, not to release any little advantage he might derive from Mr. Boffin's avowal.)

"Well," repeated Boffin, "I was a listening to you and to him. And what do you—you haven't got another stool have you? I'm rather thick in my breath."

"I haven't got another, but you're welcome to this," said Wegg, resigning it. "It's a treat to me to stand."

"Lard!" exclaimed Mr. Boffin, in a tone of great enjoyment, as he settled himself down, still nursing his stick like a baby, "it's a pleasant place, this! And then to be shut in on each side, with these ballads, like so many book-leaf blinkers! Why, it's delightful!"

"If I am not mistaken, sir," Mr. Wegg delicately hinted, resting a hand on his stall, and bending over the discursive Boffin, "you alluded to some offer or another that was in your mind?"

"I'm coming to it! All right. I'm coming to it! I was going to say that when I listened that morning, I listened with hadmiration amounting to haw. I thought to myself, 'Here's a man with a wooden leg—a literary man with——'"

"N—not exactly so, sir," said Mr. Wegg.

"Why, you know every one of these songs by name and by tune, and if you want to read or to sing any one on 'em off straight, you've only to whip on your spectacles and do it!" cried Mr. Boffin. "I see you at it!"

"Well, sir," returned Mr. Wegg, with a conscious inclination of the head; "we'll say literary, then."

"'A literary man—*with* a wooden leg—and all Print is open to him!' That's what I thought to myself, that morning," pursued Mr. Boffin, leaning forward to describe, uncramped by the clothes-horse, as large an arc as his right arm could make; "'all Print is open to him!' And it is, ain't it?"

"Why, truly, sir," Mr. Wegg admitted with modesty; "I believe you couldn't show me the piece of English print, that I wouldn't be equal to collaring and throwing."

"On the spot?" said Mr. Boffin.

"On the spot."

"I know'd it! Then consider this. Here am I, a man without a wooden leg, and yet all print is shut to me."

"Indeed, sir?" Mr. Wegg returned with increasing self-complacency. "Education neglected?"

"Neg—lected!" repeated Boffin, with emphasis. "That ain't no word for it. I don't mean to say but what if you showed me a B, I could so far give you change for it, as to answer Boffin."

"Come, come, sir," said Mr. Wegg, throwing in a little encouragement, "that's something, too."

"It's something," answered Mr. Boffin, "but I'll take my oath it ain't much."

"Perhaps it's not as much as could be wished by an inquiring mind, sir," Mr. Wegg admitted.

"Now, look here. I'm retired from business. Me and Mrs. Boffin—Henerietty Boffin—which her father's name was Henery, and her mother's name was Hetty, and so you get it—we live on a compittance, under the will of a diseased governor."

"Gentleman dead, sir?"

"Man alive, don't I tell you? A diseased governor? Now, it's too late for me to begin shovelling and sifting at alphabeds and grammar-books. I'm getting to be a old bird, and I want to take it easy. But I want some reading—some fine bold reading, some splendid book in a gorging Lord-Mayor's-Show of wollumes" (probably meaning gorgeous, but misled by association of ideas); "as'll reach right down your pint of view, and take time to go by you. How can I get that reading, Wegg? By," tapping him on the breast with the head of his thick stick, "paying a man truly qualified to do it, so much an hour (say twopence) to come and do it."

"Hem! Flattered, sir, I am sure," said Wegg, beginning to regard himself in quite a new light. "Hem! This is the offer you mentioned, sir?"

"Yes. Do you like it?"

"I am considering of it, Mr. Boffin."

"I don't," said Boffin, in a free-handed manner, "want to tie a literary man—*with* a wooden leg—down too tight. A halfpenny an hour shan't part us. The hours are your own to choose, after you've done for the day with your house here.

I live over Maiden Lane way—out Holloway direction—and you've only got to go East-and-by-North when you've finished here, and you're there. Twopence half-penny an hour," said Boffin, taking a piece of chalk from his pocket and getting off the stool to work the sum on the top of it in his own way; "two long'uns and a short'un—twopence half-penny; two short'uns is a long'un, and two two long'uns is four long'uns—making five long'uns; six nights a week at five long'uns a night," scoring them all down separately, "and you mount up to thirty long'uns. A round'un! Half-a-crown!"

Pointing to this result as a large and satisfactory one, Mr. Boffin smeared it out with his moistened glove, and sat down on the remains.

"Half a crown," said Wegg, meditating. "Yes. (It ain't much, sir.) Half a crown."

"Per week, you know."

"Per week. Yes. As to the amount of strain upon the intellect now. Was you thinking at all of poetry?" Mr. Wegg inquired, musing.

"Would it come dearer?" Mr. Boffin asked.

"It would come dearer," Mr. Wegg returned. "For when a person comes to grind off poetry night after night, it is but right he should expect to be paid for its weakening effect on his mind."

"To tell you the truth, Wegg," said Boffin, "I wasn't thinking of poetry, except in so fur as this:—If you was to happen now and then to feel yourself in the mind to tip me and Mrs. Boffin one of your ballads, why then we should drop into poetry."

"I follow you, sir," said Wegg. "But not being a regular musical professional, I should be loath to engage myself for that; and therefore when I dropped into poetry, I should ask to be considered in the light of a friend."

At this, Mr. Boffin's eyes sparkled, and he shook Silas earnestly by the hand: protesting that it was more than he could have asked, and that he took it very kindly indeed.

"What do you think of the terms, Wegg?" Mr. Boffin then demanded, with unconcealed anxiety.

Silas, who had stimulated this anxiety by his hard reserve of manner, and who had begun to understand his man very well, replied with an air; as if he were saying something extraordinarily generous and great:

"Mr. Boffin, I never bargain."

"So I should have thought of you!" said Mr. Boffin, admiringly.

"No, sir. I never did 'aggle and I never will 'aggle. Consequently I meet you at once, free and fair, with—Done, for double the money!"

Mr. Boffin seemed a little unprepared for this conclusion, but assented, with the remark, "You know better what it ought to be than I do, Wegg," and again shook hands with him upon it.

"Could you begin to-night, Wegg?" he then demanded.

"Yes, sir," said Mr. Wegg, careful to leave all the eagerness to him. "I see no difficulty if you wish it. You are provided with the needful implement—a book, sir?"

"Bought him at a sale," said Mr. Boffin. "Eight wollumes. Red and gold. Purple ribbon in every wollume, to keep the place where you leave off. Do you know him?"

"The book's name, sir?" inquired Silas.

"I thought you might have know'd him without it," said Mr. Boffin, slightly disappointed. "His name is Decline-and-Fall-Off-The-Rooshan-Empire." (Mr. Boffin went over these stones slowly and with much caution.)

"Ay indeed!" said Mr. Wegg, nodding his head with an air of friendly recognition.

"You know him, Wegg?"

"I haven't been not to say right slap through him, very lately," Mr. Wegg made answer, "having been otherways employed, Mr. Boffin. But know him? Old familiar declining and falling off the Rooshan? Rather, sir! Ever since I was not so high as your stick. Ever since my eldest brother left our cottage to enlist into the army. On which occasion, as the ballad that was made about it describes:

> "Beside that cottage door, Mr. Boffin,
> A girl was on her knees;
> She held aloft a snowy scarf, Sir,
> Which (my eldest brother noticed) fluttered in the breeze.
> She breathed a prayer for him, Mr. Boffin;
> A prayer he could not hear.
> And my eldest brother lean'd upon his sword, Mr. Boffin,
> And wiped away a tear."

Much impressed by this family circumstance, and also by the friendly disposition of Mr. Wegg, as exemplified in his so soon dropping into poetry, Mr. Boffin again shook hands with that ligneous sharper, and besought him to name his hour. Mr. Wegg named eight.

"Where I live," said Mr. Boffin, "is called The Bower. Boffin's Bower is the name Mrs. Boffin christened it when we come into it as a property. If you should meet with anybody that don't know it by that name (which hardly anybody does), when you've got nigh upon about a odd mile, or say and a quarter if you like, up Maiden Lane, Battle Bridge, ask for Harmony Jail, and you'll be put right. I shall expect you, Wegg," said Mr. Boffin, clapping him on the shoulder with the greatest enthusiasm, "most jyfully. I shall have no peace or patience till you come. Print is now opening ahead of me. This night, a literary man—*with a* wooden leg—" he bestowed an admiring look upon that decoration, as if it greatly enhanced the relish of Mr. Wegg's attainments—"will begin to lead me a new life! My fist again, Wegg. Morning, morning, morning!"

Left alone at his stall as the other ambled off, Mr. Wegg subsided into his screen, produced a small pocket-handkerchief of a penitentially-scrubbing character, and took himself by the nose with a thoughtful aspect. Also, while he still grasped that feature, he directed several thoughtful looks down the street, after the retiring figure of Mr. Boffin. But, profound gravity sat enthroned on Wegg's countenance. For, while he considered within himself that this was an old fellow of rare simplicity, that this was an opportunity to be improved, and that here might be money to be got beyond present calculation, still he compromised himself by no admission that his new engagement was at all out of his way, or involved the least element of the ridiculous. Mr. Wegg would even have picked a handsome quarrel with any one who should have challenged his deep acquaintance with those aforesaid eight volumes of Decline and Fall. His gravity was unusual, portentous, and immeasurable, not because he admitted any doubt of himself, but because he perceived it necessary to forestall any doubt of himself in others. And herein he ranged with that very numerous class of impostors, who are quite as determined to keep up appearances to themselves, as to their neighbours.

A certain loftiness, likewise, took possession of Mr. Wegg; a condescending sense of being in request as an official expounder of mysteries. It did not move him to commercial greatness, but rather to littleness, insomuch that if it had been within the possibilities of things for the wooden measure to hold fewer nuts than usual, it would have done so that day. But, when night came, and with her veiled eyes beheld him stumping towards Boffin's Bower, he was elated too.

The Bower was as difficult to find, as Fair Rosamond's without the clue. Mr

Wegg, having reached the quarter indicated, inquired for the Bower half-a-dozen times without the least success, until he remembered to ask for Harmony Jail. This occasioned a quick change in the spirits of a hoarse gentleman and a donkey, whom he had much perplexed.

"Why, yer mean Old Harmon's, do yer?" said the hoarse gentleman, who was driving his donkey in a truck, with a carrot for a whip. "Why didn't yer niver say so? Eddard and me is a goin' by *him!* Jump in."

Mr Wegg complied, and the hoarse gentleman invited his attention to the third person in company, thus;

"Now, you look at Eddard's ears. What was it as you named, agin? Whisper."

Mr. Wegg whispered, "Boffin's Bower."

"Eddard! (keep yer hi on his ears) cut away to Boffin's Bower!" Edward, with his ears lying back, remained immovable.

"Eddard! (keep yer hi on his ears) cut away to Old Harmon's."

Edward instantly pricked up his ears to their utmost, and rattled off at such a pace that Mr. Wegg's conversation was jolted out of him in a most dislocated state.

"Was-it-Ev-verajail?" asked Mr. Wegg, holding on.

"Not a proper jail, wot you and me would get committed to," returned his escort; "they giv' it the name, on accounts of Old Harmon living solitary there."

"And-why-did-they-callitharm-Ony?" asked Wegg.

"On accounts of his never agreeing with nobody. Like a speeches of chaff. Harmon's Jail; Harmony Jail. Working it round like."

"Do you know-Mist-Erboff-in?" asked Wegg.

"I should think so! Everybody do about here. Eddard knows him (Keep yer hi on his ears.) Noddy Boffin, Eddard!"

The effect of the name was so very alarming, in respect of causing a temporary disappearance of Edward's head, casting his hind hoofs in the air, greatly accelerating the pace and increasing the jolting, that Mr. Wegg was fain to devote his attention exclusively to holding on, and to relinquish his desire of ascertaining whether this homage to Boffin was to be considered complimentary or the reverse.

Presently, Edward stopped at a gateway, and Wegg discreetly lost no time in slipping out at the back of the truck. The moment he was landed, his late driver with a wave of the carrot, said "Supper, Eddard!" and he, the hind hoofs, the truck, and Edward, all seemed to fly into the air together, in a kind of apotheosis.

Pushing the gate, which stood ajar, Wegg looked into an enclosed space where certain tall dark mounds rose high against the sky, and where the pathway to the Bower was indicated, as the moonlight showed, between two lines of broken crockery set in ashes. A white figure advancing along this path, proved to be nothing more ghostly than Mr. Boffin, easily attired for the pursuit of knowledge, in an undress garment of short white smock-frock. Having received his literary friend with great cordiality, he conducted him to the interior of the Bower and there presented him to Mrs. Boffin:—a stout lady of a rubicund and cheerful aspect, dressed (to Mr. Wegg's consternation) in a low evening dress of sable satin, and a large black velvet hat and feathers.

"Mrs. Boffin, Wegg," said Boffin, "is a highflyer at Fashion. And her make is such, that she does it credit. As to myself, I ain't yet as Fash'nable as I may come to be. Henerietty, old lady, this is the gentleman that's a going to decline and fall off the Rooshan Empire."

"And I am sure I hope it'll do you both good," said Mrs. Boffin.

It was the queerest of rooms, fitted and furnished more like a luxurious amateur tap-room than anything else within the ken of Silas Wegg. There were two wooden settles by the fire, one on either side of it, with a corresponding table before each. On one of these tables, the eight volumes were ranged flat, in a row, like a galvanic battery; on the other, certain squat case-bottles of inviting appearance seemed to stand on tiptoe to exchange glances with Mr. Wegg over a front row of tumblers and a basin of white sugar. On the hob, a kettle steamed; on the hearth, a cat reposed. Facing the fire between the settles, a sofa, a footstool, and a little table formed a centrepiece devoted to Mrs. Boffin. They were garish in taste and colour, but were expensive articles of drawing-room furniture that had a very odd look beside the settles and the flaring gaslight pendent from the ceiling. There was a flowery carpet on the floor; but, instead of reaching to the fireside, its glowing vegetation stopped short at Mrs. Boffin's footstool, and gave place to a region of sand and sawdust. Mr. Wegg also noticed, with admiring eyes, that, while the flowery land displayed such hollow ornamentation as stuffed birds and waxen fruits under glass shades, there were, in the territory where vegetation ceased, compensatory shelves on which the best part of a large pie and likewise of a cold joint were plainly discernible among other solids. The room itself was large, though low; and the heavy frames of its old-fashioned windows, and the heavy beams in its crooked ceiling, seemed to indicate that it had once been a house of some mark standing alone in the country.

"Do you like it, Wegg?" asked Mr. Boffin, in his pouncing manner.

"I admire it greatly, sir," said Wegg. "Peculiar comfort at this fireside, sir."

"Do you understand it, Wegg?"

"Why, in a general way, sir," Mr. Wegg was beginning slowly and knowingly, with his head stuck on one side, as evasive people do begin, when the other cut him short:

"You *don't* understand it, Wegg, and I'll explain it. These arrangements is made by mutual consent between Mrs. Boffin and me. Mrs. Boffin, as I've mentioned, is a highflyer at Fashion; at present I'm not. I don't go higher than comfort, and comfort of the sort that I'm equal to the enjoyment of. Well then. Where would be the good of Mrs. Boffin and me quarrelling over it? We never did quarrel, before we come into Boffin's Bower as a property; why quarrel when we *have* come into Boffin's Bower as a property? So Mrs. Boffin, she keeps up her part of the room, in her way; I keep up my part of the room in mine. In consequence of which we have at once, Sociability (I should go melancholy mad without Mrs. Boffin), Fashion, and Comfort. If I get by degrees to be a highflyer at Fashion, then Mrs. Boffin will by degrees come for'arder. If Mrs. Boffin should ever be less of a dab at Fashion than she is at the present time, then Mrs. Boffin's carpet would go back'arder. If we should both continny as we are, why then *here* we are, and give us a kiss, old lady."

Mrs. Boffin, who, perpetually smiling, had approached and drawn her plump arm through her lord's, most willingly complied. Fashion, in the form of her black velvet hat and feathers, tried to prevent it; but got deservedly crushed in the endeavour.

"So now, Wegg," said Mr. Boffin, wiping his mouth with an air of much refreshment, "you begin to know us as we are. This is a charming spot, is the Bower, but you must get to appreciate it by degrees. It's a spot to find out the merits of, little by little, and a new 'un every day. There's a serpentining walk up each of the mounds, that gives you the yard and neighbourhood changing every moment. When you get to the top, there's a view of the neighbouring premises, not to be surpassed. The premises of Mrs. Boffin's late father (Canine Provision Trade), you look down into, as if they was your own. And the top of the High Mound is crowned with a lattice-work Arbour, in which, if you don't read out loud

MR. AND MRS. BOFFIN.

many a book in the summer, ay, and as a friend, drop many a time into poetry too, it shan't be my fault. Now, what'll you read on?"

"Thank you, sir," returned Wegg, as if there were nothing new in his reading at all. "I generally do it on gin and water."

"Keeps the organ moist, does it, Wegg?" asked Mr. Boffin with innocent eagerness.

"N-no, sir," replied Wegg, coolly, "I should hardly describe it so, sir. I should say, mellers it. Mellers it, is the word I should employ, Mr. Boffin."

His wooden conceit and craft kept exact pace with the delighted expectation of his victim. The visions rising before his mercenary mind, of the many ways in which this connection was to be turned to account, never obscured the foremost idea natural to a dull overreaching man, that he must not make himself too cheap.

Mrs. Boffin's Fashion, as a less inexorable deity than the idol usually worshipped under that name, did not forbid her mixing for her literary guest, or asking if he found the result to his liking. On his returning a gracious answer and taking his place at the literary settle, Mr. Boffin began to compose himself as a listener, at the opposite settle, with exultant eyes.

"Sorry to deprive you of a pipe, Wegg," he said, filling his own, "but you can't do both together. Oh! and another thing I forgot to name! When you come in here of an evening, and look round you, and notice anything on a shelf that happens to catch your fancy, mention it."

Wegg, who had been going to put on his spectacles, immediately laid them down, with the sprightly observation:

"You read my thoughts, sir. *Do* my eyes deceive me, or is that object up there a—a pie? It can't be a pie."

"Yes, it's a pie, Wegg," replied Mr. Boffin, with a glance of some little discomfiture at the Decline and Fall.

"*Have* I lost my smell for fruits, or is it a apple pie, sir?" asked Wegg.

"It's a veal and ham pie," said Mr. Boffin.

"Is it, indeed, sir? And it would be hard, sir, to name the pie that is a better pie than a weal and hammer," said Mr. Wegg, nodding his head emotionally.

"Have some, Wegg?"

"Thank you, Mr. Boffin, I think I will, at your invitation. I wouldn't at any other party's, at the present juncture; but at yours, sir!—And meaty jelly too, especially when a little salt, which is the case where there's ham, is mellering to the organ, is very mellering to the organ." Mr. Wegg did not say what organ, but spoke with a cheerful generality.

So the pie was brought down, and the worthy Mr. Boffin exercised his patience until Wegg, in the exercise of his knife and fork, had finished the dish: only profiting by the opportunity to inform Wegg that although it was not strictly Fashionable to keep the contents of a larder thus exposed to view, he (Mr. Boffin) considered it hospitable: for the reason, that instead of saying, in a comparatively unmeaning manner, to a visitor, "There are such and such edibles down-stairs; will you have anything up?" you took the bold practical course of saying, "Cast your eye along the shelves, and, if you see anything you like there, have it down."

And now, Mr. Wegg at length pushed away his plate and put on his spectacles, and Mr. Boffin lighted his pipe and looked with beaming eyes into the opening world before him, and Mrs. Boffin reclined in a fashionable manner on her sofa: as one who would be part of the audience if she found she could, and would go to sleep if she found she couldn't.

"Hem!" began Wegg. "This, Mr. Boffin and Lady, is the first chapter of the first wollume of the Decline and Fall off——" here he looked hard at the book, and stopped.

"What's the matter, Wegg?"

"Why, it comes into my mind, do you know, sir," said Wegg with an air of insinuating frankness (having first again looked hard at the book), "that you made a little mistake this morning, which I had meant to set you right in, only something put it out of my head. I think you said Rooshan Empire, sir?"

"It is Rooshan; ain't it, Wegg?"

"No, sir. Roman. Roman."

"What's the difference, Wegg?"

"The difference, sir?" Mr. Wegg was faltering and in danger of breaking down, when a bright thought flashed upon him. "The difference, sir? There you place me in a difficulty, Mr. Boffin. Suffice it to observe, that the difference is best postponed to some other occasion when Mrs. Boffin does not honour us with her company. In Mrs. Boffin's presence, sir, we had better drop it."

Mr. Wegg thus came out of his disadvantage with quite a chivalrous air, and not only that, but by dint of repeating with a manly delicacy, "In Mrs. Boffin's presence, sir, we had better drop it!" turned the disadvantage on Boffin, who felt that he had committed himself in a very painful manner.

Then, Mr. Wegg, in a dry unflinching way, entered on his task; going straight across country at everything that came before him; taking all the hard words, biographical and geographical; getting rather shaken by Hadrian, Trajan, and the Antonines; stumbling at Polybius (pronounced Polly Beeious, and supposed by Mr. Boffin to be a Roman virgin, and by Mrs. Boffin to be responsible for that necessity of dropping it); heavily unseated by Titus Antoninus Pius; up again and galloping smoothly with Augustus; finally, getting over the ground well with Commodus; who, under the appellation of Commodious, was held by Mr. Boffin to have been quite unworthy of his English origin, and "not to have acted up to his name" in his government of the Roman people. With the death of this personage, Mr. Wegg terminated his first reading; long before which consummation several total eclipses of Mrs. Boffin's candle behind her black velvet disc, would have been very alarming, but for being regularly accompanied by a potent smell of burnt pens when her feathers took fire, which acted as a restorative and woke her. Mr. Wegg having read on by rote and attached as few ideas as possible to the text, came out of the encounter fresh; but, Mr. Boffin, who had soon laid down his unfinished pipe, and had ever since sat intently staring with his eyes and mind at the confounding enormities of the Romans, was so severely punished that he could hardly wish his literary friend Good-night, and articulate "To-morrow."

"Commodious," gasped Mr. Boffin, staring at the moon, after letting Wegg out of the gate and fastening it: "Commodious fights in that wild-beast-show, seven hundred and thirty five times, in one character only! As if that wasn't stunning enough, a hundred lions is turned into the same wild-beast-show all at once! As if that wasn't stunning enough, Commodious, in another character, kills 'em all off in a hundred goes! As if that wasn't stunning enough, Vittle-us (and well named too) eats six millions' worth, English money, in seven months! Wegg takes it easy, but upon-my-soul to a old bird like myself these are scarers. And even now that Commodious is strangled, I don't see a way to our bettering ourselves." Mr. Boffin added as he turned his pensive steps towards the Bower and shook his head, "I didn't think this morning there was half so many Scarers in Print. But I'm in for it now!"

CHAPTER VI.

CUT ADRIFT.

THE Six Jolly Fellowship-Porters, already mentioned as a tavern of a dropsical appearance, had long settled down into a state of hale infirmity. In its whole constitution it had not a straight floor, and hardly a straight line; but it had outlasted, and clearly would yet outlast, many a better-trimmed building, many a sprucer public-house. Externally, it was a narrow lopsided wooden jumble of corpulent windows heaped one upon another as you might heap as many toppling oranges, with a crazy wooden verandah impending over the water; indeed the whole house, inclusive of the complaining flag-staff on the roof, impended over the water, but seemed to have got into the condition of a faint-hearted diver who has paused so long on the brink that he will never go in at all.

This description applies to the river-frontage of the Six Jolly Fellowship-Porters. The back of the establishment, though the chief entrance was there, so contracted, that it merely represented in its connection with the front, the handle of a flat-iron set upright on its broadest end. This handle stood at the bottom of a wilderness of court and alley: which wilderness pressed so hard and close upon the Six Jolly Fellowship-Porters as to leave the hostelry not an inch of ground beyond its door. For this reason, in combination with the fact that the house was all but afloat at high water, when the Porters had a family wash the linen subjected to that operation might usually be seen drying on lines stretched across the reception-rooms and bed-chambers.

The wood forming the chimney-pieces, beams, partitions, floors, and doors, of the Six Jolly Fellowship-Porters, seemed in its old age fraught with confused memories of its youth. In many places it had become gnarled and riven, according to the manner of old trees; knots started out of it; and here and there it seemed to twist itself into some likeness of boughs. In this state of second childhood, it had an air of being in its own way garrulous about its early life. Not without reason was it often asserted by the regular frequenters of the Porters, that when the light shone full upon the grain of certain panels, and particularly upon an old corner cupboard of walnut-wood in the bar, you might trace little forests there, and tiny trees like the parent tree, in full umbrageous leaf.

The bar of the Six Jolly Fellowship-Porters was a bar to soften the human breast. The available space in it was not much larger than a hackney-coach; but no one could have wished the bar bigger, that space was so girt in by corpulent little casks, and by cordial-bottles radiant with fictitious grapes in bunches, and by lemons in nets, and by biscuits in baskets, and by the polite beer-pulls that made low bows when customers were served with beer, and by the cheese in a snug corner, and by the landlady's own small table in a snugger corner near the fire, with the cloth everlastingly laid. This haven was divided from the rough world by a glass partition and a half-door with a leaden sill upon it for the convenience of resting your liquor; but, over this half-door the bar's snugness so gushed forth, that, albeit customers drank there standing, in a dark and draughty passage where they were shouldered by other customers passing in and out, they always appeared to drink under an enchanting delusion that they were in the bar itself.

For the rest, both the tap and parlour of the Six Jolly Fellowship-Porters gave upon the river, and had red curtains matching the noses of the regular customers, and were provided with comfortable fireside tin utensils, like models of sugar-loaf hats, made in that shape that they might, with their pointed ends, seek out for themselves glowing nooks in the depths of the red coals, when they mulled your ale, or heated for you those delectable drinks, Purl, Flip, and Dog's Nose. The first of these humming compounds was a speciality of the Porters, which, through an inscription on its door-posts, gently appealed to your feelings as, "The Early Purl House." For, it would seem that Purl must always be taken early; though whether for any more distinctly stomachic reason than that, as the early bird catches the worm, so the early purl catches the customer, cannot here be resolved. It only remains to add that in the handle of the flat-iron, and opposite the bar, was a very little room like a three-cornered hat, into which no direct ray of sun, moon, or star, ever penetrated, but which was superstitiously regarded as a sanctuary replete with comfort and retirement by gaslight, and on the door of which was therefore painted its alluring name: Cosy.

Miss Potterson, sole proprietor and manager of the Fellowship-Porters, reigned supreme on her throne, the Bar, and a man must have drunk himself mad drunk indeed if he thought he could contest a point with her. Being known on her own authority as Miss Abbey Potterson, some water-side heads, which (like the water) were none of the clearest, harboured muddled notions that, because of her dignity and firmness, she was named after, or in some sort related to, the Abbey at Westminster. But Abbey was only short for Abigail, by which name Miss Potterson had been christened at Limehouse Church, some sixty and odd years before.

"Now, you mind, you Riderhood," said Miss Abbey Potterson, with emphatic forefinger over the half-door, "the Fellowships don't want you at all, and would rather by far have your room than your company; but if you were as welcome here as you are not, you shouldn't even then have another drop of drink here this night, after this present pint of beer. So make the most of it."

"But you know, Miss Potterson," this was suggested very meekly though, "if I behave myself, you can't help serving me, miss."

"*Can't* I!" said Abbey, with infinite expression.

"No, Miss Potterson; because, you see, the law——"

"*I* am the law here, my man," returned Miss Abbey, "and I'll soon convince you of that, if you doubt it at all."

"I never said I did doubt it at all, Miss Abbey."

"So much the better for you."

Abbey the supreme threw the customer's halfpence into the till, and, seating herself in her fireside chair, resumed the newspaper she had been reading. She was a tall, upright, well-favoured woman, though severe of countenance, and had more of the air of a schoolmistress than mistress of the Six Jolly Fellowship-Porters. The man on the other side of the half-door, was a waterside-man with a squinting leer, and he eyed her as if he were one of her pupils in disgrace.

"You're cruel hard upon me, Miss Potterson."

Miss Potterson read her newspaper with contracted brows, and took no notice until he whispered:

"Miss Potterson! Ma'am! Might I have half a word with you?"

Deigning then to turn her eyes sideways towards the suppliant Miss Potterson beheld him knuckling his low forehead, and ducking at her with his head, as if he were asking leave to fling himself head foremost over the half-door and alight on his feet in the bar.

"Well?" said Miss Potterson, with a manner as short as she herself was long, "say your half word. Bring it out."

"Miss Potterson! Ma'am! Would you 'sxcuse me taking the liberty of asking, is it my character that you take objections to?"

"Certainly," said Miss Potterson.

"Is it that you're afraid of——"

"I am not afraid of *you*," interposed Miss Potterson, "if you mean that."

"But I humbly don't mean that, Miss Abbey."

"Then what do you mean?"

"You really are so cruel hard upon me! What I was going to make inquiries was no more than, might you have any apprehensions—leastways beliefs or suppositions—that the company's property mightn't be altogether to be considered safe, if I used the house too regular?"

"What do you want to know for?"

"Well, Miss Abbey, respectfully meaning no offence to you, it would be some satisfaction to a man's mind, to understand why the Fellowship-Porters is not to be free to such as me, and is to be free to such as Gaffer."

The face of the hostess darkened with some shadow of perplexity, as she replied: "Gaffer has never been where you have been."

"Signifying in Quod, Miss? Perhaps not. But he may have merited it. He may be suspected of far worse than ever I was."

"Who suspects him?"

"Many, perhaps. One, beyond all doubts. I do."

"*You* are not much," said Miss Abbey Potterson, knitting her brows again with disdain.

"But I was his pardner. Mind you, Miss Abbey, I was his pardner. As such I know more of the ins and outs of him than any person living does. Notice this! I am the man that was his pardner, and I am the man that suspects him."

"Then," suggested Miss Abbey, though with a deeper shade of perplexity than before, "you criminate yourself."

"No I don't, Miss Abbey. For how does it stand? It stands this way. When I was his pardner, I couldn't never give him satisfaction. Why couldn't I never give him satisfaction? Because my luck was bad; because I couldn't find many enough of 'em. How was his luck? Always good. Notice this! Always good! Ah! There's a many games, Miss Abbey, in which there's chance, but there's a many others in which there's skill too, mixed along with it."

"That Gaffer has a skill in finding what he finds, who doubts, man?" asked Miss Abbey.

"A skill in purwiding what he finds, perhaps," said Riderhood, shaking his evil head.

Miss Abbey knitted her brow at him, as he darkly leered at her.

"If you're out upon the river pretty nigh every tide, and if you want to find a man or woman in the river, you'll greatly help your luck, Miss Abbey, by knocking a man or woman on the head aforehand and pitching 'em in."

"Gracious Lud!" was the involuntary exclamation of Miss Potterson.

"Mind you!" returned the other, stretching forward over the half-door to throw his words into the bar; for his voice was as if the head of his boat's mop were down his throat; "I say so, Miss Abbey! And mind you! I'll follow him up, Miss Abbey! And mind you! I'll bring him to book at last, if it's twenty year hence, I will! Who's he, to be favoured along of his daughter? Ain't I got a daughter of my own!"

With that flourish, and seeming to have talked himself rather more drunk and much more ferocious than he had begun by being, Mr. Riderhood took up his pint pot and swaggered off to the tap-room.

Gaffer was not there, but a pretty strong muster of Miss Abbey's pupils were, who exhibited, when occasion required, the greatest docility. On the clock's striking ten, and Miss Abbey's appearing at the door, and addressing a certain person in a faded scarlet jacket, with "George Jones, your time's up! I told your wife you should be punctual," Jones submissively rose, gave the company good-night, and retired. At half-past ten, on Miss Abbey's looking in again, and saying, "William Williams, Bob Glamour, and Jonathan, you are all due," Williams, Bob, and Jonathan with similar meekness took their leave and evaporated. Greater wonder than these, when a bottle-nosed person in a glazed hat had after some considerable hesitation ordered another glass of gin and water of the attendant potboy, and when Miss Abbey, instead of sending it, appeared in person, saying, "Captain Joey, you have had as much as will do you good," not only did the captain feebly rub his knees and contemplate the fire without offering a word of protest, but the rest of the company murmured, "Ay, ay, Captain! Miss Abbey's right; you be guided by Miss Abbey, Captain." Nor was Miss Abbey's vigilance in anywise abated by this submission, but rather sharpened; for, looking round on the deferential faces of her school, and descrying two other young persons in need of admonition, she thus bestowed it: "Tom Tootle, it's time for a young fellow who's going to be married next month, to be at home and asleep. And you needn't nudge him, Mr. Jack Mullins, for I know your work begins early to-morrow, and I say the same to you. So come! Good-night, like good lads!" Upon which the blushing Tootle looked to Mullins, and the blushing Mullins looked to Tootle, on the question who should rise first, and finally both rose together and went out on the broad grin, followed by Miss Abbey; in whose presence the company did not take the liberty of grinning likewise.

In such an establishment, the white-aproned potboy, with his shirt-sleeves arranged in a tight roll on each bare shoulder, was a mere hint of the possibility of physical force, thrown out as a matter of state and form. Exactly at the closing hour, all the guests who were left, filed out in the best order; Miss Abbey standing at the half-door of the bar, to hold a ceremony of review and dismissal. All wished Miss Abbey good-night, and Miss Abbey wished good-night to all, except Riderhood. The sapient potboy, looking on officially, then had the conviction borne in upon his soul, that the man was evermore outcast and excommunicate from the Six Jolly Fellowship-Porters.

"You Bob Glibbery," said Miss Abbey to this potboy, "run round to Hexam's and tell his daughter Lizzie that I want to speak to her."

With exemplary swiftness Bob Glibbery departed, and returned. Lizzie, following him, arrived as one of the two female domestics of the Fellowship-Porters arranged on the snug little table by the bar fire, Miss Potterson's supper of hot sausages and mashed potatoes.

"Come in and sit ye down, girl," said Miss Abbey. "Can you eat a bit?"

"No thank you, Miss. I have had my supper."

"I have had mine too, I think," said Miss Abbey, pushing away the untasted dish, "and more than enough of it. I am put out, Lizzie."

"I am very sorry for it, Miss."

"Then why, in the name of Goodness," quoth Miss Abbey, sharply, "do you do it?"

"*I* do it, Miss!"

"There, there. Don't look astonished. I ought to have begun with a word of explanation, but it's my way to make short cuts at things. I always was a pepperer. You Bob Glibbery there, put the chain upon the door and get ye down to your supper."

With an alacrity that seemed no less referable to the pepperer fact than to the supper fact, Bob obeyed, and his boots were heard descending towards the bed of the river.

"Lizzie Hexam, Lizzie Hexam," then began Miss Potterson, "how often have I held out to you the opportunity of getting clear of your father, and doing well?"

"Very often, Miss."

"Very often? Yes! And I might as well have spoken to the iron funnel of the strongest sea-going steamer that passes the Fellowship-Porters."

"No, Miss," Lizzie pleaded, "because that would not be thankful, and I am."

"I vow and declare I am half ashamed of myself for taking such an interest in you," said Miss Abbey, pettishly, "for I don't believe I should do it if you were not good-looking. Why ain't you ugly?"

Lizzie merely answered this difficult question with an apologetic glance.

"However, you ain't," resumed Miss Potterson, "so it's no use going into that. I must take you as I find you. Which indeed is what I've done. And you mean to say you are still obstinate?"

"Not obstinate, Miss, I hope."

"Firm (I suppose you call it) then?"

"Yes, Miss. Fixed like."

"Never was an obstinate person yet, who would own to the word!" remarked Miss Potterson, rubbing her vexed nose: "I'm sure I would, if I was obstinate; but I am a pepperer, which is different. Lizzie Hexam, Lizzie Hexam, think again. Do you know the worst of your father?"

"Do I know the worst of father!" she repeated, opening her eyes.

"Do you know the suspicions to which your father makes himself liable? Do you know the suspicions that are actually about, against him?"

The consciousness of what he habitually did, oppressed the girl heavily, and she slowly cast down her eyes.

"Say, Lizzie. Do you know?" urged Miss Abbey.

"Please to tell me what the suspicions are, Miss," she asked after a silence, with her eyes upon the ground.

"It's not an easy thing to tell a daughter, but it must be told. It is thought by some, then, that your father helps to their death a few of those that he finds dead."

The relief of hearing what she felt sure was a false suspicion, in place of the expected real and true one, so lightened Lizzie's breast for the moment, that Miss Abbey was amazed at her demeanour. She raised her eyes quickly, shook her head, and, in a kind of triumph, almost laughed.

"They little know father who talk like that."

("She takes it," thought Miss Abbey, "very quietly. She takes it with extraordinary quietness!")

"And perhaps," said Lizzie, as a recollection flashed upon her, "it is some one who has a grudge against father; some one who has threatened father! Is it Riderhood, Miss?"

"Well; yes it is."

"Yes! He was father's partner, and father broke with him, and now he revenges himself. Father broke with him when I was by, and he was very angry at it. And besides, Miss Abbey!—Will you never, without strong reason, let pass your lips what I am going to say?"

She bent forward to say it in a whisper.

"I promise," said Miss Abbey.

"It was on the night when the Harmon murder was found out, through father, just above bridge. And just below bridge, as we were sculling home, Riderhood crept out of the dark in his boat. And many and many times afterwards, when such great pains were taken to come to the bottom of the crime, and it never could be come near, I thought in my own thoughts, could Riderhood himself have done the murder, and did he purposely let father find the body? It seemed a'most wicked and cruel to so much as think such a thing; but now that he tries to throw it upon father, I go back to it as if it was a truth. Can it be a truth? That was put into my mind by the dead?"

She asked this question, rather of the fire than of the hostess of the Fellowship-Porters, and looked round the little bar with troubled eyes.

But, Miss Potterson, as a ready schoolmistress accustomed to bring her pupils to book, set the matter in a light that was essentially of this world.

"You poor deluded girl," she said, "don't you see that you can't open your mind to particular suspicions of one of the two, without opening your mind to general suspicions of the other? They had worked together. Their goings-on had been going on for some time. Even granting that it was as you have had in your thoughts, what the two had done together would come familiar to the mind of one."

"You don't know father, Miss, when you talk like that. Indeed, indeed, you don't know father."

"Lizzie, Lizzie," said Miss Potterson. "Leave him. You needn't break with him altogether, but leave him. Do well away from him; not because of what I have told you to-night—we'll pass no judgment upon that, and we'll hope it may not be—but because of what I have urged on you before. No matter whether it's owing to your good looks or not, I like you and I want to serve you. Lizzie, come under my direction. Don't fling yourself away, my girl, but be persuaded into being respectable and happy."

In the sound good feeling and good sense of her entreaty, Miss Abbey had softened into a soothing tone, and had even drawn her arm round the girl's waist. But, she only replied, "Thank you, thank you! I can't. I won't. I must not think of it. The harder father is borne upon, the more he needs me to lean on."

And then Miss Abbey, who, like all hard people when they do soften, felt that there was considerable compensation owing to her, underwent reaction and became frigid.

"I have done what I can," she said, "and you must go your way. You make your bed, and you must lie on it. But tell your father one thing: he must not come here any more."

"Oh, Miss, will you forbid him the house where I know he is safe?"

"The Fellowships," returned Miss Abbey, "has itself to look to, as well as others. It has been hard work to establish order here, and make the Fellowships what it is, and it is daily and nightly hard work to keep it so. The Fellowships must not have a taint upon it that may give it a bad name. I forbid the house to Riderhood, and I forbid the house to Gaffer. I forbid both, equally. I find from Riderhood and you together, that there are suspicions against both men, and I'm not going to take upon myself to decide betwixt them. They are both tarred with a dirty brush, and I can't have the Fellowships tarred with the same brush. That's all *I* know."

"Good-night, Miss!" said Lizzie Hexam, sorrowfully.

"Hah!—Good-night!" returned Miss Abbey with a shake of her head.

"Believe me, Miss Abbey, I am truly grateful all the same."

"I can believe a good deal," returned the stately Abbey, "so I'll try to believe that too, Lizzie."

No supper did Miss Potterson take that night, and only half her usual tumbler of hot Port Negus. And the female domestics—two robust sisters with staring black eyes, shining flat red faces, blunt noses, and strong black curls, like dolls—interchanged the sentiment that Missis had had her hair combed the wrong way by somebody. And the potboy afterwards remarked, that he hadn't been

"so rattled to bed," since his late mother had systematically accelerated **his retirement** to rest with a poker.

The chaining of the door behind her, as she went forth, disenchanted Lizzie Hexam of that first relief she had felt. The night was black and shrill, the river-side wilderness was melancholy, and there was a sound of casting-out, in the rattling of the iron-links, and the grating of the bolts and staples under Miss Abbey's hand. As she came beneath the lowering sky, a sense of being involved in a murky shade of Murder dropped upon her; and, as the tidal swell of the river broke at her feet without her seeing how it gathered, so, her thoughts startled her by rushing out of an unseen void and striking at her heart.

Of her father's being groundlessly suspected, she felt sure. Sure. Sure. And yet, repeat the words inwardly as often as she would, the attempt to reason out and prove that she was sure, always came after it and failed. Riderhood had done the deed, and entrapped her father. Riderhood had not done the deed, but had resolved in his malice to turn against her father, the appearances that were ready to his hand to distort. Equally and swiftly upon either putting of the case, followed the frightful possibility that her father, being innocent, yet might come to be believed guilty. She had heard of people suffering Death for bloodshed of which they were afterwards proved pure, and those ill-fated persons were not, first, in that dangerous wrong in which her father stood. Then at the best, the beginning of his being set apart, whispered against, and avoided, was a certain fact. It dated from that very night. And as the great black river with its dreary shores was soon lost to her view in the gloom, so, she stood on the river's brink unable to see into the vast blank misery of a life suspected, and fallen away from by good and bad, but knowing that it lay there dim before her, stretching away to the great ocean, Death.

One thing only was clear to the girl's mind. Accustomed from her very babyhood promptly to do the thing that could be done—whether to keep out weather, to ward off cold, to postpone hunger, or what not—she started out of her meditation, and ran home.

The room was quiet, and the lamp burnt on the table. In the bunk in the corner, her brother lay asleep. She bent over him, softly kissed him, and came to the table.

"By the time of Miss Abbey's closing, and by the run of the tide, it must be one. Tide's running up. Father at Chiswick, wouldn't think of coming down till after the turn, and that's at half after four. I'll call Charley at six. I shall hear the church clock strike, as I sit here."

Very quietly, she placed a chair before the scanty fire, and sat down in it, drawing her shawl about her.

"Charley's hollow down by the flare is not there now. Poor Charley!"

The clock struck two, and the clock struck three, and the clock struck four, and she remained there, with a woman's patience and her own purpose. When the morning was well on between four and five, she slipped off her shoes (that her going about might not wake Charley), trimmed the fire sparingly, put water on to boil, and set the table for breakfast. Then she went up the ladder, lamp in hand, and came down again, and glided about and about, making a little bundle. Lastly, from her pocket, and from the chimney-piece, and from an inverted basin on the highest shelf, she brought halfpence, a few sixpences, fewer shillings, and fell to laboriously and noiselessly counting them, and setting aside one little heap. She was still so engaged, when she was startled by:

"Hal-loa!" From her brother, sitting up in bed.

"You made me jump, Charley."

"Jump! Didn't you make *me* jump, when I opened my eyes a moment ago, and saw you sitting there, like the ghost of a girl-miser, in the dead of the night."

"It's not the dead of the night, Charley. It's nigh six in the morning."

"Is it though? But what are you up to, Liz?"

"Still telling your fortune, Charley."

"It seems to be a precious small one, if that's it," said the boy. "What are you putting that little pile of money by itself for?"

"For you, Charley."

"What do you mean?"

"Get out of bed, Charley, and get washed and dressed, and then I'll tell you."

Her composed manner, and her low distinct voice, always had an influence over him. His head was soon in a basin of water, and out of it again, and staring at her through a storm of towelling.

"I never," towelling at himself as if he were his bitterest enemy, "saw such a girl as you are. What *is* the move, Liz?"

"Are you almost ready for breakfast, Charley?"

"You can pour it out. Hal-loa! I say? And a bundle?"

"And a bundle, Charley."

"You don't mean it's for me, too?"

"Yes, Charley; I do, indeed."

More serious of face, and more slow of action, than he had been, the boy completed his dressing, and came and sat down at the little breakfast-table, with his eyes amazedly directed to her face.

"You see, Charley dear, I have made up my mind that this is the right time for your going away from us. Over and above all the blessed change of by-and-by, you'll be much happier, and do much better, even so soon as next month. Even so soon as next week."

"How do you know I shall?"

"I don't quite know how, Charley, but I do." In spite of her unchanged manner of speaking, and her unchanged appearance of composure, she scarcely trusted herself to look at him, but kept her eyes employed on the cutting and buttering of his bread, and on the mixing of his tea, and other such little preparations. "You must leave father to me, Charley—I will do what I can with him—but you must go."

"You don't stand upon ceremony, I think," grumbled the boy, throwing his bread and butter about, in an ill-humour.

She made him no answer.

"I tell you what," said the boy, then bursting out into an angry whimpering, "you're a selfish jade, and you think there's not enough for three of us, and you want to get rid of me."

"If you believe so, Charley,—yes, then I believe too, that I am a selfish jade, and that I think there's not enough for three of us, and that I want to get rid of you."

It was only when the boy rushed at her, and threw his arms round her neck, that she lost her self-restraint. But she lost it then, and wept over him.

"Don't cry, don't cry! I am satisfied to go, Liz; I am satisfied to go. I know you send me away for my good."

"O, Charley, Charley, Heaven above us knows I do!"

"Yes, yes. Don't mind what I said. Don't remember it. Kiss me."

After a silence, she loosed him to dry her eyes, and regain her strong quiet influence.

"Now listen, Charley dear. We both know it must be done, and I alone know there is good reason for its being done at once. Go straight to the school, and say that you and I agreed upon it—that we can't overcome father's opposition—that father will never trouble them, but will never take you back. You are a credit to the school, and you will be a greater credit to it yet, and they will help you to get a living. Show what clothes you have brought, and what money, and say that I will send some more money. If I can get some in no other way, I will ask a little help of those two gentlemen who came here that night."

"I say!" cried her brother, quickly. "Don't you have it of that chap that took hold of me by the chin! Don't you have it of that Wrayburn one!"

Perhaps a slight additional tinge of red flashed up into her face and brow, as with a nod she laid a hand upon his lips to keep him silently attentive.

"And above all things, mind this, Charley! Be sure you always speak well of father. Be sure you always give father his full due. You can't deny that because father has no learning himself he is set against it in you; but favour nothing else against him, and be sure you say—as you know—that your sister is devoted to him. And if you should ever happen to hear anything said against father that is new to you, it will not be true. Remember, Charley! It will not be true."

The boy looked at her with some doubt and surprise, but she went on again without heeding it.

"Above all things remember! It will not be true. I have nothing more to say, Charley dear, except, be good, and get learning, and only think of some things in the old life here, as if you had dreamed them in a dream last night. Good-bye, my Darling!"

Though so young, she infused into these parting words a love that was far more like a mother's than a sister's, and before which the boy was quite bowed down. After holding her to his breast with a passionate cry, he took up his bundle and darted out at the door, with an arm across his eyes.

The white face of the winter day came sluggishly on, veiled in a frosty mist; and the shadowy ships in the river slowly changed to black substances; and the sun, blood-red on the eastern marshes behind dark masts and yards, seemed filled with the ruins of a forest it had set on fire. Lizzie, looking for her father, saw him coming, and stood upon the causeway that he might see her.

He had nothing with him but his boat, and came on apace. A knot of those amphibious human creatures who appear to have some mysterious power of extracting a subsistence out of tidal water by looking at it, were gathered together about the causeway. As her father's boat grounded, they became contemplative of the mud, and dispersed themselves. She saw that the mute avoidance had begun.

Gaffer saw it, too, in so far that he was moved when he set foot on shore, to stare around him. But, he promptly set to work to haul up his boat, and make her fast, and take the sculls and rudder and rope out of her. Carrying these, with Lizzie's aid, he passed up to his dwelling.

"Sit close to the fire, father, dear, while I cook your breakfast. It's all ready for cooking, and only been waiting for you. You must be frozen."

"Well, Lizzie, I ain't of a glow; that's certain. And my hands seemed nailed through to the sculls. See how dead they are!" Something suggestive in their colour, and perhaps in her face, struck him as he held them up; he turned his shoulder and held them down to the fire.

"You were not out in the perishing night, I hope, father?"

"No, my dear. Lay aboard a barge, by a blazing coal-fire.—Where's that boy?"

"There's a drop of brandy for your tea, father, if you'll put it in while I turn this bit of meat. If the river was to get frozen, there would be a deal of distress; wouldn't there, father?"

"Ah! there's always enough of that," said Gaffer, dropping the liquor into his cup from a squat black bottle, and dropping it slowly that it might seem more; "distress is for ever a going about like sut in the air.—Ain't that boy up yet?"

"The meat's ready now, father. Eat it while it's hot and comfortable. After you have finished, we'll turn round to the fire and talk."

But, he perceived that he was evaded, and, having thrown a hasty angry glance towards the bunk, plucked at a corner of her apron and asked:

"What's gone with that boy?"

"Father, if you'll begin your breakfast, I'll sit by and tell you."

He looked at her, stirred his tea and took two or three gulps, then cut at his piece of hot steak with his case-knife, and said, eating:

"Now then. What's gone with that boy?"

"Don't be angry, dear. It seems, father, that he has quite a gift of learning."

"Unnat'ral young beggar!" said the parent, shaking his knife in the air.

"—And that having this gift, and not being equally good at other things, he has made shift to get some schooling."

"Unnat'ral young beggar!" said the parent again, with his former action.

"—And that knowing you have nothing to spare, father, and not wishing to be a burden on you, he gradually made up his mind to go seek his fortune out of learning. He went away this morning, father, and he cried very much at going, and he hoped you would forgive him."

"Let him never come a nigh me to ask me my forgiveness," said the father, again emphasizing his words with the knife. "Let him never come within sight of my eyes, nor yet within reach of my arm. His own father ain't good enough for him. He's disowned his own father. His own father, therefore, disowns him for ever and ever, as a unnat'ral young beggar."

He had pushed away his plate. With the natural need of a strong rough man in anger, to do something forcible, he now clutched his knife overhand and struck downward with it at the end of every succeeding sentence. As he would have struck with his own clenched fist if there had chanced to be nothing in it.

"He's welcome to go. He's more welcome to go than to stay. But let him never come back. Let him never put his head inside that door. And let you never speak a word more in his favour, or you'll disown your own father, likewise, and what your father says of him he'll have to come to say of you. Now I see why them men yonder held aloof from me. They says to one another, 'Here comes the man as ain't good enough for his own son!' Lizzie——!"

But, she stopped him with a cry. Looking at her he saw her, with a face quite strange to him, shrinking back against the wall, with her hands before her eyes.

"Father, don't! I can't bear to see you striking with it. Put it down!"

He looked at the knife; but in his astonishment he still held it.

"Father, it's too horrible. O put it down, put it down!"

Confounded by her appearance and exclamation, he tossed it away, and stood up with his open hands held out before him.

"What's come to you, Liz? Can you think I would strike at you with a knife?"

"No, father, no; you would never hurt me."

"What should I hurt?"

"Nothing, dear father. On my knees, I am certain, in my heart and soul I am certain, nothing! But it was too dreadful to bear; for it looked——" her hands covering her face again, "O it looked——"

"What did it look like?"

The recollection of his murderous figure, combining with her trial of last night, and her trial of the morning, caused her to drop at his feet, without having answered.

He had never seen her so before. He raised her with the utmost tenderness, calling her the best of daughters, and "my poor pretty creetur," and laid her head upon his knee, and tried to restore her. But failing, he laid her head gently down again, got a pillow and placed it under her dark hair, and sought on the table for a spoonful of brandy. There being none left, he hurriedly caught up the empty bottle, and ran out at the door.

He returned as hurriedly as he had gone, with the bottle still empty. He kneeled down by her, took her head on his arm, and moistened her lips with a little water into which he had dipped his fingers: saying, fiercely, as he looked around, now over this shoulder, now over that:

"Have we got a pest in the house? Is there summ'at deadly sticking to my clothes? What's let loose upon us? Who loosed it?"

CHAPTER VII.

MR. WEGG LOOKS AFTER HIMSELF.

SILAS WEGG, being on his road to the Roman Empire, approaches it by way of Clerkenwell. The time is early in the evening; the weather moist and raw. Mr. Wegg finds leisure to make a little circuit, by reason that he folds his screen early, now that he combines another source of income with it, and also that he feels it due to himself to be anxiously expected at the Bower. "Boffin will get all the eagerer for waiting a bit," says Silas, screwing up, as he stumps along, first his right eye, and then his left. Which is something superfluous in him, for Nature has already screwed both pretty tight.

"If I get on with him as I expect to get on," Silas pursues, stumping and meditating, "it wouldn't become me to leave it here. It wouldn't be respectable." Animated by this reflection, he stumps faster, and looks a long way before him, as a man with an ambitious project in abeyance often will do.

Aware of a working-jeweller population taking sanctuary about the church in Clerkenwell, Mr. Wegg is conscious of an interest in, and a respect for, the neighbourhood. But his sensations in this regard halt as to their strict morality, as he halts in his gait; for they suggest the delights of a coat of invisibility in which to walk off safely with the precious stones and watch-cases, but stop short of any compunction for the people who would lose the same.

Not, however, towards the "shops" where cunning artificers work in pearls and diamonds and gold and silver, making their hands so rich, that the enriched water in which they wash them is bought for the refiners;—not towards these does Mr. Wegg stump, but towards the poorer shops of small retail traders in commodities to eat and drink and keep folks warm, and of Italian frame-makers, and of barbers, and of brokers, and of dealers in dogs and singing-birds. From these, in a narrow and a dirty street devoted to such callings, Mr. Wegg selects one dark shop-window with a tallow candle dimly burning in it, surrounded by a muddle of objects, vaguely resembling pieces of leather and dry stick, but among which nothing is resolvable into anything distinct, save the candle itself in its old tin candlestick, and two preserved frogs fighting a small-sword duel. Stumping with fresh vigour, he goes in at the dark greasy entry, pushes a little greasy dark reluctant side-door, and follows the door into the little dark greasy shop. It is so dark that nothing can be made out in it, over a little counter, but another tallow candle in another old tin candlestick, close to the face of a man stooping low in a chair.

Mr. Wegg nods to the face, "Good evening."

The face looking up is a sallow face with weak eyes, surmounted by a tangle of reddish-dusty hair. The owner of the face has no cravat on, and has opened his tumbled shirt-collar to work with the more ease. For the same reason he has no coat on: only a loose waistcoat over his yellow linen. His eyes are like the over-tried eyes of an engraver, but he is not that; his expression and stoop are like those of a shoemaker, but he is not that.

"Good evening, Mr. Venus. Don't you remember?"

With slowly dawning remembrance, Mr. Venus rises, and holds his candle over the little counter, and holds it down towards the legs, natural and artificial, of Mr. Wegg.

"To be *sure!*" he says, then. "How do you do?"

"Wegg, you know," that gentleman explains.

"Yes, yes," says the other. "Hospital amputation?"

"Just so," says Mr. Wegg.

"Yes, yes," quoth Venus. "How do you do? Sit down by the fire, and warm your—your other one."

The little counter being so short a counter that it leaves the fireplace, which would have been behind it if it had been longer, accessible, Mr. Wegg sits down on a box in front of the fire, and inhales a warm and comfortable smell which is not the smell of the shop. "For that," Mr. Wegg inwardly decides, as he takes a corrective sniff or two, "is musty, leathery, feathery, cellary, gluey, gummy, and," with another sniff, "as it might be, strong of old pairs of bellows."

"My tea is drawing, and my muffin is on the hob, Mr. Wegg; will you partake?"

It being one of Mr. Wegg's guiding rules in life always to partake, he says he will. But, the little shop is so excessively dark, is stuck so full of black shelves and brackets and nooks and corners, that he sees Mr. Venus's cup and saucer only because it is close under the candle, and does not see from what mysterious recess Mr. Venus produces another for himself, until it is under his nose. Concurrently, Wegg perceives a pretty little dead bird lying on the counter, with its head drooping on one side against the rim of Mr. Venus's saucer, and a long stiff wire piercing its breast. As if it were Cock Robin, the hero of the ballad, and Mr. Venus were the sparrow with his bow and arrow, and Mr. Wegg were the fly with his little eye.

Mr. Venus dives, and produces another muffin, yet untoasted; taking the arrow out of the breast of Cock Robin, he proceeds to toast it on the end of that cruel instrument. When it is brown, he dives again and produces butter, with which he completes his work.

Mr. Wegg, as an artful man who is sure of his supper by-and-by, presses muffin on his host to soothe him into a compliant state of mind, or, as one might say, to grease his works. As the muffins disappear, little by little, the black shelves and nooks and corners begin to appear, and Mr. Wegg gradually acquires an imperfect notion that over against him on the chimney-piece is a Hindoo baby in a bottle, curved up with his big head tucked under him, as though he would instantly throw a summersault if the bottle were large enough.

When he deems Mr. Venus's wheels sufficiently lubricated, Mr. Wegg approaches his object by asking, as he lightly taps his hands together, to express an undesigning frame of mind:

"And how have I been going on, this long time, Mr. Venus?"

"Very bad," says Mr. Venus, uncompromisingly.

"What? Am I still at home?" asks Wegg, with an air of surprise.

"Always at home."

This would seem to be secretly agreeable to Wegg, but he veils his feelings, and observes, "Strange. To what do you attribute it?"

"I don't know," replies Venus, who is a haggard melancholy man, speaking in a weak voice of querulous complaint, "to what to attribute it, Mr. Wegg. I can't work you into a miscellaneous one, nohow. Do what I will, you can't be got to fit. Anybody with a passable knowledge would pick you out at a look, and say—'No go! Don't match!'"

"Well, but hang it, Mr. Venus," Wegg expostulates with some little irritation, "that can't be personal and peculiar in *me*. It must often happen with miscellaneous ones."

"With ribs (I grant you) always. But not else. When I prepare a miscellaneous one, I know beforehand that I can't keep to nature, and be miscellaneous with ribs, because every man has his own ribs, and no other man's will go with them; but elseways I can be miscellaneous. I have just sent home a Beauty—a perfect Beauty—to a school of art. One leg Belgian, one leg English, and the pickings of eight other people in it. Talk of not being qualified to be miscellaneous! By rights you *ought* to be, Mr. Wegg."

Silas looks as hard at his one leg as he can in the dim light, and after a pause sulkily opines "that it must be the fault of the other people. Or how do you mean to say it comes about?" he demands impatiently.

"I don't know how it comes about. Stand up a minute. Hold the light." Mr. Venus takes from a corner by his chair, the bones of a leg and foot, beautifully pure, and put together with exquisite neatness. These he compares with Mr. Wegg's leg; that gentleman looking on, as if he were being measured for a riding-boot. "No, I don't know how it is, but so it is. You have got a twist in that bone, to the best of my belief. *I* never saw the likes of you."

Mr. Wegg having looked distrustfully at his own limb, and suspiciously at the pattern with which it has been compared, makes the point:

"I'll bet a pound that ain't an English one!"

"An easy wager, when we run so much into foreign! No, it belongs to that French gentleman."

As he nods towards a point of darkness behind Mr. Wegg, the latter, with a slight start, looks round for "that French gentleman," whom he at length descries to be represented (in a very workmanlike manner) by his ribs only, standing on a shelf in another corner, like a piece of armour or a pair of stays.

"Oh!" says Mr. Wegg, with a sort of sense of being introduced; "I dare say you were all right enough in your own country, but I hope no objections will be taken to my saying that the Frenchman was never yet born as I should wish to match."

At this moment the greasy door is violently pushed inward, and a boy follows it, who says, after having let it slam:

"Come for the stuffed canary."

"It's three and ninepence," returns Venus; "have you got the money?"

The boy produces four shillings. Mr. Venus, always in exceedingly low spirits, and making whimpering sounds, peers about for the stuffed canary. On his taking the candle to assist his search, Mr. Wegg observes that he has a convenient little shelf near his knees, exclusively appropriated to skeleton hands, which have very much the appearance of wanting to lay hold of him. From these Mr. Venus rescues the canary in a glass case, and shows it to the boy.

"There!" he whimpers. "There's animation! On a twig, making up his mind to hop! Take care of him; he's a lovely specimen.—And three is four."

The boy gathers up his change and has pulled the door open by a leather strap nailed to it for the purpose, when Venus cries out:

"Stop him! Come back, you young villain! You've got a tooth among them halfpence."

"How was I to know I'd got it? You giv it me. I don't want none of your teeth, I've got enough of my own." So the boy pipes, as he selects it from his change, and throws it on the counter.

"Don't sauce *me*, in the wicious pride of your youth," Mr. Venus retorts pathetically. "Don't hit *me* because you see I'm down. I'm low enough without that. It dropped into the till, I suppose. They drop into everything. There was two in the coffee-pot at breakfast-time. Molars."

"Very well, then," argues the boy, "what do you call names for?"

To which Mr. Venus only replies, shaking his shock of dusty hair, and winking his weak eyes, "Don't sauce *me*, in the wicious pride of your youth; don't hit *me* because you see I'm down. You've no idea how small you'd come out, if I had the articulating of you."

This consideration seems to have its effect upon the boy, for he goes out grumbling.

"Oh dear me, dear me!" sighs Mr. Venus, heavily, snuffing the candle, "the world that appeared so flowery has ceased to blow! You're casting your eye round the shop, Mr. Wegg. Let me show you a light. My working bench. My young man's bench. A Wice. Tools. Bones, warious. Skulls, warious. Preserved Indian baby. African ditto. Bottled preparations, warious. Everything within reach of your hand, in good preservation. The mouldy ones a-top. What's in those hampers over them again, I don't quite remember. Say, human warious. Cats. Articulated English baby. Dogs. Ducks. Glass eyes, warious. Mummied bird. Dried cuticle, warious. Oh dear me! That's the general panoramic view."

Having so held and waved the candle as that all these heterogeneous objects seemed to come forward obediently when they were named, and then retire again, Mr. Venus despondently repeats, "Oh dear me, dear me!" resumes his seat, and with drooping despondency upon him, falls to pouring himself out more tea.

"Where am I?" asks Mr. Wegg.

"You're somewhere in the back shop across the yard, sir; and speaking quite candidly, I wish I'd never bought you of the Hospital Porter."

"Now, look here, what did you give for me?"

"Well," replies Venus, blowing his tea: his head and face peering out of the darkness, over the smoke of it, as if he were modernising the old original rise in his family: "you were one of a warious lot, and I don't know."

Silas puts his point in the improved form of "What will you take for me?"

"Well," replies Venus, still blowing his tea, "I'm not prepared, at a moment's notice, to tell you, Mr. Wegg."

"Come! According to your own account, I'm not worth much," Wegg reasons persuasively.

"Not for miscellaneous working in, I grant you, Mr. Wegg; but you might turn out valuable yet, as a——" here Mr. Venus takes a gulp of tea, so hot that it makes him choke, and sets his weak eyes watering: "as a Monstrosity, if you'll excuse me."

Repressing an indignant look, indicative of anything but a disposition to excuse him, Silas pursues his point.

"I think you know me, Mr. Venus, and I think you know I never bargain."

Mr. Venus takes gulps of hot tea, shutting his eyes at every gulp, and opening them again in a spasmodic manner; but does not commit himself to assent.

"I have a prospect of getting on in life and elevating myself by my own independent exertions," says Wegg, feelingly, "and I shouldn't like—I tell you openly

I should *not* like—under such circumstances, to be what I may call dispersed, a part of me here, and a part of me there, but should wish to collect myself like a genteel person."

"It's a prospect at present, is it, Mr. Wegg? Then you haven't got the money for a deal about you? Then I'll tell you what I'll do with you; I'll hold you over. I am a man of my word, and you needn't be afraid of my disposing of you. I'll hold you over. That's a promise. Oh dear me, dear me!"

Fain to accept his promise, and wishing to propitiate him, Mr. Wegg looks on as he sighs and pours himself out more tea, and then says, trying to get a sympathetic tone into his voice:

"You seem very low, Mr. Venus. Is business bad?"

"Never was so good."

"Is your hand out at all?"

"Never was so well in. Mr. Wegg, I'm not only first in the trade, but I'm *the* trade. You may go and buy a skeleton at the West End if you like, and pay the West End price, but it'll be my putting together. I've as much to do as I can possibly do, with the assistance of my young man, and I take a pride and a pleasure in it."

Mr. Venus thus delivers himself, his right hand extended, his smoking saucer in his left hand, protesting as though he were going to burst into a flood of tears.

"That ain't a state of things to make you low, Mr. Venus."

"Mr. Wegg, I know it ain't. Mr. Wegg, not to name myself as a workman without an equal, I've gone on improving myself in my knowledge of Anatomy, till both by sight and by name I'm perfect. Mr. Wegg, if you was brought here loose in a bag to be articulated, I'd name your smallest bones blindfold equally with your largest, as fast as I could pick 'em out, and I'd sort 'em all, and sort your wertebræ, in a manner that would equally surprise and charm you."

"Well," remarks Silas (though not quite so readily as last time), "*that* ain't a state of things to be low about.—Not for *you* to be low about, leastways."

"Mr. Wegg, I know it ain't; Mr. Wegg, I know it ain't. But it's the heart that lowers me, it is the heart! Be so good as take and read that card out loud."

Silas receives one from his hand, which Venus takes from a wonderful litter in a drawer, and putting on his spectacles, reads:

"'Mr. Venus,'"

"Yes. Go on."

"'Preserver of Animals and Birds,'"

"Yes. Go on."

"'Articulator of human bones.'"

"That's it," with a groan. "That's it! Mr. Wegg, I'm thirty-two, and a bachelor. Mr. Wegg, I love her. Mr. Wegg, she is worthy of being loved by a Potentate!" Here Silas is rather alarmed by Mr. Venus springing to his feet in the hurry of his spirits, and haggardly confronting him with his hand on his coat collar; but Mr. Venus, begging pardon, sits down again, saying, with the calmness of despair, "She objects to the business."

"Does she know the profits of it?"

"She knows the profits of it, but she don't appreciate the art of it, and she objects to it. 'I do not wish,' she writes in her own hand-writing, 'to regard myself, nor yet to be regarded, in that bony light.'"

Mr. Venus pours himself out more tea, with a look and in an attitude of the deepest desolation.

"And so a man climbs to the top of the tree, Mr. Wegg, only to see that there's no look-out when he's up there! I sit here of a night surrounded by the lovely trophies of my art, and what have they done for me? Ruined me. Brought me to the pass of being informed that 'she does not wish to regard herself, nor yet to be regarded, in that bony light!'" Having repeated the fatal expressions, Mr. Venus drinks more tea by gulps, and offers an explanation of his doing so.

"It lowers me. When I'm equally lowered all over, lethargy sets in. By sticking to it till one or two in the morning, I get oblivion. Don't let me detain you, Mr. Wegg. I'm not company for any one."

"It is not on that account," says Silas, rising, "but because I've got an appointment. It's time I was at Harmon's."

"Eh?" said Mr. Venus. "Harmon's, up Battle Bridge way?"

Mr. Wegg admits that he is bound for that port.

"You ought to be in a good thing, if you've worked yourself in there. There's lots of money going there."

"To think," says Silas, "that you should catch it up so quick, and know about it. Wonderful!"

"Not at all, Mr. Wegg. The old gentleman wanted to know the nature and worth of everything that was found in the dust; and many's the bone, and feather, and what not, that he's brought to me."

"Really, now!"

"Yes. (Oh dear me, dear me!) And he's buried quite in this neighbourhood, you know. Over yonder."

Mr. Wegg does not know, but he makes as if he did, by responsively nodding his head. He also follows with his eyes, the toss of Venus's head: as if to seek a direction to over yonder.

"I took an interest in that discovery in the river," says Venus. "(She hadn't written her cutting refusal at that time.) I've got up there——never mind, though."

He had raised the candle at arm's length towards one of the dark shelves, and Mr. Wegg had turned to look, when he broke off.

"The old gentleman was well known all round here. There used to be stories about his having hidden all kinds of property in those dust mounds. I suppose there was nothing in 'em. Probably you know, Mr. Wegg?"

"Nothing in 'em," says Wegg, who has never heard a word of this before.

"Don't let me detain you. Good-night!"

The unfortunate Mr. Venus gives him a shake of the hand with a shake of his own head, and drooping down in his chair, proceeds to pour himself out more tea.

Mr. Wegg, looking back over his shoulder as he pulls the door open by the strap, notices that the movement so shakes the crazy shop, and so shakes a momentary flare out of the candle, as that the babies—Hindoo, African, and British—the "human warious," the French gentleman, the green glass-eyed cats, the dogs, the ducks, and all the rest of the collection, show for an instant as if paralytically animated; while even poor little Cock Robin at Mr. Venus's elbow turns over on his innocent side. Next moment, Mr. Wegg is stumping under the gaslights and through the mud.

CHAPTER VIII.

MR. BOFFIN IN CONSULTATION.

WHOSOEVER had gone out of Fleet Street into the Temple at the date of this history, and had wandered disconsolate about the Temple until he stumbled on a dismal churchyard, and had looked up at the dismal windows commanding that churchyard until at the most dismal window of them all he saw a dismal boy, would in him have beheld, at one grand comprehensive swoop of the eye, the managing clerk, junior clerk, common-law clerk, conveyancing clerk, chancery clerk, every refinement and department of clerk, of Mr. Mortimer Lightwood, erewhile called in the newspapers eminent solicitor.

Mr. Boffin having been several times in communication with this clerkly essence, both on its own ground and at the Bower, had no difficulty in identifying it when he saw it up in its dusty eyrie. To the second floor on which the window was situated, he ascended, much pre-occupied in mind by the uncertainties besetting the Roman Empire, and much regretting the death of the amiable Pertinax: who only last night had left the Imperial affairs in a state of great confusion, by falling a victim to the fury of the prætorian guards.

"Morning, morning, morning!" said Mr. Boffin, with a wave of his hand, as the office door was opened by the dismal boy, whose appropriate name was Blight. "Governor in?"

"Mr. Lightwood gave you an appointment, sir, I think?"

"I don't want him to give it, you know," returned Mr. Boffin; "I'll pay my way, my boy."

"No doubt, sir. Would you walk in? Mr. Lightwood ain't in at the present moment, but I expect him back very shortly. Would you take a seat in Mr. Lightwood's room, sir, while I look over our Appointment Book?" Young Blight made a great show of fetching from his desk a long thin manuscript volume with a brown paper cover, and running his finger down the day's appointments, murmuring, "Mr. Aggs, Mr. Baggs, Mr. Caggs, Mr. Daggs, Mr. Faggs, Mr. Gaggs, Mr. Boffin. Yes, sir, quite right. You are a little before your time, sir. Mr. Lightwood will be in directly."

"I'm not in a hurry," said Mr. Boffin.

"Thank you, sir. I'll take the opportunity, if you please, of entering your name in our Callers' Book for the day." Young Blight made another great show of changing the volume, taking up a pen, sucking it, dipping it, and running over previous entries before he wrote. As, "Mr. Alley, Mr. Balley, Mr. Calley, Mr. Dalley, Mr. Falley, Mr. Galley, Mr. Halley, Mr. Lalley, Mr. Malley. And Mr. Boffin."

"Strict system here; eh, my lad?" said Mr. Boffin, as he was booked.

"Yes, sir," returned the boy. "I couldn't get on without it."

By which he probably meant that his mind would have been shattered to pieces without this fiction of an occupation. Wearing in his solitary confinement no fetters that he could polish, and being provided with no drinking-cup that he could carve, he had fallen on the device of ringing alphabetical changes into the two volumes in question, or of entering vast numbers of persons out of the Directory as transacting business with Mr. Lightwood. It was the more necessary for his spirits, because, being of a sensitive temperament, he was apt to consider it personally disgraceful to himself that his master had no clients.

"How long have you been in the law, now?" asked Mr. Boffin, with a pounce, in his usual inquisitive way.

"I've been in the law, now, sir, about three years."

"Must have been as good as born in it!" said Mr. Boffin, with admiration. "Do you like it?"

"I don't mind it much," returned Young Blight, heaving a sigh, as if its bitterness were past.

"What wages do you get?"

"Half what I could wish," replied young Blight.

"What's the whole that you could wish?"

"Fifteen shillings a week," said the boy.

"About how long might it take you now, at a average rate of going, to be a Judge?" asked Mr. Boffin, after surveying his small stature in silence.

The boy answered that he had not yet quite worked out that little calculation.

"I suppose there's nothing to prevent your going in for it?" said Mr. Boffin.

The boy virtually replied that as he had the honour to be a Briton who never, never, never, there was nothing to prevent his going in for it. Yet he seemed inclined to suspect that there might be something to prevent his coming out with it.

"Would a couple of pound help you up at all?" asked Mr. Boffin.

On this head, young Blight had no doubt whatever, so Mr. Boffin made him a present of that sum of money, and thanked him for his attention to his (Mr. Boffin's) affairs, which, he added, were now, he believed, as good as settled.

Then Mr. Boffin, with his stick at his ear, like a Familiar Spirit explaining the office to him, sat staring at a little bookcase of Law Practice and Law Reports, and at a window, and at an empty blue bag, and at a stick of sealing-wax, and a pen, and a box of wafers, and an apple, and a writing-pad—all very dusty—and at a number of inky smears and blots, and at an imperfectly-disguised gun-case pretending to be something legal, and at an iron box labelled HARMON ESTATE, until Mr. Lightwood appeared.

Mr. Lightwood explained that he came from the proctor's, with whom he had been engaged in transacting Mr. Boffin's affairs.

"And they seem to have taken a deal out of you!" said Mr. Boffin, with commiseration.

Mr. Lightwood, without explaining that his weariness was chronic, proceeded with his exposition that, all forms of law having been at length complied with, will of Harmon deceased having been proved, death of Harmon next inheriting having been proved, &c., and so forth, Court of Chancery having been moved, &c., and so forth, he, Mr. Lightwood, had now the great gratification, honour, and happiness, again &c. and so forth, of congratulating Mr. Boffin on coming into possession, as residuary legatee, of upwards of one hundred thousand pounds, standing in the books of the Governor and Company of the Bank of England, again &c. and so forth.

"And what is particularly eligible in the property, Mr. Boffin, is, that it involves no trouble. There are no estates to manage, no rents to return so much per cent. upon in bad times (which is an extremely dear way of getting your name into the newspapers), no voters to become parboiled in hot water with, no agents to take the cream off the milk before it comes to table. You could put the whole in a cash-box to-morrow morning, and take it with you to—say, to the Rocky Mountains. Inasmuch as every man," concluded Mr. Lightwood, with an indolent smile, "appears to be under a fatal spell which obliges him, sooner or later, to mention the Rocky Mountains in a tone of extreme familiarity to some other man, I hope you'll excuse my pressing you into the service of that gigantic range of geographical bores."

Without following this last remark very closely, Mr. Boffin cast his perplexed gaze first at the ceiling, and then at the carpet.

"Well," he remarked, "I don't know what to say about it, I am sure. I was a'most as well as I was. It's a great lot to take care of."

"My dear Mr. Boffin, then *don't* take care of it!"

"Eh?" said that gentleman.

"Speaking now," returned Mortimer, "with the irresponsible imbecility of a private individual, and not with the profundity of a professional adviser, I should say that if the circumstance of its being too much, weighs upon your mind, you have the haven of consolation open to you that you can easily make it less. And if you should be apprehensive of the trouble of doing so, there is the further haven of consolation that any number of people will take the trouble off your hands."

"Well! I don't quite see it," retorted Mr. Boffin, still perplexed. "That's not satisfactory, you know, what you're a-saying."

"Is Anything satisfactory, Mr. Boffin?" asked Mortimer, raising his eyebrows.

"I used to find it so," answered Mr. Boffin, with a wistful look. "While I was foreman at the Bower—afore it *was* the Bower—I considered the business very satisfactory. The old man was a awful Tartar (saying it, I'm sure, without disrespect to his memory), but the business was a pleasant one to look after, from before daylight to past dark. It's a'most a pity," said Mr. Boffin, rubbing his ear, "that he ever went and made so much money. It would have been better for him if he hadn't so given himself up to it. You may depend upon it," making the discovery all of a sudden, "that *he* found it a great lot to take care of!"

Mr. Lightwood coughed, not convinced.

"And speaking of satisfactory," pursued Mr. Boffin, "why, Lord save us! when we come to take it to pieces, bit by bit, where's the satisfactoriness of the money as yet? When the old man does right the poor boy after all, the poor boy gets no good of it. He gets made away with, at the moment when he's lifting (as one may say) the cup and sarser to his lips. Mr. Lightwood, I will now name to you, that on behalf of the poor dear boy, me and Mrs. Boffin have stood out against the old man times out of number, till he has called us every name he could lay his tongue to. I have seen him, after Mrs. Boffin has given him her mind respecting the claims of the nat'ral affections, catch off Mrs. Boffin's bonnet (she wore, in general, a black straw, perched as a matter of convenience on the top of her head), and send it spinning across the yard. I have indeed. And once, when he did this in a manner that amounted to personal, I should have given him a rattler for himself, if Mrs. Boffin hadn't thrown herself betwixt us, and received flush on the temple. Which dropped her, Mr. Lightwood. Dropped her."

Mr. Lightwood murmured "Equal honour—Mrs. Boffin's head and heart."

"You understand; I name this," pursued Mr. Boffin, "to show you, now the affairs are wound up, that me and Mrs. Boffin have ever stood, as we were in Christian honour bound, the children's friend. Me and Mrs. Boffin stood the poor girl's friend; me and Mrs. Boffin stood the poor boy's friend; me and Mrs. Boffin up and faced the old man when we momently expected to be turned out for our pains. As to Mrs. Boffin," said Mr. Boffin, lowering his voice, "she mightn't wish it mentioned now she's Fashionable, but she went so far as to tell him, in my presence, he was a flinty-hearted rascal."

Mr. Lightwood murmured "Vigorous Saxon spirit—Mrs. Boffin's ancestors—bowmen—Agincourt and Cressy."

"The last time me and Mrs. Boffin saw the poor boy," said Mr. Boffin, warming (as fat usually does), with a tendency to melt, "he was a child of seven year old. For when he come back to make intercession for his sister, me and Mrs. Boffin were away overlooking a country contract which was to be sifted before carted, and he was come and gone in a single hour. I say he was a child of seven year old. He was going away, all alone and forlorn, to that foreign school, and he come into our place, situate up the yard of the present Bower, to have a warm at our fire. There was his little scanty travelling clothes upon him. There was his little scanty box outside in the shivering wind, which I was going to carry for him down to the steamboat, as the old man wouldn't hear of allowing a sixpence coach-money. Mrs. Boffin, then quite a young woman and a pictur of a full-blown rose, stands him by her, kneels down at the fire, warms her two open hands, and falls to rubbing his cheeks; but seeing the tears come into the child's eyes, the tears come fast into her own, and she holds him round the neck, like as if she was protecting him, and cries to me, 'I'd give the wide wide world, I would, to run away with him!' I don't say but what it cut me, and but what it at the same time heightened my feelings of admiration for Mrs. Boffin. The poor child clings to her for awhile, as she clings to him, and then, when the old man calls, he says 'I must go! God bless you!' and for a moment rests his heart against her bosom, and looks up at both of us, as if it was in pain—in agony. Such a look! I went aboard with him (I gave him first what little treat I thought he'd like), and I left him when he had fallen asleep in his berth, and I came back to Mrs. Boffin. But tell her what I would of how I had left him, it all went for nothing, for, according to her thoughts, he never changed that look that he had looked up at us two. But it did one piece of good. Mrs. Boffin and me had no child of our own, and had sometimes wished that how we had one. But not now. 'We might both of us die,' says Mrs. Boffin, 'and other eyes might see that lonely look in our child.' So of a night, when it was very cold, or when the wind roared, or the rain dripped heavy, she would wake sobbing, and call out in a fluster, 'Don't you see the poor child's face? O shelter the poor child!'—till in course of years it gently wore out, as many things do."

"My dear Mr. Boffin, everything wears to rags," said Mortimer, with a light laugh.

"I won't go so far as to say everything," returned Mr. Boffin, on whom his manner seemed to grate, "because there's some things that I never found among the dust. Well, sir. So Mrs. Boffin and me grow older and older in the old man's service, living and working pretty hard in it, till the old man is discovered dead in his bed. Then Mrs. Boffin and me seal up his box, always standing on the table at the side of his bed, and having frequently heerd tell of the Temple as a spot where lawyer's dust is contracted for, I come down here in search of a lawyer to advise, and I see your young man up at this present elevation, chopping at the flies on the window-sill with his penknife, and I give him a Hoy! not then having the pleasure of your acquaintance, and by that means come to gain the honour. Then you, and the gentleman in the uncomfortable neckcloth under the little archway in Saint Paul's Churchyard——"

"Doctors' Commons," observed Lightwood.

"I understood it was another name," said Mr. Boffin, pausing, "But you know best. Then you and Doctor Scommons, you go to work, and you do the thing that's proper, and you and Doctor S. take steps for finding out the poor boy, and at last you do find out the poor boy, and me and Mrs. Boffin often exchange the observation, 'We shall see him again, under happy circumstances.' But it was never to be; and the want of satisfactoriness is, that after all the money never gets to him."

"But it gets," remarked Lightwood, with a languid inclination of the head, "into excellent hands."

"It gets into the hands of me and Mrs. Boffin only this very day and hour, and that's what I'm working round to, having waited for this day and hour a' purpose. Mr. Lightwood, here has been a wicked cruel murder. By that murder me and Mrs. Boffin mysteriously profit. For the apprehension and conviction of the murderer, we offer a reward of one tithe of the property—a reward of Ten Thousand Pound."

"Mr. Boffin, it's too much."

"Mr. Lightwood, me and Mrs. Boffin have fixed the sum together, and we stand to it."

"But let me represent to you," returned Lightwood, "speaking now with professional profundity, and not with individual imbecility, that the offer of such an immense reward is a temptation to forced suspicion, forced construction of circumstances, strained accusation, a whole tool-box of edged tools."

"Well," said Mr. Boffin, a little staggered, "that's the sum we put o' one side for the purpose. Whether it shall be openly declared in the new notices that must now be put about in our names——"

"In your name, Mr. Boffin; in your name."

"Very well; in my name, which is the same as Mrs. Boffin's, and means both of us, *is* to be considered in drawing 'em up. But this is the first instruction that I, as the owner of the property, give to my lawyer on coming into it."

"Your lawyer, Mr. Boffin," returned Lightwood, making a very short note of it with a very rusty pen, "has the gratification of taking the instruction. There is another?"

"There is just one other, and no more. Make me as compact a little will as can be reconciled with tightness, leaving the whole of the property to 'my beloved wife, Henerietty Boffin, sole executrix.' Make it as short as you can, using those words; but make it tight."

At some loss to fathom Mr. Boffin's notions of a tight will, Lightwood felt his way.

"I beg your pardon, but professional profundity must be exact. When you say tight——"

"I mean tight," Mr. Boffin explained.

"Exactly so. And nothing can be more laudable. But is the tightness to bind Mrs. Boffin to any and what conditions?"

"Bind Mrs. Boffin?" interposed her husband. "No! What are you thinking of? What I want is, to make it all hers so tight as that her hold of it can't be loosed."

"Hers freely, to do what she likes with? Hers absolutely?"

"Absolutely?" repeated Mr. Boffin, with a short sturdy laugh. "Hah! I should think so! It would be handsome in me to begin to bind Mrs. Boffin at this time of day!"

So that instruction, too, was taken by Mr. Lightwood; and Mr. Lightwood, having taken it, was in the act of showing Mr. Boffin out, when Mr. Eugene Wrayburn almost jostled him in the doorway. Consequently Mr. Lightwood said, in his cool manner, "Let me make you two known to one another," and further signified that Mr. Wrayburn was counsel learned in the law, and that, partly in the way of business and partly in the way of pleasure, he had imparted to Mr. Wrayburn some of the interesting facts of Mr. Boffin's biography.

"Delighted," said Eugene—though he didn't look so—"to know Mr. Boffin."

"Thankee, sir, thankee," returned that gentleman. "And how do *you* like the law?"

"A——not particularly," returned Eugene.

"Too dry for you, eh? Well, I suppose it wants some years of sticking to, before you master it. But there's nothing like work. Look at the bees."

"I beg your pardon," returned Eugene, with a reluctant smile, "but will you excuse my mentioning that I always protest against being referred to the bees?"

"Do you!" said Mr. Boffin.

"I object on principle," said Eugene, "as a biped——"

"As a what?" asked Mr. Boffin.

"As a two-footed creature;—I object on principle, as a two-footed creature, to being constantly referred to insects and four-footed creatures. I object to being required to model my proceedings according to the proceedings of the bee, or the dog, or the spider, or the camel. I fully admit that the camel, for instance, is an excessively temperate person; but he has several stomachs to entertain himself with, and I have only one. Besides, I am not fitted up with a convenient cool cellar to keep my drink in."

"But I said, you know," urged Mr. Boffin, rather at a loss for an answer, "the bee."

"Exactly. And may I represent to you that it's injudicious to say the bee? For the whole case is assumed. Conceding for a moment that there is any analogy between a bee and a man in a shirt and pantaloons (which I deny), and that it is settled that the man is to learn from the bee (which I also deny), the question still remains, what is he to learn? To imitate? Or to avoid? When your friends the bees worry themselves to that highly fluttered extent about their sovereign, and become perfectly distracted touching the slightest monarchical movement, are we men to learn the greatness of Tuft-hunting, or the littleness of the Court Circular? I am not clear, Mr. Boffin, but that the hive may be satirical."

"At all events, they work," said Mr. Boffin.

"Ye-es," returned Eugene, disparagingly, "they work; but don't you think they overdo it? They work so much more than they need—they make so much more than they can eat—they are so incessantly boring and buzzing at their one idea till Death comes upon them—that don't you think they overdo it? And are human labourers to have no holidays, because of the bees? And am I never to have change of air, because the bees don't? Mr. Boffin, I think honey excellent at breakfast; but regarded in the light of my conventional schoolmaster and moralist, I protest against the tyrannical humbug of your friend the bee. With the highest respect for you."

"Thankee," said Mr. Boffin. "Morning, morning!"

But, the worthy Mr. Boffin jogged away with a comfortless impression he could have dispensed with, that there was a deal of unsatisfactoriness in the world, besides what he had recalled as appertaining to the Harmon property. And he was still jogging along Fleet Street in this condition of mind, when he became aware that he was closely tracked and observed by a man of genteel appearance.

"Now then?" said Mr. Boffin, stopping short, with his meditations brought to an abrupt check, "what's the next article?"

"I beg your pardon, Mr. Boffin."

"My name too, eh? How did you come by it? I don't know you."

"No, sir, you don't know me."

Mr. Boffin looked full at the man, and the man looked full at him.

"No," said Mr. Boffin, after a glance at the pavement, as if it were made of faces and he were trying to match the man's, "I *don't* know you."

"I am nobody," said the stranger, "and not likely to be known; but Mr. Boffin's wealth——"

"Oh! that's got about already, has it?" muttered Mr. Boffin.

"—And his romantic manner of acquiring it, make him conspicuous. You were pointed out to me the other day."

"Well," said Mr. Boffin, "I should say I was a disappintment to you when I *was* pinted out, if your politeness would allow you to confess it, for I am well aware I am not much to look at. What might you want with me? Not in the law, are you?"

"No, sir."

"No information to give, for a reward?"

"No, sir."

There may have been a momentary mantling in the face of the man as he made the last answer, but it passed directly.

"If I don't mistake, you have followed me from my lawyer's and tried to fix my attention. Say out! Have you? Or haven't you?" demanded Mr. Boffin, rather angry.

"Yes."

"Why have you?"

"If you will allow me to walk beside you, Mr. Boffin, I will tell you. Would you object to turn aside into this place—I think it is called Clifford's Inn—where we can hear one another better than in the roaring street?"

("Now," thought Mr. Boffin, "if he proposes a game at skittles, or meets a country gentleman just come into property, or produces any article of jewellery he has found, I'll knock him down!" With this discreet reflection, and carrying his stick in his arms much as Punch carries his, Mr. Boffin turned into Clifford's Inn aforesaid.)

"Mr. Boffin, I happened to be in Chancery Lane this morning, when I saw you going along before me. I took the liberty of following you, trying to make up my mind to speak to you, till you went into your lawyer's. Then I waited outside till you came out."

("Don't quite sound like skittles, nor yet country gentleman, nor yet jewellery," thought Mr. Boffin, "but there's no knowing.")

"I am afraid my object is a bold one, I am afraid it has little of the usual practical world about it, but I venture it. If you ask me, or if you ask yourself—which is more likely—what emboldens me, I answer, I have been strongly assured that you are a man of rectitude and plain dealing, with the soundest of sound hearts, and that you are blessed in a wife distinguished by the same qualities."

"Your information is true of Mrs. Boffin, anyhow," was Mr. Boffin's answer, as he surveyed his new friend again. There was something repressed in the strange man's manner, and he walked with his eyes on the ground—though conscious, for all that, of Mr. Boffin's observation—and he spoke in a subdued voice. But his words came easily, and his voice was agreeable in tone, albeit constrained.

"When I add, I can discern for myself what the general tongue says of you—that you are quite unspoiled by Fortune, and not uplifted—I trust you will not, as a man of an open nature, suspect that I mean to flatter you, but will believe that all I mean is to excuse myself, these being my only excuses for my present intrusion."

("How much?" thought Mr. Boffin. "It must be coming to money. How much?")

"You will probably change your manner of living, Mr. Boffin, in your changed circumstances. You will probably keep a larger house, have many matters to arrange, and be beset by numbers of correspondents. If you would try me as your Secretary——"

"As *what?*" cried Mr. Boffin, with his eyes wide open.

"Your Secretary."

"Well," said Mr. Boffin, under his breath, "that's a queer thing!"

"Or," pursued the stranger, wondering at Mr. Boffin's wonder, "if you would try me as your man of business under any name, I know you would find me faithful and grateful, and I hope you would find me useful. You may naturally think that my immediate object is money. Not so, for I would willingly serve you a year—two years—any term you might appoint—before that should begin to be a consideration between us."

"Where do you come from?" asked Mr. Boffin.

"I come" returned the other, meeting his eye, "from many countries."

Mr. Boffin's acquaintance with the names and situations of foreign lands being limited in extent and somewhat confused in quality, he shaped his next question on an elastic model.

"From—any particular place?"

"I have been in many places."

"What have you been?" asked Mr. Boffin.

Here again he made no great advance, for the reply was, "I have been a student and a traveller."

"But if it ain't a liberty to plump it out," said Mr. Boffin, "what do you do for your living?"

"I have mentioned," returned the other, with another look at him, and a smile, "what I aspire to do. I have been superseded as to some slight intentions I had, and I may say that I have now to begin life."

Not very well knowing how to get rid of this applicant, and feeling the more embarrassed because his manner and appearance claimed a delicacy in which the worthy Mr. Boffin feared he himself might be deficient, that gentleman glanced into the mouldy little plantation, or cat-preserve, of Clifford's Inn, as it was that day, in search of a suggestion. Sparrows were there, cats were there, dry-rot and wet-rot were there, but it was not otherwise a suggestive spot.

"All this time," said the stranger, producing a little pocket-book and taking out a card, "I have not mentioned my name. My name is Rokesmith. I lodge at one Mr. Wilfer's, at Holloway."

Mr. Boffin stared again.

"Father of Miss Bella Wilfer?" said he.

"My landlord has a daughter named Bella. Yes; no doubt."

Now, this name had been more or less in Mr. Boffin's thoughts all the morning, and for days before, therefore he said:

"That's singular, too!" unconsciously staring again, past all bounds of good manners, with the card in his hand. "Though, by-the-bye, I suppose it was one of that family that pinted me out?"

"No. I have never been in the streets with one of them."

"Heard me talked of among 'em, though?"

"No. I occupy my own rooms, and have held scarcely any communication with them."

"Odder and odder!" said Mr. Boffin. "Well, sir, to tell you the truth, I don't know what to say to you."

"Say nothing," returned Mr. Rokesmith; "allow me to call on you in a few days. I am not so unconscionable as to think it likely that you would accept me on trust at first sight, and take me out of the very street. Let me come to you for your further opinion, at your leisure."

"That's fair, and I don't object," said Mr. Boffin; "but it must be on condition that it's fully understood that I no more know that I shall ever be in want of any gentleman as Secretary—it *was* Secretary you said; wasn't it?"

"Yes."

Again Mr. Boffin's eyes opened wide, and he stared at the applicant from head to foot, repeating, "Queer!—You're sure it was Secretary? Are you?"

"I am sure I said so."

"—As Secretary," repeated Mr. Boffin, meditating upon the word; "I no more know that I may ever want a Secretary, or what not, than I do that I shall ever be in want of the man in the moon. Me and Mrs. Boffin have not even settled that we shall make any change in our way of life. Mrs. Boffin's inclinations certainly do tend towards Fashion; but, being already set up in a fashionable way at the Bower, she may not make further alterations. However, sir, as you don't press yourself, I wish to meet you so far as saying, by all means call at the Bower if you like. Call in the course of a week or two. At the same time, I consider that I ought to name, in addition to what I have already named, that I have in my employment a literary man—*with* a wooden leg—as I have no thoughts of parting from."

"I regret to hear I am in some sort anticipated," Mr. Rokesmith answered, evidently having heard it with surprise; "but perhaps other duties might arise?"

"You see," returned Mr. Boffin, with a confidential sense of dignity, "as to my literary man's duties, they're clear. Professionally he declines and he falls, and as a friend he drops into poetry."

Without observing that these duties seemed by no means clear to Mr. Rokesmith's astonished comprehension, Mr. Boffin went on:

"And now, sir, I'll wish you good-day. You can call at the Bower any time in a week or two. It's not above a mile or so from you, and your landlord can direct you to it. But as he may not know it by its new name of Boffin's Bower, say, when you inquire of him, it's Harmon's; will you?"

"Harmoon's," repeated Mr. Rokesmith, seeming to have caught the sound imperfectly, "Harmarn's. How do you spell it?"

"Why, as to the spelling of it," returned Mr. Boffin, with great presence of mind, "that's *your* look out. Harmon's is all you've got to say to *him*. Morning, morning, morning!" And so departed, without looking back.

CHAPTER IX.

MR. AND MRS. BOFFIN IN CONSULTATION.

BETAKING himself straight homeward, Mr. Boffin, without further let or hindrance, arrived at the Bower, and gave Mrs. Boffin (in a walking dress of black velvet and feathers, like a mourning coach-horse) an account of all he had said and done since breakfast.

"This brings us round, my dear," he then pursued, "to the question we left unfinished: namely, whether there's to be any new go-in for Fashion."

"Now, I'll tell you what I want, Noddy," said Mrs. Boffin, "smoothing her dress with an air of immense enjoyment, "I want Society."

"Fashionable Society, my dear?"

"Yes!" cried Mrs. Boffin, laughing with the glee of a child. "Yes! It's no good my being kept here like Wax-Work; is it now?"

"People have to pay to see Wax-Work, my dear," returned her husband, "whereas (though you'd be cheap at the same money) the neighbours is welcome to see *you* for nothing."

"But it don't answer," said the cheerful Mrs. Boffin. "When we worked like the neighbours, we suited one another. Now we have left work off, we have left off suiting one another."

"What, do you think of beginning work again?" Mr. Boffin hinted.

"Out of the question! We have come into a great fortune, and we must do what's right by our fortune; we must act up to it."

Mr. Boffin, who had a deep respect for his wife's intuitive wisdom, replied, though rather pensively: "I suppose we must."

"It's never been acted up to yet, and, consequently, no good has come of it," said Mrs. Boffin.

"True, to the present time," Mr. Boffin assented, with his former pensiveness, as he took his seat upon his settle. "I hope good may be coming of it in the future time. Towards which, what's your views, old lady?"

Mrs. Boffin, a smiling creature, broad of figure and simple of nature, with her hands folded in her lap, and with buxom creases in her throat, proceeded to expound her views.

"*I* say a good house in a good neighbourhood, good things about us, good living, and good society. *I* say, live like our means, without extravagance, and be happy."

"Yes. *I* say be happy, too," assented the still pensive Mr. Boffin.

"Lor-a-mussy!" exclaimed Mrs. Boffin, laughing and clapping her hands, and gaily rocking herself to and fro, "when I think of me in a light yellow chariot and pair, with silver boxes to the wheels——"

"Oh! you was thinking of that, was you, my dear?"

"Yes!" cried the delighted creature. "And with a footman up behind, with a bar across, to keep his legs from being poled!. And with a coachman up in front, sinking down into a seat big enough for three of him, all covered with upholstery in green and white! And with two bay horses tossing their heads and stepping higher than they trot long-ways! And with you and me leaning back inside, as grand as ninepence! Oh-h-h-h My! Ha ha ha ha ha!"

Mrs. Boffin clapped her hands again, rocked herself again, beat her feet upon the floor, and wiped the tears of laughter from her eyes.

"And what, my old lady," inquired Mr. Boffin, when he also had sympathetically laughed: "what's your views on the subject of the Bower?"

"Shut it up. Don't part with it, but put somebody in it, to keep it."

"Any other views?"

"Noddy," said Mrs. Boffin, coming from her fashionable sofa to his side on the plain settle, and hooking her comfortable arm through his, "Next I think—and I really have been thinking early and late—of the disappointed girl; her that was so cruelly disappointed, you know, both of her husband and his riches. Don't you think we might do something for her? Have her to live with us? Or something of that sort?"

"Ne-ver once thought of the way of doing it!" cried Mr. Boffin, smiting the table in his admiration. "What a thinking steam-ingein this old lady is. And she don't know how she does it. Neither does the ingein!"

Mrs. Boffin pulled his nearest ear, in acknowledgment of this piece of philosophy, and then said, gradually toning down to a motherly strain: "Last, and not least, I have taken a fancy. You remember dear little John Harmon, before he went to school? Over yonder across the yard, at our fire? Now that he is past all benefit of the money, and it s come to us, I should like to find some orphan child, and take the boy and adopt him and give him John's name, and provide for him. Somehow, it would make me easier, I fancy. Say it's only a whim——"

"But I don't say so," interposed her husband.

"No, but deary, if you did——"

"I should be a Beast if I did," her husband interposed again.

"That's as much as to say you agree? Good and kind of you, and like you, deary! And don't you begin to find it pleasant now," said Mrs. Boffin, once more radiant in her comely way from head to foot, and once more smoothing her dress with immense enjoyment, "don't you begin to find it pleasant already, to think that a child will be made brighter, and better, and happier, because of that poor sad child that day? And isn't it pleasant to know that the good will be done with the poor sad child's own money?"

"Yes; and it's pleasant to know that you are Mrs. Boffin," said her husband, "and it's been a pleasant thing to know this many and many a year!" It was ruin to Mrs. Boffin's aspirations, but, having so spoken, they sat side by side, a hopelessly Unfashionable pair.

These two ignorant and unpolished people had guided themselves so far on in their journey of life, by a religious sense of duty and desire to do right. Ten thousand weaknesses and absurdities might have been detected in the breasts of both; ten thousand vanities additional, possibly, in the breast of the woman. But the hard wrathful and sordid nature that had wrung as much work out of them as could be got in their best days, for as little money as could be paid to hurry on their worst, had never been so warped but that it knew their moral straightness and respected it. In its own despite, in a constant conflict with itself and them, it had done so. And this is the eternal law. For, Evil often stops short at itself and dies with the doer of it; but Good, never.

Through his most inveterate purposes, the dead Jailer of Harmony Jail had known these two faithful servants to be honest and true. While he raged at them and reviled them for opposing him with the speech of the honest and true, it had scratched his stony heart, and he had perceived the powerlessness of all his wealth to buy them if he had addressed himself to the attempt. So, even while he was their griping taskmaster and never gave them a good word, he had written their names down in his will. So, even while it was his daily declaration that he mistrusted all mankind—and sorely indeed he did mistrust all who bore any resemblance to himself—he was as certain that these two people, surviving him, would be trustworthy in all things from the greatest to the least, as he was that he must surely die.

Mr. and Mrs. Boffin, sitting side by side, with Fashion withdrawn to an immeasurable distance, fell to discussing how they could best find their orphan. Mrs. Boffin suggested advertisement in the newspapers, requesting orphans answering annexed description to apply at the Bower on a certain day; but Mr. Boffin wisely apprehending obstruction of the neighbouring thoroughfares by orphan swarms, this course was negatived. Mrs. Boffin next suggested application to their clergyman for a likely orphan. Mr. Boffin thinking better of this scheme, they resolved to call upon the reverend gentleman at once, and to take the same opportunity of making acquaintance with Miss Bella Wilfer. In order that these visits might be visits of state, Mrs. Boffin's equipage was ordered out.

This consisted of a long hammer-headed old horse, formerly used in the business, attached to a four-wheeled chaise of the same period, which had long been exclusively used by the Harmony Jail poultry as the favourite laying-place of several discreet hens. An unwonted application of corn to the horse, and of paint and varnish to the carriage, when both fell in as a part of the Boffin legacy, had made what Mr. Boffin considered a neat turn-out of the whole; and a driver being added, in the person of a long hammer-headed young man who was a very good match for the horse, left nothing to be desired. He, too, had been formerly used in the business, but was now entombed by an honest jobbing tailor of the district in a perfect Sepulchre of coat and gaiters, sealed with ponderous buttons.

Behind this domestic, Mr. and Mrs. Boffin took their seats in the back compartment of the vehicle: which was sufficiently commodious, but had an undignified and alarming tendency, in getting over a rough crossing, to hiccup itself away from the front compartment. On their being descried emerging from the gates of the Bower, the neighbourhood turned out at door and window to salute the Boffins. Among those who were ever and again left behind, staring after the equipage, were many youthful spirits, who hailed it in stentorian tones with such congratulations as "Nod-dy Bof-fin!" "Bof-fin's mon-ey!" "Down with the dust, Bof-fin!" and other similar compliments. These, the hammer-headed young man took in such ill part that he often impaired the majesty of the progress by pulling up short, and making as though he would alight to exterminate the offenders; a purpose from which he only allowed himself to be dissuaded after long and lively arguments with his employers.

At length the Bower district was left behind, and the peaceful dwelling of the Reverend Frank Milvey was gained. The Reverend Frank Milvey's abode was a very modest abode, because his income was a very modest income. He was officially accessible to every blundering old woman who had incoherence to bestow upon him, and readily received the Boffins. He was quite a young man, expensively educated and wretchedly paid, with quite a young wife and half-a-dozen quite young children. He was under the necessity of teaching and translating from the classics, to eke out his scanty means, yet was generally expected to have more time to spare than the idlest person in the parish, and more money than the richest. He accepted the needless inequalities and inconsistencies of his life, with a kind of conventional submission that was almost slavish; and any daring layman who would have adjusted such burdens as his, more decently and graciously, would have had small help from him.

With a ready patient face and manner, and yet with a latent smile that showed a quick enough observation of Mrs. Boffin's dress, Mr. Milvey, in his little back-room—charged with sounds and cries as though the six children above were coming down through the ceiling, and the roasting leg of mutton below were coming up through the floor—listened to Mrs. Boffin's statement of her want of an orphan.

"I think," said Mr. Milvey, "that you have never had a child of your own, Mr. and Mrs. Boffin?"

Never.

"But, like the Kings and Queens in the Fairy Tales, I suppose you have wished for one?"

In a general way, yes.

Mr. Milvey smiled again, as he remarked to himself, "Those kings and queens were always wishing for children." It occurred to him, perhaps, that if they had been Curates, their wishes might have tended in the opposite direction.

"I think," he pursued, "we had better take Mrs. Milvey into our Council. She is indispensable to me. If you please, I'll call her."

So, Mr. Milvey called, "Margaretta, my dear!" and Mrs. Milvey came down. A pretty, bright little woman, something worn by anxiety, who had repressed many pretty tastes and bright fancies, and substituted in their stead, schools, soup, flannel, coals, and all the week-day cares and Sunday coughs of a large population, young and old. As gallantly had Mr. Milvey repressed much in himself that naturally belonged to his old studies and old fellow-students, and taken up among the poor and their children with the hard crumbs of life.

"Mr. and Mrs. Boffin, my dear, whose good fortune you have heard of."

Mrs. Milvey, with the most unaffected grace in the world, congratulated them, and was glad to see them. Yet her engaging face, being an open as well as a perceptive one, was not without her husband's latent smile.

"Mrs. Boffin wishes to adopt a little boy, my dear."

Mrs. Milvey looking rather alarmed, her husband added:

"An orphan, my dear."

"Oh!" said Mrs. Milvey, reassured for her own little boys.

"And I was thinking, Margaretta, that perhaps old Mrs. Goody's grandchild might answer the purpose."

"Oh, my *dear* Frank! I *don't* think that would do!"

"No?"

"Oh *no!*"

The smiling Mrs. Boffin, feeling it incumbent on her to take part in the conversation, and being charmed with the emphatic little wife and her ready interest, here offered her acknowledgments and inquired what there was against him?

"I *don't* think," said Mrs. Milvey, glancing at the Reverend Frank—"and I believe my husband will agree with me when he considers it again—that you could possibly keep that orphan clean from snuff. Because his grandmother takes so *many* ounces, and drops it over him."

"But he would not be living with his grandmother then, Margaretta," said Mr. Milvey.

"No, Frank, but it would be impossible to keep her from Mrs. Boffin's house; and the *more* there was to eat and drink there, the oftener she would go. And she *is* an inconvenient woman. I *hope* it's not uncharitable to remember that last Christmas Eve she drank eleven cups of tea, and grumbled all the time. And she is *not* a grateful woman, Frank. You recollect her addressing a crowd outside this house, about her wrongs, when, one night after we had gone to bed, she brought back the petticoat of new flannel that had been given her, because it was too short."

"That's true," said Mr. Milvey. "I don't think that would do. Would little Harrison——"

"Oh, *Frank!*" remonstrated his emphatic wife.

"He has no grandmother, my dear."

"No, but I *don't* think Mrs. Boffin would like an orphan who squints so *much*."

"That's true again," said Mr. Milvey, becoming haggard with perplexity. "If a little girl would do——"

"But, my *dear* Frank, Mrs. Boffin wants a boy."

"That's true again," said Mr. Milvey. "Tom Bocker is a nice boy" (thoughtfully).

"But I *doubt*, Frank," Mrs. Milvey hinted, after a little hesitation, "if Mrs. Boffin wants an orphan *quite* nineteen, who drives a cart and waters the roads."

Mr. Milvey referred the point to Mrs. Boffin in a look; on that smiling lady's shaking her black velvet bonnet and bows, he remarked, in lower spirits, "That's true again."

"I am sure," said Mrs. Boffin, concerned at giving so much trouble, "that if I had known you would have taken so much pains, sir—and you too, ma'am—I don't think I would have come."

"*Pray* don't say that!" urged Mrs. Milvey.

"No, don't say that," assented Mr. Milvey, "because we are so much obliged to you for giving us the preference." Which Mrs. Milvey confirmed; and really the kind, conscientious couple spoke as if they kept some profitable orphan warehouse and were personally patronised. "But it is a responsible trust," added Mr. Milvey, "and difficult to discharge. At the same time, we are naturally very unwilling to lose the chance you so kindly give us, and if you could afford us a day or two to look about us,—you know, Margaretta, we might carefully examine the workhouse, and the Infant School, and your District."

"To be *sure!*" said the emphatic little wife.

"We have orphans, I know," pursued Mr. Milvey, quite with the air as if he might have added, "in stock," and quite as anxiously as if there were great competition in the business and he were afraid of losing an order, "over at the claypits; but they are employed by relations or friends, and I am afraid it would come at last to a transaction in the way of barter. And even if you exchanged blankets for the child—or books and firing—it would be impossible to prevent their being turned into liquor."

Accordingly, it was resolved that Mr. and Mrs. Milvey should search for an orphan likely to suit, and as free as possible from the foregoing objections, and should communicate again with Mrs. Boffin. Then, Mr. Boffin took the liberty of mentioning to Mr. Milvey that if Mr. Milvey would do him the kindness to be perpetually his banker to the extent of "a twenty pound note or so," to be expended without any reference to him, he would be heartily obliged. At this, both

Mr. Milvey and Mrs. Milvey were quite as much pleased as if they had no wants of their own, but only knew what poverty was, in the persons of other people; and so the interview terminated with satisfaction and good opinion on all sides.

"Now, old lady," said Mr. Boffin, as they resumed their seats behind the hammer-headed horse and man: "having made a very agreeable visit there, we'll try Wilfer's."

It appeared, on their drawing up at the family gate, that to try Wilfer's was a thing more easily projected than done, on account of the extreme difficulty of getting into that establishment; three pulls at the bell producing no external result, though each was attended by audible sounds of scampering and rushing within. At the fourth tug—vindictively administered by the hammer-headed young man—Miss Lavinia appeared, emerging from the house in an accidental manner, with a bonnet and parasol, as designing to take a contemplative walk. The young lady was astonished to find visitors at the gate, and expressed her feelings in appropriate action.

"Here's Mr. and Mrs. Boffin!" growled the hammer-headed young man through the bars of the gate, and at the same time shaking it, as if he were on view in a Menagerie; "they've been here half-an-hour."

"Who did you say?" asked Miss Lavinia.

"Mr. and Mrs. BOFFIN!" returned the young man, rising into a roar.

Miss Lavinia tripped up the steps to the house-door, tripped down the steps with the key, tripped across the little garden, and opened the gate. "Please to walk in," said Miss Lavinia, haughtily. "Our servant is out."

Mr. and Mrs. Boffin complying, and pausing in the little hall until Miss Lavinia came up to show them where to go next, perceived three pairs of listening legs upon the stairs above. Mrs. Wilfer's legs, Miss Bella's legs, Mr. George Sampson's legs.

"Mr. and Mrs. Boffin, I think?" said Lavinia, in a warning voice.

Strained attention on the part of Mrs. Wilfer's legs, of Miss Bella's legs, of Mr. George Sampson's legs.

"Yes, miss."

"If you'll step this way—down these stairs—I'll let Ma know."

Excited flight of Mrs. Wilfer's legs, of Miss Bella's legs, of Mr. George Sampson's legs.

After waiting some quarter of an hour alone in the family sitting-room, which presented traces of having been so hastily arranged after a meal, that one might have doubted whether it was made tidy for visitors, or cleared for blindman's buff, Mr. and Mrs. Boffin became aware of the entrance of Mrs. Wilfer, majestically faint, and with a condescending stitch in her side: which was her company manner.

"Pardon me," said Mrs. Wilfer, after the first salutations, and as soon as she had adjusted the handkerchief under her chin, and waved her gloved hands, "to what am I indebted for this honour?"

"To make short of it, ma'am," returned Mr. Boffin, "perhaps you may be acquainted with the names of me and Mrs. Boffin, as having come into a certain property."

"I have heard, sir," returned Mrs. Wilfer, with a dignified bend of her head, "of such being the case."

"And I dare say, ma'am," pursued Mr. Boffin, while Mrs. Boffin added confirmatory nods and smiles, "you are not very much inclined to take kindly to us?"

"Pardon me," said Mrs. Wilfer. "'Twere unjust to visit upon Mr. and Mrs. Boffin a calamity which was doubtless a dispensation." These words were rendered the more effective by a serenely heroic expression of suffering.

"That's fairly meant, I am sure," remarked the honest Mr. Boffin; "Mrs. Boffin and me, ma'am, are plain people, and we don't want to pretend to anything, nor yet to go round and round at anything: because there's always a straight way to everything. Consequently, we make this call to say, that we shall be glad to have the honour and pleasure of your daughter's acquaintance, and that we shall be rejiced if your daughter will come to consider our house in the light of her home equally with this. In short, we want to cheer your daughter, and to give her the opportunity of sharing such pleasures as we are a-going to take ourselves. We want to brisk her up, and brisk her about, and give her a change."

"That's it!" said the open-hearted Mrs. Boffin. "Lor! Let's be comfortable."

Mrs. Wilfer bent her head in a distant manner to her lady visitor, and with majestic monotony replied to the gentleman:

"Pardon me. I have several daughters. Which of my daughters am I to understand is thus favoured by the kind intentions of Mr. Boffin and his lady?"

"Don't you see?" the ever-smiling Mrs. Boffin put in. "Naturally, Miss Bella, you know."

"Oh-h!" said Mrs. Wilfer, with a severely unconvinced look. "My daughter Bella is accessible and shall speak for herself." Then opening the door a little way, simultaneously with a sound of scuttling outside it, the good lady made the proclamation, "Send Miss Bella to me!" Which proclamation, though grandly formal, and one might almost say heraldic, to hear, was in fact enunciated with her maternal eyes reproachfully glaring on that young lady in the flesh—and in so much of it that she was retiring with difficulty into the small closet under the stairs, apprehensive of the emergence of Mr. and Mrs. Boffin.

"The avocations of R. W., my husband," Mrs. Wilfer explained, on resuming her seat, "keep him fully engaged in the City at this time of the day, or he would have had the honour of participating in your reception beneath our humble roof."

"Very pleasant premises!" said Mr. Boffin, cheerfully.

"Pardon me, sir," returned Mrs. Wilfer, correcting him, "it is the abode of conscious though independent Poverty."

Finding it rather difficult to pursue the conversation down this road, Mr. and Mrs. Boffin sat staring at mid-air, and Mrs. Wilfer sat silently giving them to understand that every breath she drew required to be drawn with a self-denial rarely paralleled in history, until Miss Bella appeared: whom Mrs. Wilfer presented, and to whom she explained the purpose of the visitors.

"I am much obliged to you, I am sure," said Miss Bella, coldly shaking her curls, "but I doubt if I have the inclination to go out at all."

"Bella!" Mrs. Wilfer admonished her; "Bella, you must conquer this."

"Yes, do what your Ma says, and conquer it, my dear," urged Mrs. Boffin, "because we shall be so glad to have you, and because you are much too pretty to keep yourself shut up." With that, the pleasant creature gave her a kiss, and patted her on her dimpled shoulders; Mrs. Wilfer sitting stiffly by, like a functionary presiding over an interview, previous to an execution.

"We are going to move into a nice house," said Mrs. Boffin, who was woman enough to compromise Mr. Boffin on that point, when he couldn't very well contest it; "and we are going to set up a nice carriage, and we'll go everywhere and see everything. And you mustn't," seating Bella beside her, and patting her hand, "you mustn't feel a dislike to us to begin with, because we couldn't help it, you know, my dear."

With the natural tendency of youth to yield to candour and sweet temper, Miss Bella was so touched by the simplicity of this address that she frankly returned Mrs. Boffin's kiss. Not at all to the satisfaction of that good woman of the world, her mother, who sought to hold the advantageous ground of obliging the Boffins instead of being obliged.

"My youngest daughter, Lavinia," said Mrs. Wilfer, glad to make a diversion, as that young lady reappeared. "Mr. George Sampson, a friend of the family."

The friend of the family was in that stage of the tender passion which bound him to regard everybody else as the foe of the family. He put the round head of his cane in his mouth, like a stopper, when he sat down. As if he felt himself full to the throat with affronting sentiments. And he eyed the Boffins with implacable eyes.

"If you like to bring your sister with you when you come to stay with us," said Mrs. Boffin, "of course we shall be glad. The better you please yourself, Miss Bella, the better you'll please us."

"Oh, my consent is of no consequence at all, I suppose?" cried Miss Lavinia.

"Lavvy," said her sister, in a low voice, "have the goodness to be seen and not heard."

"No, I won't," replied the sharp Lavinia. "I'm not a child, to be taken notice of by strangers."

"You *are* a child."

"I'm not a child, and I won't be taken notice of. 'Bring your sister,' indeed!"

"Lavinia!" said Mrs. Wilfer. "Hold! I will not allow you to utter in my presence the absurd suspicion that any strangers—I care not what their names—can patronize my child. Do you dare to suppose, you ridiculous girl, that Mr. and Mrs. Boffin would enter these doors upon a patronizing errand; or, if they did, would remain within them, only for one single instant, while your mother had the strength yet remaining in her vital frame to request them to depart? You little know your mother, if you presume to think so."

"It's all very fine," Lavinia began to grumble, when Mrs. Wilfer repeated:

"Hold! I will not allow this. Do you not know what is due to guests? Do you not comprehend that in presuming to hint that this lady and gentleman could have any idea of patronizing any member of your family—I care not which—you accuse them of an impertinence little less than insane?"

"Never mind me and Mrs. Boffin, ma'am," said Mr. Boffin, smilingly; "we don't care."

"Pardon me, but *I* do," returned Mrs. Wilfer.

Miss Lavinia laughed a short laugh as she muttered, "Yes, to be sure."

"And I require my audacious child," proceeded Mrs. Wilfer, with a withering look at her youngest, on whom it had not the slightest effect, "to please to be just to her sister Bella; to remember that her sister Bella is much sought after; and that when her sister Bella accepts an attention, she considers herself to be conferring qui-i-ite as much honour,"—this with an indignant shiver,—"as she receives."

But here Miss Bella repudiated, and said quietly, "I can speak for myself, you know, Ma. You needn't bring *me* in, please."

"And it's all very well aiming at others through convenient me," said the irrepressible Lavinia, spitefully; "but I should like to ask George Sampson what *he* says to it."

"Mr. Sampson," proclaimed Mrs. Wilfer, seeing that young gentleman take his stopper out, and so darkly fixing him with her eyes as that he put it in again: "Mr. Sampson, as a friend of this family, and a frequenter of this house, is, I am persuaded, far too well-bred to interpose on such an invitation."

This exaltation of the young gentleman moved the conscientious Mrs. Boffin to repentance for having done him an injustice in her mind, and consequently to saying that she and Mr. Boffin would at any time be glad to see him; an attention which he handsomely acknowledged by replying, with his stopper unremoved, "Much obliged to you, but I'm always engaged, day and night."

However, Bella compensating for all drawbacks by responding to the advances of the Boffins in an engaging way, that easy pair were on the whole well satisfied, and proposed to the said Bella that as soon as they should be in a condition to receive her in a manner suitable to their desires, Mrs. Boffin should return with notice of the fact. This arrangement Mrs. Wilfer sanctioned with a stately inclination of her head and wave of her gloves, as who should say, "Your demerits shall be overlooked, and you shall be mercifully gratified, poor people."

"By-the-bye, ma'am," said Mr. Boffin, turning back as he was going, "you have a lodger?"

"A gentleman," Mrs. Wilfer answered, qualifying the low expression, "undoubtedly occupies our first floor."

"I may call him Our Mutual Friend," said Mr. Boffin. "What sort of a fellow *is* Our Mutual Friend, now? Do you like him?"

"Mr. Rokesmith is very punctual, very quiet, a very eligible inmate."

"Because," Mr. Boffin explained, "you must know that I am not particularly well acquainted with Our Mutual Friend, for I have only seen him once. You give a good account of him. Is he at home?"

"Mr. Rokesmith is at home," said Mrs. Wilfer; "indeed," pointing through the window, "there he stands at the garden gate. Waiting for you, perhaps?"

"Perhaps so," replied Mr. Boffin. "Saw me come in, maybe."

Bella had closely attended to this short dialogue. Accompanying Mrs. Boffin to the gate, she as closely watched what followed.

"How are you, sir, how are you?" said Mr. Boffin. "This is Mrs. Boffin. Mr. Rokesmith, that I told you of, my dear."

She gave him good day, and he bestirred himself and helped her to her seat, and the like, with a ready hand.

"Good-bye for the present, Miss Bella," said Mrs. Boffin, calling out a hearty parting. "We shall meet again soon! And then I hope I shall have my little John Harmon to show you."

Mr. Rokesmith, who was at the wheel adjusting the skirts of her dress, suddenly looked behind him, and around him, and then looked up at her, with a face so pale that Mrs. Boffin cried:

"Gracious!" And after a moment, "What's the matter, sir?"

"How can you show her the Dead?" returned Mr. Rokesmith.

"It's only an adopted child. One I have told her of. One I'm going to give the name to!"

"You took me by surprise," said Mr. Rokesmith, "and it sounded like an omen, that you should speak of showing the Dead to one so young and blooming."

Now, Bella suspected by this time that Mr. Rokesmith admired her. Whether the knowledge (for it was rather that than suspicion) caused her to incline to him a little more, or a little less, than she had done at first; whether it rendered her eager to find out more about him, because she sought to establish reason for her distrust, or because she sought to free him from it, was as yet dark to her own heart. But at most times he occupied a great amount of her attention, and she had set her attention closely on this incident.

That he knew it as well as she, she knew as well as he, when they were left together standing on the path by the garden gate.

"Those are worthy people, Miss Wilfer."

"Do you know them well?" asked Bella.

He smiled, reproaching her, and she coloured, reproaching herself—both, with the knowledge that she had meant to entrap him into an answer not true—when he said "I know *of* them."

"Truly, he told us he had seen you but once."

"Truly, I supposed he did."

Bella was nervous now, and would have been glad to recall her question.

"You thought it strange that, feeling much interested in you, I should start at what sounded like a proposal to bring you into contact with the murdered man who lies in his grave. I might have known—of course in a moment should have known—that it could not have that meaning. But my interest remains."

Re-entering the family room in a meditative state, Miss Bella was received by the irrepressible Lavinia with:

"There, Bella! At last I hope you have got your wishes realized—by your Boffins. You'll be rich enough now—with your Boffins. You can have as much flirting as you like—at your Boffins'. But you won't take *me* to your Boffins, I can tell you—you and your Boffins too!"

"If," quoth Mr. George Sampson, moodily pulling his stopper out, "Miss Bella's Mr. Boffin comes any more of his nonsense to *me*, I only wish him to understand, as betwixt man and man, that he does it at his per——" and was going to say peril; but Miss Lavinia having no confidence in his mental powers, and feeling his oration to have no definite application to any circumstances, jerked his stopper in again, with a sharpness that made his eyes water.

And now the worthy Mrs. Wilfer, having used her youngest daughter as a lay figure for the edification of these Boffins, became bland to her, and proceeded to develop her last instance of force of character, which was still in reserve. This was to illuminate the family with her remarkable powers as a physiognomist; powers that terrified R. W. whenever let loose, as being always fraught with gloom and evil which no inferior prescience was aware of. And this Mrs. Wilfer now did, be it observed, in jealousy of these Boffins, in the very same moments when she was already reflecting how she would flourish these very same Boffins and the state they kept, over the heads of her Boffinless friends.

"Of their manners," said Mrs. Wilfer, "I say nothing. Of their appearance, I say nothing. Of the disinterestedness of their intentions towards Bella, I say nothing. But the craft, the secrecy, the dark deep underhanded plotting, written in Mrs. Boffin's countenance, make me shudder."

As an incontrovertible proof that those baleful attributes were all there, Mrs. Wilfer shuddered on the spot.

CHAPTER X.

A MARRIAGE CONTRACT.

THERE is excitement in the Veneering mansion. The mature young lady is going to be married (powder and all) to the mature young gentleman, and she is to be married from the Veneering house, and the Veneerings are to give the breakfast. The Analytical, who objects as a matter of principle to everything that occurs on the premises, necessarily objects to the match; but his consent has been dispensed with, and a spring van is delivering its load of greenhouse plants at the door, in order that to-morrow's feast may be crowned with flowers.

The mature young lady is a lady of property. The mature young gentleman is a gentleman of property. He invests his property. He goes, in a condescending amateurish way, into the City, attends meetings of Directors, and has to do with traffic in Shares. As is well known to the wise in their generation, traffic in Shares is the one thing to have to do with in this world. Have no antecedents, no established character, no cultivation, no ideas, no manners; have Shares. Have Shares enough to be on Boards of Direction in capital letters, oscillate on mysterious business between London and Paris, and be great. Where does he come from? Shares. Where is he going to? Shares. What are his tastes? Shares. Has he any principles? Shares. What squeezes him into Parliament? Shares. Perhaps he never of himself achieved success in anything, never originated anything, never produced anything! Sufficient answer to all; Shares. O mighty Shares! To set those blaring images so high, and to cause us smaller vermin, as under the influence of henbane or opium, to cry out night and day, "Relieve us of our money, scatter it for us, buy us and sell us, ruin us, only we beseech ye take rank among the powers of the earth, and fatten on us!"

While the Loves and Graces have been preparing this torch for Hymen, which is to be kindled to-morrow, Mr. Twemlow has suffered much in his mind. It would seem that both the mature young lady and the mature young gentleman must indubitably be Veneering's oldest friends. Wards of his, perhaps? Yet that can scarcely be, for they are older than himself. Veneering has been in their confidence throughout, and has done much to lure them to the altar. He has mentioned to Twemlow how he said to Mrs. Veneering, "Anastatia, this must be a match." He has mentioned to Twemlow how he regards Sophronia Akershem (the mature young lady) in the light of a sister, and Alfred Lammle (the mature young gentleman) in the light of a brother. Twemlow has asked him whether he went to school as a junior with Alfred? He has answered, "Not exactly." Whether Sophronia was adopted by his mother? He has answered, "Not precisely so." Twemlow's hand has gone to his forehead with a lost air.

But, two or three weeks ago, Twemlow, sitting over his newspaper, and over his dry toast and weak tea, and over the stable-yard in Duke Street, St. James's, received a highly-perfumed cocked-hat and monogram from Mrs. Veneering, entreating her dearest Mr. T., if not particularly engaged that day, to come like a charming soul and make a fourth at dinner with dear Mr. Podsnap, for the discussion of an interesting family topic; the last three words doubly underlined and pointed with a note of admiration. And Twemlow, replying, "Not engaged, and more than delighted," goes, and this takes place:

"My dear Twemlow," says Veneering, "your ready response to Anastatia's unceremonious invitation is truly kind, and like an old, old friend. You know our dear friend Podsnap?"

Twemlow ought to know the dear friend Podsnap who covered him with so much confusion, and he says he does know him, and Podsnap reciprocates. Apparently, Podsnap has been so wrought upon in a short time, as to believe that he has been intimate in the house many, many, many years. In the friendliest manner he is making himself quite at home with his back to the fire, executing a statuette of the Colossus at Rhodes. Twemlow has before noticed in his feeble way how soon the Veneering guests become infected with the Veneering fiction. Not, however, that he has the least notion of its being his own case.

"Our friends, Alfred and Sophronia," pursues Veneering the veiled prophet: "our friends, Alfred and Sophronia, you will be glad to hear, my dear fellows, are going to be married. As my wife and I make it a family affair, the entire direction of which we take upon ourselves, of course our first step is to communicate the fact to our family friends."

("Oh!" thinks Twemlow, with his eyes on Podsnap, "then there are only two of us, and he's the other.")

"I did hope," Veneering goes on, "to have had Lady Tippins to meet you; but she is always in request, and is unfortunately engaged."

("Oh!" thinks Twemlow, with his eyes wandering, "then there are three of us, and *she's* the other.")

"Mortimer Lightwood," resumes Veneering, "whom you both know, is out of town; but he writes in his whimsical manner, that as we ask him to be bridegroom's best man when the ceremony takes place, he will not refuse, though he doesn't see what he has to do with it."

("Oh!" thinks Twemlow, with his eyes rolling, "then there are four of us, and *he's* the other.")

"Boots and Brewer," observes Veneering, "whom you also know, I have not asked to-day; but I reserve them for the occasion."

("Then," thinks Twemlow, with his eyes shut, "there are si——" But here collapses and does not completely recover until dinner is over and the Analytical has been requested to withdraw.)

"We now come," says Veneering, "to the point, the real point, of our little family consultation. Sophronia, having lost both father and mother, has no one to give her away."

"Give her away yourself," says Podsnap.

"My dear Podsnap, no. For three reasons. Firstly, because I couldn't take so much upon myself when I have respected family friends to remember. Secondly, because I am not so vain as to think that I look the part. Thirdly, because Anastatia is a little superstitious on the subject and feels averse to my giving away anybody until baby is old enough to be married."

"What would happen if he did?" Podsnap inquires of Mrs. Veneering.

"My dear Mr. Podsnap, it's very foolish, I know, but I have an instinctive presentiment that if Hamilton gave away anybody else first, he would never give away baby." Thus Mrs. Veneering, with her open hands pressed together, and each of her eight aquiline fingers looking so very like her one aquiline nose that the bran-new jewels on them seemed necessary for distinction's sake.

"But, my dear Podsnap," quoth Veneering, "there *is* a tried friend of our family who, I think and hope you will agree with me, Podsnap, is the friend on whom this agreeable duty almost naturally devolves. That friend," saying the words as if the company were about a hundred and fifty in number, "is now among us. That friend is Twemlow."

"Certainly!" from Podsnap.

"That friend," Veneering repeats with greater firmness, "is our dear good Twemlow. And I cannot sufficiently express to you, my dear Podsnap, the pleasure I feel in having this opinion of mine and Anastatia's so readily confirmed by you, that other equally familiar and tried friend who stands in the proud position—I mean who proudly stands in the position—or I ought rather to say, who places Anastatia and myself in the proud position of himself standing in the simple position—of baby's godfather." And, indeed, Veneering is much relieved in mind to find that Podsnap betrays no jealousy of Twemlow's elevation.

So, it has come to pass that the spring-van is strewing flowers on the rosy hours and on the staircase, and that Twemlow is surveying the ground on which he is to play his distinguished part to-morrow. He has already been to the church, and taken note of the various impediments in the aisle, under the auspices of an extremely dreary widow who opens the pews, and whose left hand appears to be in a state of acute rheumatism, but is in fact voluntarily doubled up to act as a money-box.

And now Veneering shoots out of the Study wherein he is accustomed, when contemplative, to give his mind to the carving and gilding of the Pilgrims going to Canterbury, in order to show Twemlow the little flourish he has prepared for the trumpets of fashion, describing how that on the seventeenth instant, at St. James's

Church, the Reverend Blank Blank, assisted by the Reverend Dash Dash, united in the bonds of matrimony, Alfred Lammle, Esquire, of Sackville Street, Piccadilly, to Sophronia, only daughter of the late Horatio Akershem, Esquire, of Yorkshire. Also how the fair bride was married from the house of Hamilton Veneering, Esquire, of Stucconia, and was given away by Melvin Twemlow, Esquire, of Duke Street, St. James's, second cousin to Lord Snigsworth, of Snigsworthy Park. While perusing which composition, Twemlow makes some opaque approach to perceiving that if the Reverend Blank Blank and the Reverend Dash Dash fail, after this introduction, to become enrolled in the list of Veneering's dearest and oldest friends, they will have none but themselves to thank for it.

After which, appears Sophronia (whom Twemlow has seen twice in his lifetime), to thank Twemlow for counterfeiting the late Horatio Akershem, Esquire, broadly of Yorkshire. And after her, appears Alfred (whom Twemlow has seen once in his lifetime), to do the same, and to make a pasty sort of glitter, as if he were constructed for candlelight only, and had been let out into daylight by some grand mistake. And after that, comes Mrs. Veneering, in a pervadingly aquiline state of figure, and with transparent little knobs on her temper, like the little transparent knob on the bridge of her nose, "Worn out by worry and excitement," as she tells her dear Mr. Twemlow, and reluctantly revived with curaçoa by the Analytical. And after that, the bridesmaids begin to come by railroad from various parts of the country, and to come like adorable recruits enlisted by a sergeant not present; for, on arriving at the Veneering depôt, they are in a barrack of strangers.

So, Twemlow goes home to Duke Street, St. James's, to take a plate of mutton broth with a chop in it, and a look at the marriage service, in order that he may cut in at the right place to-morrow; and he is low, and feels it dull over the livery stable-yard, and is distinctly aware of a dint in his heart, made by the most adorable of the adorable bridesmaids. For, the poor little harmless gentleman once had his fancy, like the rest of us, and she didn't answer (as she often does not), and he thinks the adorable bridesmaid is like the fancy as she was then (which she is not at all), and that if the fancy had not married some one else for money, but had married him for love, he and she would have been happy (which they wouldn't have been), and that she has a tenderness for him still (whereas her toughness is a proverb). Brooding over the fire, with his dried little head in his dried little hands, and his dried little elbows on his dried little knees, Twemlow is melancholy. "No Adorable to bear me company here!" thinks he. "No Adorable at the club! A waste, a waste, a waste, my Twemlow!" And so drops asleep, and has galvanic starts all over him.

Betimes next morning, that horrible old Lady Tippins (relict of the late Sir Thomas Tippins, knighted in mistake for somebody else by His Majesty King George the Third, who, while performing the ceremony, was graciously pleased to observe, "What, what, what? Who, who, who? Why, why, why?") begins to be dyed and varnished for the interesting occasion. She has a reputation for giving smart accounts of things, and she must be at these people's early, my dear, to lose nothing of the fun. Whereabout in the bonnet and drapery announced by her name, any fragment of the real woman may be concealed, is perhaps known to her maid; but you could easily buy all you see of her, in Bond Street: or you might scalp her, and peel her, and scrape her, and make two Lady Tippinses out of her, and yet not penetrate to the genuine article. She has a large gold eye-glass, has Lady Tippins, to survey the proceedings with. If she had one in each eye, it might keep that other drooping lid up, and look more uniform. But perennial youth is in her artificial flowers, and her list of lovers is full.

"Mortimer, you wretch," says Lady Tippins, turning the eye-glass about and about, "where is your charge, the bridegroom?"

"Give you my honour," returns Mortimer, "I don't know, and I don't care."

"Miserable! Is that the way you do your duty?"

"Beyond an impression that he is to sit upon my knee and be seconded at some point of the solemnities, like a principal at a prize-fight, I assure you I have no notion what my duty is," returns Mortimer.

Eugene is also in attendance, with a pervading air upon him of having presupposed the ceremony to be a funeral, and of being disappointed. The scene is the Vestry-room of St. James's Church, with a number of leathery old registers on shelves, that might be bound in Lady Tippinses.

But, hark! A carriage at the gate, and Mortimer's man arrives, looking rather like a spurious Mephistopheles and an unacknowledged member of that gentleman's family. Whom Lady Tippins, surveying through her eye-glass, considers a fine man, and quite a catch, and of whom Mortimer remarks, in the lowest spirits, as he approaches, "I believe this is my fellow, confound him!" More carriages at the gate, and lo, the rest of the characters. Whom Lady Tippins, standing on a cushion, surveying through the eye-glass, thus checks off: "Bride; five-and-forty if a day, thirty shillings a yard, veil fifteen pounds, pocket-handkerchief a present. Bridesmaids; kept down for fear of outshining bride, consequently not girls, twelve and sixpence a yard, Veneering's flowers, snub-nosed one rather pretty but too conscious of her stockings, bonnets three pound ten. Twemlow; blessed release for the dear man if she really was his daughter, nervous even under the pretence that she is, well he may be. Mrs. Veneering; never saw such velvet, say two thousand pounds as she stands, absolute jeweller's window, father must have been a pawnbroker, or how could these people do it? Attendant unknowns; pokey."

Ceremony performed, register signed, Lady Tippins escorted out of sacred edifice by Veneering, carriages rolling back to Stucconia, servants with favours and flowers, Veneering's house reached, drawing-rooms most magnificent. Here, the Podsnaps await the happy party; Mr. Podsnap, with his hair-brushes made the most of; that imperial rocking-horse, Mrs. Podsnap, majestically skittish. Here, too, are Boots and Brewer, and the two other Buffers; each Buffer with a flower in his button-hole, his hair curled, and his gloves buttoned on tight, apparently come prepared, if anything had happened to the bridegroom, to be married instantly. Here, too, the bride's aunt, and next relation; a widowed female of a Medusa sort, in a stony cap, glaring petrifaction at her fellow-creatures. Here, too, the bride's trustee; an oilcake-fed style of business-gentleman with mooney spectacles, and an object of much interest. Veneering launching himself upon this trustee as his oldest friend (which makes seven, Twemlow thought), and confidentially retiring with him into the conservatory, it is understood that Veneering is his co-trustee, and that they are arranging about the fortune. Buffers are even overheard to whisper Thir-ty Thou-sand Pou-nds! with a smack and a relish suggestive of the very finest oysters. Pokey unknowns, amazed to find how intimately they know Veneering, pluck up spirit, fold their arms, and begin to contradict him before breakfast. What time Mrs. Veneering, carrying baby dressed as a bridesmaid, flits about among the company, emitting flashes of many-coloured lightning from diamonds, emeralds, and rubies.

The Analytical, in course of time achieving what he feels to be due to himself in bringing to a dignified conclusion several quarrels he has on hand with the pastrycook's men, announces breakfast. Dining-room no less magnificent than drawing-room; tables superb; all the camels out, and all laden. Splendid cake, covered with Cupids, silver, and true-lovers' knots. Splendid bracelet, produced by Veneering before going down, and clasped upon the arm of bride. Yet nobody seems to think much more of the Veneerings than if they were a tolerable landlord and landlady doing the thing in the way of business at so much a head. The bride and bridegroom talk and laugh apart, as has always been their manner; and the Buffers work their way through the dishes with systematic perseverance, as has always been *their* manner; and the pokey unknowns are exceedingly benevolent to one another in invitations to take glasses of champagne; but Mrs. Podsnap, arching her mane and rocking her grandest, has a far more deferential audience than Mrs. Veneering; and Podsnap all but does the honours.

Another dismal circumstance is, that Veneering, having the captivating Tippins on one side of him and the bride's aunt on the other, finds it immensely difficult to keep the peace. For, Medusa, besides unmistakingly glaring petrifaction at the fascinating Tippins, follows every lively remark made by that dear creature with an audible snort: which may be referable to a chronic cold in the head, but may also be referable to indignation and contempt. And this snort being regular in its reproduction, at length comes to be expected by the company, who make embarrassing pauses when it is falling due, and by waiting for it, render it more emphatic when it comes. The stony aunt has likewise an injurious way of rejecting all dishes whereof Lady Tippins partakes: saying aloud when they are proffered to her, "No, no, no, not for me. Take it away!" As with a set purpose of implying a misgiving that if nourished upon similar meats she might come to be like that charmer, which would be a fatal consummation. Aware of her enemy, Lady Tippins tries a youthful sally or two, and tries the eye-glass; but, from the impenetrable cap and snorting armour of the stony aunt all weapons rebound powerless.

Another objectionable circumstance is, that the pokey unknowns support each other in being unimpressible. They persist in not being frightened by the gold and silver camels, and they are banded together to defy the elaborately chased ice-pails. They even seem to unite in some vague utterance of the sentiment that the landlord and landlady will make a pretty good profit out of this, and they almost carry themselves like customers. Nor is there compensating influence in the adorable bridesmaids; for, having very little interest in the bride, and none at all in one another, those lovely beings become, each one on her own account, depreciatingly contemplative of the millinery present. While the bridegroom's man, exhausted, in the back of his chair, appears to be improving the occasion by penitentially contemplating all the wrong he has ever done; the difference between him and his friend Eugene being, that the latter, in the back of *his* chair, appears to be contemplating all the wrong he would like to do—particularly to the present company.

In which state of affairs, the usual ceremonies rather droop and flag, and the spendid cake when cut by the fair hand of the bride has but an indigestible appearance. However, all the things indispensable to be said are said, and all the things indispensable to be done are done (including Lady Tippins's yawning, falling asleep, and waking insensible), and there is hurried preparation for the nuptial journey to the Isle of Wight, and the outer air teems with brass bands and spectators. In full sight of whom, the malignant star of the Analytical has pre-ordained that pain and ridicule shall befall him. For he, standing on the doorsteps to grace the departure, is suddenly caught a most prodigious thump on the side of his head with a heavy shoe, which a Buffer in the hall, champagne-flushed and wild of aim, has borrowed on the spur of the moment from the pastrycook's porter, to cast after the departing pair as an auspicious omen.

So they all go up again into the gorgeous drawing-rooms—all of them flushed with breakfast, as having taken scarlatina sociably—and there the combined unknowns do malignant things with their legs to ottomans, and take as much as possible out of the splendid furniture. And so, Lady Tippins, quite undetermined whether to-day is the day before yesterday, or the day after to-morrow, or the week after next, fades away; and Mortimer Lightwood and Eugene fade away, and Twemlow fades away, and the stony aunt goes away—she declines to fade, proving rock to the last—and even the unknowns are slowly strained off, and it is all over.

All over, that is to say, for the time being. But, there is another time to come, and it comes in about a fortnight, and it comes to Mr. and Mrs. Lammle on the sands at Shanklin, in the Isle of Wight.

Mr. and Mrs. Lammle have walked for some time on the Shanklin sands, and one may see by their footprints that they have not walked arm in arm, and that they have not walked in a straight track, and that they have walked in a moody humour; for, the lady has prodded little spirting holes in the damp sand before her with her parasol, and the gentleman has trailed his stick after him. As if he were of the Mephistopheles family indeed, and had walked with a drooping tail.

"Do you mean to tell me, then, Sophronia——"

Thus he begins after a long silence, when Sophronia flashes fiercely, and turns upon him.

"Don't put it upon *me*, sir. I ask you, do *you* mean to tell me?"

Mr. Lammle falls silent again, and they walk as before. Mrs. Lammle opens her nostrils and bites her under-lip; Mr. Lammle takes his gingerous whiskers in his left hand, and bringing them together, frowns furtively at his beloved, out of a thick gingerous bush.

"Do *I* mean to say!" Mrs. Lammle after a time repeats, with indignation. "Putting it on me! The unmanly disingenuousness!"

Mr. Lammle stops, releases his whiskers, and looks at her. "The what?"

Mrs. Lammle haughtily replies, without stopping, and without looking back. "The meanness."

He is at her side again in a pace or two, and he retorts, "That is not what you said. You said disingenuousness."

"What if I did?"

"There is no 'if' in the case. You did."

"I did, then. And what of it?"

"What of it?" says Mr. Lammle. "Have you the face to utter the word to me?"

"The face, too!" replied Mrs. Lammle, staring at him with cold scorn. "Pray, how dare you, sir, utter the word to me?"

"I never did."

As this happens to be true, Mrs. Lammle is thrown on the feminine resource of saying, "I don't care what you uttered or did not utter."

After a little more walking and a little more silence, Mr. Lammle breaks the latter.

"You shall proceed in your own way. You claim a right to ask me do I mean to tell you. Do I mean to tell you what?"

"That you are a man of property?"

"No."

"Then you married me on false pretences?"

"So be it. Next comes what you mean to say. Do you mean to say you are a woman of property?"

"No."

"Then you married me on false pretences."

"If you were so dull a fortune hunter that you deceived yourself, or if you were so greedy and grasping that you were over-willing to be deceived by appearances, is it my fault, you adventurer?" the lady demands, with great asperity.

"I asked Veneering, and he told me you were rich."

"Veneering!" with great contempt. "And what does Veneering know about me?"

"Was he not your trustee?"

"No. I have no trustee, but the one you saw on the day when you fraudulently married me. And his trust is not a very difficult one, for it is only an annuity of a hundred and fifteen pounds. I think there are some odd shillings or pence, if you are very particular."

Mr. Lammle bestows a by no means loving look upon the partner of his joys and sorrows, and he mutters something; but checks himself.

"Question for question. It is my turn again, Mrs. Lammle. What made you suppose me a man of property?"

"You made me suppose you so. Perhaps you will deny that you always presented yourself to me in that character?"

"But you asked somebody, too. Come, Mrs. Lammle, admission for admission. You asked somebody?"

"I asked Veneering."

"And Veneering knew as much of me as he knew of you, or as anybody knows of him."

After more silent walking, the bride stops short, to say in a passionate manner:

"I never will forgive the Veneerings for this!"

"Neither will I," returns the bridegroom.

With that, they walk again; she, making those angry spirts in the sand, he, dragging that dejected tail. The tide is low, and seems to have thrown them together high on the bare shore. A gull comes sweeping by their heads, and flouts them. There was a golden surface on the brown cliffs but now, and behold they are only damp earth. A taunting roar comes from the sea, and the far-out rollers mount upon one another, to look at the entrapped impostors, and to join in impish and exultant gambols.

"Do you pretend to believe," Mrs. Lammle resumes, sternly, "when you talk of my marrying you for worldly advantages, that it was within the bounds of reasonable probability that I would have married you for yourself?"

"Again there are two sides to the question, Mrs. Lammle. What do you pretend to believe?"

"So you first deceive me and then insult me!" cries the lady, with a heaving bosom.

"Not at all. I have originated nothing. The double-edged question was yours."

"Was mine!" the bride repeats, and her parasol breaks in her angry hand.

His colour has turned to a livid white, and ominous marks have come to light about his nose, as if the finger of the very devil himself had, within the last few moments, touched it here and there. But he has repressive power, and she has none.

"Throw it away," he coolly recommends as to the parasol; "you have made it useless; you look ridiculous with it."

Whereupon she calls him in her rage, "a deliberate villain," and so casts the broken thing from her as that it strikes him in falling. The finger-marks are something whiter for the instant, but he walks on at her side.

She bursts into tears, declaring herself the wretchedest, the most deceived, the worst-used of women. Then she says that if she had the courage to kill herself, she would do it. Then she calls him vile impostor. Then she asks him, why, in the disappointment of his base speculation, he does not take her life with his own hand, under the present favourable circumstances. Then she cries again. Then she is enraged again, and makes some mention of swindlers. Finally, she sits down crying on a block of stone, and is in all the known and unknown humours of her sex at once. Pending her changes, those aforesaid marks in his face have come and gone, now here now there, like white stops of a pipe on which the diabolical performer has played a tune. Also his livid lips are parted at last, as if he were breathless with running. Yet he is not.

"Now, get up, Mrs. Lammle, and let us speak reasonably."

She sits upon her stone, and takes no heed of him.

"Get up, I tell you."

Raising her head, she looks contemptuously in his face, and repeats, "You tell me! Tell me, forsooth!"

She affects not to know that his eyes are fastened on her as she droops her head again; but her whole figure reveals that she knows it uneasily.

"Enough of this. Come! Do you hear? Get up!"

Yielding to his hand, she rises, and they walk again; but this time with their faces turned towards their place of residence.

"Mrs. Lammle, we have both been deceiving, and we have both been deceived We have both been biting, and we have both been bitten. In a nut-shell, there's the state of the case."

"You sought me out——"

"Tut! Let us have done with that. *We* know very well how it was. Why should you and I talk about it, when you and I can't disguise it? To proceed. I am disappointed and cut a poor figure."

"Am I no one?"

"Some one—and I was coming to you, if you had waited a moment. You, too, are disappointed and cut a poor figure."

"An injured figure!"

"You are now cool enough, Sophronia, to see that you can't be injured without my being equally injured; and that therefore the mere word is not to the purpose. When I look back, I wonder how I can have been such a fool as to take you to so great an extent upon trust."

"And when I look back——" the bride cries, interrupting.

"And when you look back, you wonder how you can have been—you'll excuse the word?"

"Most certainly, with so much reason."

"—Such a fool as to take *me* to so great an extent upon trust. But the folly is committed on both sides. I cannot get rid of you; you cannot get rid of me. What follows?"

"Shame and misery," the bride bitterly replies.

"I don't know. A mutual understanding follows, and I think it may carry us through. Here I split my discourse (give me your arm, Sophronia) into three heads, to make it shorter and plainer. Firstly, it's enough to have been done, without the mortification of being known to have been done. So we agree to keep the fact to ourselves. You agree?"

"If it is possible, I do."

"Possible! We have pretended well enough to one another. Can't we, united, pretend to the world? Agreed. Secondly, we owe the Veneerings a grudge, and we owe all other people the grudge of wishing them to be taken in, as we ourselves have been taken in. Agreed?"

"Yes. Agreed."

"We come smoothly to thirdly. You have called me an adventurer, Sophronia. So I am. In plain uncomplimentary English, so I am. So are you, my dear. So are many people. We agree to keep our own secret, and to work together in furtherance of our own schemes."

"What schemes?"

"Any scheme that will bring us money. By our own schemes, I mean our joint interest. Agreed?"

She answers, after a little hesitation, "I suppose so. Agreed."

"Carried at once, you see! Now, Sophronia, only half-a-dozen words more. We know one another perfectly. Don't be tempted into twitting me with the past knowledge that you have of me, because it is identical with the past knowledge that I have of you, and in twitting me, you twit yourself, and I don't want to hear you do it. With this good understanding established between us, it is better never done. To wind up all:—You have shown temper to-day, Sophronia. Don't be betrayed into doing so again, because I have a Devil of a temper myself."

So, the happy pair, with this hopeful marriage contract thus signed, sealed, and delivered, repair homeward. If, when those infernal fingermarks were on the white and breathless countenance of Alfred Lammle, Esquire, they denoted that he conceived the purpose of subduing his dear wife Mrs. Alfred Lammle, by at once divesting her of any lingering reality or pretence of self-respect, the purpose would seem to have been presently executed. The mature young lady has mighty little need of powder, now, for her downcast face, as he escorts her in the light of the setting sun to their abode of bliss.

CHAPTER XI.

PODSNAPPERY.

MR. PODSNAP was well to do, and stood very high in Mr. Podsnap's opinion. Beginning with a good inheritance, he had married a good inheritance, and had thriven exceedingly in the Marine Insurance way, and was quite satisfied. He never could make out why everybody was not quite satisfied, and he felt conscious that he set a brilliant social example in being particularly well satisfied with most things, and, above all other things, with himself.

Thus happily acquainted with his own merit and importance, Mr. Podsnap settled that whatever he put behind him he put out of existence. There was a dignified conclusiveness—not to add a grand convenience—in this way of getting rid of disagreeables, which had done much towards establishing Mr. Podsnap in his lofty place in Mr. Podsnap's satisfaction. "I don't want to know about it; I don't choose to discuss it; I don't admit it!" Mr. Podsnap had even acquired a peculiar flourish of his right arm in often clearing the world of its most difficult problems, by sweeping them behind him (and consequently sheer away) with those words and a flushed face. For they affronted him.

Mr. Podsnap's world was not a very large world, morally; no, nor even geographically: seeing that although his business was sustained upon commerce with other countries, he considered other countries, with that important reservation, a mistake, and of their manners and customs would conclusively observe, "Not English!" when, PRESTO! with a flourish of the arm, and a flush of the face, they were swept away. Elsewise, the world got up at eight, shaved close at a quarter-past, breakfasted at nine, went to the City at ten, came home at half-past five, and dined at seven. Mr. Podsnap's notions of the Arts in their integrity might have been stated thus. Literature; large print, respectively descriptive of getting up at eight, shaving close at a quarter-past, breakfasting at nine, going to the City at ten, coming home at half-past five, and dining at seven. Painting and Sculpture; models and portraits representing Professors of getting up at eight, shaving close at a quarter-past, breakfasting at nine, going to the City at ten, coming home at half-past five, and dining at seven. Music; a respectable performance (without variations) on stringed and wind instruments, sedately expressive of getting up at eight, shaving close at a quarter-past, breakfasting at nine, going to the City at ten, coming home at half-past five, and dining at seven. Nothing else to be permitted to those same vagrants the Arts, on pain of excommunication. Nothing else To Be—anywhere!

As a so eminently respectable man, Mr. Podsnap was sensible of its being required of him to take Providence under his protection. Consequently he always knew exactly what Providence meant. Inferior and less respectable men might fall short of that mark, but Mr. Podsnap was always up to it. And it was very remarkable (and must have been very comfortable) that what Providence meant, was invariably what Mr. Podsnap meant.

These may be said to have been the articles of a faith and school which the present chapter takes the liberty of calling, after its representative man, Podsnappery. They were confined within close bounds, as Mr. Podsnap's own head was confined by his shirt-collar; and they were enunciated with a sounding pomp that smacked of the creaking of Mr. Podsnap's own boots.

There was a Miss Podsnap. And this young rocking-horse was being trained in her mother's art of prancing in a stately manner without ever getting on. But the high parental action was not yet imparted to her, and in truth she was but an under-sized damsel, with high shoulders, low spirits, chilled elbows, and a rasped surface of nose, who seemed to take occasional frosty peeps out of childhood into womanhood, and to shrink back again, overcome by her mother's head-dress and her father from head to foot—crushed by the mere dead-weight of Podsnappery.

A certain institution in Mr. Podsnap's mind which he called "the young person" may be considered to have been embodied in Miss Podsnap, his daughter. It was an inconvenient and exacting institution, as requiring everything in the universe to be filed down and fitted to it. The question about everything was, would it bring a blush into the cheek of the young person? And the inconvenience of the young person was, that, according to Mr. Podsnap, she seemed always liable to burst into blushes when there was no need at all. There appeared to be no line of demarcation between the young person's excessive innocence, and another person's guiltiest knowledge. Take Mr. Podsnap's word for it, and the soberest tints of drab, white, lilac, and grey, were all flaming red to this troublesome Bull of a young person.

The Podsnaps lived in a shady angle adjoining Portman Square. They were a kind of people certain to dwell in the shade, wherever they dwelt. Miss Podsnap's life had been, from her first appearance on this planet, altogether of a shady order; for, Mr. Podsnap's young person was likely to get little good out of association with other young persons, and had therefore been restricted to companionship with not very congenial older persons, and with massive furniture. Miss Podsnap's early views of life being principally derived from the reflections of it in her father's boots, and in the walnut and rosewood tables of the dim drawing-rooms, and in their swarthy giants of looking-glasses, were of a sombre cast; and it was not wonderful that now, when she was on most days solemnly tooled through the Park by the side of her mother in a great tall custard-coloured phaeton, she showed above the apron of that vehicle like a dejected young person sitting up in bed to take a startled look at things in general, and very strongly desiring to get her head under the counterpane again.

Said Mr. Podsnap to Mrs. Podsnap, "Georgiana is almost eighteen."

Said Mrs. Podsnap to Mr. Podsnap, assenting, "Almost eighteen."

Said Mr. Podsnap then to Mrs. Podsnap, "Really I think we should have some people on Georgiana's birthday."

Said Mrs. Podsnap then to Mr. Podsnap, "Which will enable us to clear off all those people who are due."

So it came to pass that Mr. and Mrs. Podsnap requested the honour of the company of seventeen friends of their souls at dinner; and that they substituted other friends of their souls for such of the seventeen original friends of their souls as deeply regretted that a prior engagement prevented their having the honour of dining with Mr. and Mrs. Podsnap, in pursuance of their kind invitation; and that Mrs. Podsnap said of all these inconsolable personages, as she checked them off with a pencil in her list, "Asked, at any rate, and got rid of;" and that they successfully disposed of a good many friends of their souls in this way, and felt their consciences much lightened.

There were still other friends of their souls who were not entitled to be asked to dinner, but had a claim to be invited to come and take a haunch of mutton vapour-bath at half-past nine. For the clearing off of these worthies, Mrs. Podsnap added a small and early evening to the dinner, and looked in at the music-shop to bespeak a well-conducted automaton to come and play quadrilles for a carpet dance.

Mr. and Mrs. Veneering, and Mr. and Mrs. Veneering's bran-new bride and bridegroom, were of the dinner company; but the Podsnap establishment had nothing else in common with the Veneerings. Mr. Podsnap could tolerate taste in a mushroom man who stood in need of that sort of thing, but was far above it himself. Hideous solidity was the characteristic of the Podsnap plate. Everything was made to look as heavy as it could, and to take up as much room as possible. Everything said boastfully, "Here you have as much of me in my ugliness as if I were only lead; but I am so many ounces of precious metal worth so much an ounce;—wouldn't you like to melt me down?" A corpulent straddling epergne, blotched all over as if it had broken out in an eruption rather than been ornamented, delivered this address from an unsightly silver platform in the centre of the table. Four silver wine-coolers, each furnished with four staring heads, each head obtrusively carrying a big silver ring in each of its ears, conveyed the sentiment up and down the table, and handed it on to the pot-bellied silver salt-cellars. All the big silver spoons and forks widened the mouths of the company expressly for the purpose of thrusting the sentiment down their throats with every morsel they ate.

The majority of the guests were like the plate, and included several heavy articles weighing ever so much. But there was a foreign gentleman among them: whom Mr. Podsnap had invited after much debate with himself—believing the whole European continent to be in mortal alliance against the young person—and there was a droll disposition, not only on the part of Mr. Podsnap, but of everybody else, to treat him as if he were a child who was hard of hearing.

As a delicate concession to this unfortunately-born foreigner, Mr. Podsnap, in receiving him, had presented his wife as "Madame Podsnap;" also his daughter as "Mademoiselle Podsnap," with some inclination to add "ma fille," in which bold venture, however, he checked himself. The Veneerings being at that time the only other arrivals, he had added (in a condescendingly explanatory manner), "Monsieur Vey-nair-reeng," and had then subsided into English.

"How Do You Like London?" Mr. Podsnap now inquired from his station of host, as if he were administering something in the nature of a powder or potion to the deaf child; "London, Londres, London?"

The foreign gentleman admired it.

"You find it Very Large?" said Mr. Podsnap, spaciously.

The foreign gentleman found it very large.

"And Very Rich?"

The foreign gentleman found it, without doubt, enormément riche.

"Enormously Rich, We say," returned Mr. Podsnap, in a condescending manner. "Our English adverbs do Not terminate in Mong, and We Pronounce the 'ch' as if there were a 't' before it. We Say Ritch."

"Reetch," remarked the foreign gentleman.

"And Do You Find, Sir," pursued Mr. Podsnap, with dignity, "Many Evidences that Strike You, of our British Constitution in the Streets Of The World's Metropolis, London, Londres, London?"

The foreign gentleman begged to be pardoned, but did not altogether understand.

"The Constitution Britannique," Mr. Podsnap explained, as if he were teaching in an infant school. "We Say British, But You Say Britannique, You Know" (forgivingly, as if that were not his fault). "The Constitution, Sir."

The foreign gentleman said, "Mais, yees; I know eem."

A youngish sallowish gentleman in spectacles, with a lumpy forehead, seated in a supplementary chair at a corner of the table, here caused a profound sensation by saying, in a raised voice, "ESKER," and then stopping dead.

"Mais oui," said the foreign gentleman, turning towards him. "Est-ce que? Quoi donc?"

But the gentleman with the lumpy forehead having for the time delivered himself of all that he found behind his lumps, spake for the time no more.

"I Was Inquiring," said Mr. Podsnap, resuming the thread of his discourse, "Whether You Have Observed in our Streets as We should say, Upon our Pavvy as You would say, any Tokens——"

The foreign gentleman with patient courtesy entreated pardon "But what was tokenz?"

"Marks," said Mr. Podsnap; "Signs, you know, Appearances—Traces."

"Ah! Of a Orse?" inquired the foreign gentleman.

"We call it Horse," said Mr. Podsnap, with forbearance. "In England, Angleterre, England, We Aspirate the 'H,' and We Say 'Horse.' Only our Lower Classes Say 'Orse!'"

"Pardon," said the foreign gentleman; "I am alwiz wrong!"

"Our Language," said Mr. Podsnap, with a gracious consciousness of being always right, "is Difficult. Ours is a Copious Language, and Trying to Strangers. I will not Pursue my Question."

But the lumpy gentleman, unwilling to give it up, again madly said, "ESKER," and again spake no more.

"It merely referred," Mr. Podsnap explained, with a sense of meritorious proprietorship, "to Our Constitution, Sir. We Englishmen are Very Proud of our Constitution, Sir. It Was Bestowed Upon Us By Providence. No Other Country is so Favoured as This Country."

"And ozer countries?—" the foreign gentleman was beginning, when Mr. Podsnap put him right again.

"We do not say Ozer; we say Other: the letters are 'T' and 'H;' you say Tay and Aish, You Know;" (still with clemency). "The sound is 'th'—'th!'"

"And *oth*er countries," said the foreign gentleman. "They do how?"

"They do, Sir," returned Mr. Podsnap, gravely shaking his head; "they do —I am sorry to be obliged to say it—*as* they do."

"It was a little particular of Providence," said the foreign gentleman, laughing; "for the frontier is not large."

"Undoubtedly," assented Mr. Podsnap; "But So it is. It was the Charter of the Land. This Island was Blest, Sir, to the Direct Exclusion of such Other

Countries as—as there may happen to be. And if we were all Englishmen present, I would say," added Mr. Podsnap, looking round upon his compatriots, and sounding solemnly with his theme, "that there is in the Englishman a combination of qualities, a modesty, an independence, a responsibility, a repose, combined with an absence of everything calculated to call a blush into the cheek of a young person, which one would seek in vain among the Nations of the Earth."

Having delivered this little summary, Mr. Podsnap's face flushed, as he thought of the remote possibility of its being at all qualified by any prejudiced citizen of any other country; and, with his favourite right-arm flourish, he put the rest of Europe and the whole of Asia, Africa, and America nowhere.

The audience were much edified by this passage of words; and Mr. Podsnap, feeling that he was in rather remarkable force to-day, became smiling and conversational.

"Has anything more been heard, Veneering," he inquired, "of the lucky legatee?"

"Nothing more," returned Veneering, "than that he has come into possession of the property. I am told people now call him The Golden Dustman. I mentioned to you some time ago, I think, that the young lady whose intended husband was murdered is daughter to a clerk of mine?"

"Yes, you told me that," said Podsnap; "and by-the-bye, I wish you would tell it again here, for it's a curious coincidence—curious that the first news of the discovery should have been brought straight to your table (when I was there), and curious that one of your people should have been so nearly interested in it. Just relate that, will you?"

Veneering was more than ready to do it, for he had prospered exceedingly upon the Harmon Murder, and had turned the social distinction it conferred upon him to the account of making several dozen of bran-new bosom-friends. Indeed, such another lucky hit would almost have set him up in that way to his satisfaction. So, addressing himself to the most desirable of his neighbours, while Mrs. Veneering secured the next most desirable, he plunged into the case, and emerged from it twenty minutes afterwards with a Bank Director in his arms. In the mean time, Mrs. Veneering had dived into the same waters for a wealthy Ship-Broker, and had brought him up, safe and sound, by the hair. Then Mrs. Veneering had to relate, to a larger circle, how she had been to see the girl, and how she was really pretty, and (considering her station) presentable. And this she did with such a successful display of her eight aquiline fingers and their encircling jewels, that she happily laid hold of a drifting General Officer, his wife and daughter, and not only restored their animation which had become suspended, but made them lively friends within an hour.

Although Mr. Podsnap would in a general way have highly disapproved of Bodies in rivers as ineligible topics with reference to the cheek of the young person, he had, as one may say, a share in this affair which made him a part proprietor. As its returns were immediate, too, in the way of restraining the company from speechless contemplation of the wine-coolers, it paid, and he was satisfied.

And now the haunch of mutton vapour-bath having received a gamey infusion, and a few last touches of sweets and coffee, was quite ready, and the bathers came; but not before the discreet automaton had got behind the bars of the piano music-desk, and there presented the appearance of a captive languishing in a rosewood jail. And who now so pleasant or so well assorted as Mr. and Mrs. Alfred Lammle, he all sparkle, she all gracious contentment, both at occasional intervals exchanging looks like partners at cards, who played a game against All England.

There was not much youth among the bathers, but there was no youth (the young person always excepted) in the articles of Podsnappery. Bald bathers folded their arms and talked to Mr. Podsnap on the hearthrug; sleek-whiskered bathers, with hats in their hands, lunged at Mrs. Podsnap and retreated; prowling bathers went about looking into ornamental boxes and bowls as if they had suspicions of larceny on the part of the Podsnaps, and expected to find something they had lost at the bottom; bathers of the gentler sex sat silently comparing ivory shoulders. All this time and always, poor little Miss Podsnap, whose tiny efforts (if she had made any) were swallowed up in the magnificence of her mother's rocking, kept herself as much out of sight and mind as she could, and appeared to be counting on many dismal returns of the day. It was somehow understood, as a secret article in the state proprieties of Podsnappery, that nothing must be said about the day. Consequently this young damsel's nativity was hushed up and looked over, as if it were agreed on all hands that it would have been better that she had never been born.

The Lammles were so fond of the dear Veneerings that they could not for some time detach themselves from those excellent friends; but at length, either a very open smile on Mr. Lammle's part, or a very secret elevation of one of his gingerous eyebrows—certainly the one or the other—seemed to say to Mrs. Lammle, "Why don't you play?" . And so, looking about her, she saw Miss Podsnap, and seeming to say responsively, "That card?" and to be answered "Yes," went and sat beside Miss Podsnap.

Mrs. Lammle was overjoyed to escape into a corner for a little quiet talk.

It promised to be a very quiet talk, for Miss Podsnap replied in a flutter, "Oh! Indeed, it's very kind of you, but I am afraid I *don't* talk."

"Let us make a beginning," said the insinuating Mrs. Lammle, with her best smile.

"Oh! I am afraid you'll find me very dull. But Ma talks!"

That was plainly to be seen, for Ma was talking then at her usual canter, with arched head and mane, opened eyes and nostrils.

"Fond of reading perhaps?"

"Yes. At least I—don't mind that so much," returned Miss Podsnap.

"M—m—m—m—music." So insinuating was Mrs. Lammle that she got half-a-dozen ms into the word before she got it out.

"I haven't nerve to play even if I could. Ma plays."

(At exactly the same canter, and with a certain flourishing appearance of doing something, Ma did, in fact, occasionally take a rock upon the instrument.)

"Of course you like dancing?"

"Oh no, I don't," said Miss Podsnap.

"No? With your youth and attractions? Truly, my dear, you surprise me!"

"I can't say," observed Miss Podsnap, after hesitating considerably, and stealing several timid looks at Mrs. Lammle's carefully arranged face, "how I might have liked it if I had been a—you won't mention it, *will* you?"

"My dear! Never!"

"No, I am sure you won't. I can't say then how I should have liked it, if I had been a chimney-sweep on May-day."

"Gracious!" was the exclamation which amazement elicited from Mrs. Lammle.

"There! I knew you'd wonder. But you won't mention it, will you?"

"Upon my word, my love," said Mrs. Lammle, "you make me ten times more desirous, now I talk to you, to know you well, than I was when I sat over yonder looking at you. How I wish we could be real friends! Try me as a real friend. Come! Don't fancy me a frumpy old married woman, my dear; I was married but the other day, you know; I am dressed as a bride now, you see. About the chimney-sweeps?"

"Hush! Ma'll hear."

"She can't hear from where she sits."

"Don't you be too sure of that," said Miss Podsnap, in a lower voice. "Well, what I mean is, that they seem to enjoy it."

"And that perhaps you would have enjoyed it, if you had been one of them?"

Miss Podsnap nodded significantly.

"Then you don't enjoy it now?"

"How is it possible?" said Miss Podsnap. "Oh, it is such a dreadful thing! If I was wicked enough—and strong enough—to kill anybody, it should be my partner."

This was such an entirely new view of the Terpsichorean art as socially practised, that Mrs. Lammle looked at her young friend in some astonishment. Her young friend sat nervously twiddling her fingers in a pinioned attitude, as if she were trying to hide her elbows. But this latter Utopian object (in short sleeves) always appeared to be the great inoffensive aim of her existence.

"It sounds horrid, don't it?" said Miss Podsnap, with a penitential face.

Mrs. Lammle, not very well knowing what to answer, resolved herself into a look of smiling encouragement.

"But it is, and it always has been," pursued Miss Podsnap, "such a trial to me! I so dread being awful. And it is so awful! No one knows what I suffered at Madame Sauteuse's, where I learnt to dance and make presentation-curtseys, and other dreadful things—or at least where they tried to teach me. Ma can do it."

"At any rate, my love," said Mrs. Lammle, soothingly, "that's over."

"Yes, it's over," returned Miss Podsnap, "but there's nothing gained by that. It's worse here than at Madame Sauteuse's. Ma was there, and Ma's here; but Pa wasn't there, and company wasn't there, and there were not real partners there. Oh, there's Ma speaking to the man at the piano! Oh, there's Ma going up to somebody! Oh, I know she's going to bring him to me! Oh, please don't, please don't, please don't! Oh, keep away, keep away, keep away!" These pious ejaculations Miss Podsnap uttered with her eyes closed, and her head leaning back against the wall.

But the Ogre advanced under the pilotage of Ma, and Ma said, "Georgiana, Mr. Grompus," and the Ogre clutched his victim and bore her off to his castle in the top couple. Then the discreet automaton who had surveyed his ground, played a blossomless tuneless "set," and sixteen disciples of Podsnappery went through the figures of—1, Getting up at eight and shaving close at a quarter-past—2, Breakfasting at nine—3, Going to the City at ten—4, Coming home at half-past five—5, Dining at seven, and the grand chain.

While these solemnities were in progress, Mr. Alfred Lammle (most loving of husbands) approached the chair of Mrs. Alfred Lammle (most loving of wives), and bending over the back of it, trifled for some few seconds with Mrs. Lammle's bracelet. Slightly in contrast with this brief airy toying, one might have noticed a certain dark attention in Mrs. Lammle's face as she said some words with her eyes on Mr. Lammle's waistcoat, and seemed in return to receive some lesson. But it was all done as a breath passes from a mirror.

And now, the grand chain riveted to the last link, the discreet automaton ceased, and the sixteen, two and two, took a walk among the furniture. And herein the unconsciousness of the Ogre Grompus was pleasantly conspicuous; for, that complacent monster, believing that he was giving Miss Podsnap a treat, prolonged to the utmost stretch of possibility a peripatetic account of an archery meeting; while his victim, heading the procession of sixteen as it slowly circled about, like a revolving funeral, never raised her eyes except once to steal a glance at Mrs. Lammle, expressive of intense despair.

At length the procession was dissolved by the violent arrival of a nutmeg, before which the drawing-room door bounced open as if it were a cannon-ball; and while that fragrant article, dispersed through several glasses of coloured warm water, was going the round of society, Miss Podsnap returned to her seat by her new friend.

"Oh, my goodness," said Miss Podsnap. "*That's* over! I hope you didn't look at me."

"My dear, why not?"

"Oh, I know all about myself," said Miss Podsnap.

"I'll tell you something *I* know about you, my dear," returned Mrs. Lammle in her winning way, "and that is, you are most unnecessarily shy."

"Ma ain't," said Miss Podsnap. "—I detest you! Go along!" This shot was levelled under her breath at the gallant Grompus for bestowing an insinuating smile upon her in passing.

"Pardon me if I scarcely see, my dear Miss Podsnap," Mrs. Lammle was beginning when the young lady interposed.

"If we are going to be real friends (and I suppose we are, for you are the only person who ever proposed it) don't let us be awful. It's awful enough to *be* Miss Podsnap, without being called so. Call me Georgiana."

"Dearest Georgiana——" Mrs. Lammle began again.

"Thank you," said Miss Podsnap.

"Dearest Georgiana, pardon me if I scarcely see, my love, why your mamma's not being shy is a reason why you should be."

"Don't you really see that?" asked Miss Podsnap, plucking at her fingers in a troubled manner, and furtively casting her eyes now on Mrs. Lammle, now on the ground. "Then perhaps it isn't?"

"My dearest Georgiana, you defer much too readily to my poor opinion. Indeed it is not even an opinion, darling, for it is only a confession of my dulness."

"Oh, *you* are not dull," returned Miss Podsnap. "*I* am dull, but you couldn't have made me talk if you were."

Some little touch of conscience answering this perception of her having gained a purpose, called bloom enough into Mrs. Lammle's face to make it look brighter as she sat smiling her best smile on her dear Georgiana, and shaking her head with an affectionate playfulness. Not that it meant anything, but that Georgiana seemed to like it.

"What I mean is," pursued Georgiana, "that Ma being so endowed with awfulness, and Pa being so endowed with awfulness, and there being so much awfulness everywhere—I mean, at least, everywhere where I am—perhaps it makes me who am so deficient in awfulness, and frightened at it—I say it very badly—I don't know whether you can understand what I mean?"

"Perfectly, dearest Georgiana!" Mrs. Lammle was proceeding with every re-assuring wile, when the head of that young lady suddenly went back against the wall again, and her eyes closed.

"Oh! there's Ma being awful with somebody with a glass in his eye! Oh, I know she's going to bring him here! Oh, don't bring him, don't bring him! Oh, he'll be my partner with his glass in his eye! Oh, what shall I do!" This time Georgiana accompanied her ejaculations with taps of her feet upon the floor, and was altogether in quite a desperate condition. But, there was no escape from the majestic Mrs. Podsnap's production of an ambling stranger, with one eye screwed up into extinction and the other framed and glazed, who, having looked down out of that organ, as if he descried Miss Podsnap at the bottom of some perpendicular shaft, brought her to the surface, and ambled off with her. And then the captive at the piano played another "set," expressive of his mournful aspirations after freedom, and other sixteen went through the former melancholy motions, and the ambler took Miss Podsnap for a furniture walk, as if he had struck out an entirely original conception.

In the mean time a stray personage of a meek demeanour, who had wandered to the hearthrug and got among the heads of tribes assembled there in conference with Mr. Podsnap, eliminated Mr. Podsnap's flush and flourish by a highly unpolite remark; no less than a reference to the circumstance that some half-dozen people had lately died in the streets, of starvation. It was clearly ill-timed, after dinner. It was not adapted to the cheek of the young person. It was not in good taste.

"I don't believe it," said Mr. Podsnap, putting it behind him.

The meek man was afraid we must take it as proved, because there were the Inquests and the Registrar's returns.

"Then it was their own fault," said Mr. Podsnap.

Veneering and other elders of tribes commended this way out of it. At once a short cut and a broad road.

The man of meek demeanour intimated that truly it would seem from the facts as if starvation had been forced upon the culprits in question—as if, in their wretched manner, they had made their weak protests against it—as if they would have taken the liberty of staving it off if they could—as if they would rather not have been starved upon the whole, if perfectly agreeable to all parties.

"There is not," said Mr. Podsnap, flushing angrily, "there is not a country in the world, sir, where so noble a provision is made for the poor as in this country."

The meek man was quite willing to concede that, but perhaps it rendered the matter even worse, as showing that there must be something appallingly wrong somewhere.

"Where?" said Mr. Podsnap.

The meek man hinted Wouldn't it be well to try, very seriously, to find out where?

"Ah!" said Mr. Podsnap. "Easy to say somewhere; not so easy to say where! But I see what you are driving at. I knew it from the first. Centralization. No. Never with my consent. Not English."

An approving murmur arose from the heads of tribes; as saying, "There you have him! Hold him!"

He was not aware (the meek man submitted of himself) that he was driving at any ization. He had no favourite ization that he knew of. But he certainly was more staggered by these terrible occurrences than he was by names, of howsoever so many syllables. Might he ask, was dying of destitution and neglect necessarily English?

"You know what the population of London is, I suppose," said Mr. Podsnap.

The meek man supposed he did, but supposed that had absolutely nothing to do with it, if its laws were well administered.

"And you know; at least I hope you know," said Mr. Podsnap, with severity, "that Providence has declared that you shall have the poor always with you?"

The meek man also hoped he knew that.

"I am glad to hear it," said Mr. Podsnap, with a portentous air. "I am glad to hear it. It will render you cautious how you fly in the face of Providence."

In reference to that absurd and irreverent conventional phrase, the meek man said, for which Mr. Podsnap was not responsible, he the meek man had no fear of doing anything so impossible; but——

But Mr. Podsnap felt that the time had come for flushing and flourishing this meek man down for good. So he said:

"I must decline to pursue this painful discussion. It is not pleasant to my feelings. It is repugnant to my feelings. I have said that I do not admit these things. I have also said that if they do occur (not that I admit it), the fault lies with the sufferers themselves. It is not for *me*"—Mr. Podsnap pointed "me" forcibly, as adding by implication though it may be all very well for *you*—"it is not for me to impugn the workings of Providence. I know better than that, I trust, and I have mentioned what the intentions of Providence are. Besides," said Mr. Podsnap, flushing high up among his hair-brushes, with a strong consciousness of personal affront, "the subject is a very disagreeable one. I will go so far as to say it is an odious one. It is not one to be introduced among our wives and young persons, and I——" He finished with that flourish of his arm which added more expressively than any words, And I remove it from the face of the earth.

Simultaneously with this quenching of the meek man's ineffectual fire, Georgiana having left the ambler up a lane of sofa, in a No Thoroughfare of back drawing-room, to find his own way out, came back to Mrs. Lammle. And who should be with Mrs. Lammle, but Mr. Lammle. So fond of her!

"Alfred, my love, here is my friend. Georgiana, dearest girl, you must like my husband next to me."

Mr. Lammle was proud to be so soon distinguished by this special commendation to Miss Podsnap's favour. But if Mr. Lammle were prone to be jealous of his dear Sophronia's friendships, he would be jealous of her feeling towards Miss Podsnap.

"Say Georgiana, darling," interposed his wife.

"Towards—shall I?—Georgiana." Mr. Lammle uttered the name, with a delicate curve of his right hand, from his lips outward. "For never have I known Sophronia (who is not apt to take sudden likings) so attracted and so captivated as she is by——shall I once more?—Georgiana."

The object of this homage sat uneasily enough in receipt of it, and then said, turning to Mrs. Lammle, much embarrassed:

"I wonder what you like me for! I am sure I can't think."

"Dearest Georgiana, for yourself. For your difference from all around you."

"Well! That may be. For I think I like you for your difference from all around me," said Georgiana with a smile of relief.

"We must be going with the rest," observed Mrs. Lammle, rising with a show of unwillingness, amidst a general dispersal. "We are real friends, Georgiana dear."

"Real."

"Good-night, dear girl!"

She had established an attraction over the shrinking nature upon which her smiling eyes were fixed, for Georgiana held her hand while she answered in a secret and half-frightened tone:

"Don't forget me when you are gone away. And come again soon. Good-night!"

Charming to see Mr. and Mrs. Lammle taking leave so gracefully, and going down the stairs so lovingly and sweetly. Not quite so charming to see their smiling faces fall and brood as they dropped moodily into separate corners of their little carriage. But to be sure that was a sight behind the scenes, which nobody saw, and which nobody was meant to see.

Certain big, heavy vehicles, built on the model of the Podsnap plate, took away the heavy articles of guests weighing ever so much; and the less valuable articles got away after their various manners; and the Podsnap plate was put to bed. As Mr. Podsnap stood with his back to the drawing-room fire, pulling up his shirt-collar, like a veritable cock of the walk literally pluming himself in the midst of his possessions, nothing would have astonished him more than an intimation that Miss

Podsnap, or any other young person properly born and bred, could not be exactly put away like the plate, brought out like the plate, polished like the plate, counted, weighed, and valued like the plate. That such a young person could possibly have a morbid vacancy in the heart for anything younger than the plate, or less monotonous than the plate; or that such a young person's thoughts could try to scale the region bounded on the north, south, east, and west, by the plate; was a monstrous imagination which he would on the spot have flourished into space. This perhaps in some sort arose from Mr. Podsnap's blushing young person being, so to speak, all cheek: whereas there is a possibility that there may be young persons of a rather more complex organization.

If Mr. Podsnap, pulling up his shirt-collar, could only have heard himself called "that fellow" in a certain short dialogue which passed between Mr. and Mrs. Lammle in their opposite corners of their little carriage, rolling home!

"Sophronia, are you awake?"

"Am I likely to be asleep, sir?"

"Very likely, I should think, after that fellow's company. Attend to what I am going to say."

"I have attended to what you have already said, have I not? What else have I been doing all night?"

"Attend, I tell you" (in a raised voice), "to what I am going to say. Keep close to that idiot girl. Keep her under your thumb. You have her fast, and you are not to let her go. Do you hear?"

"I hear you."

"I foresee there is money to be made out of this, besides taking that fellow down a peg. We owe each other money, you know."

Mrs. Lammle winced a little at the reminder, but only enough to shake her scents and essences anew into the atmosphere of the little carriage, as she settled herself afresh into her own dark corner.

CHAPTER XII.

THE SWEAT OF AN HONEST MAN'S BROW.

MR. MORTIMER LIGHTWOOD and Mr. Eugene Wrayburn took a coffee-house dinner together in Mr. Lightwood's office. They had newly agreed to set up a joint establishment together. They had taken a bachelor cottage near Hampton, on the brink of the Thames, with a lawn, and a boat-house, and all things fitting, and were to float with the stream through the summer and the Long Vacation.

It was not summer yet, but spring; and it was not gentle spring ethereally mild, as in Thomson's Seasons, but nipping spring with an easterly wind, as in Johnson's, Jackson's, Dickson's, Smith's, and Jones's Seasons. The grating wind sawed rather than blew; and as it sawed, the sawdust whirled about the sawpit. Every street was a sawpit, and there were no top-sawyers; every passenger was an under-sawyer, with the sawdust blinding him and choking him.

That mysterious paper currency which circulates in London when the wind blows, gyrated here and there and everywhere. Whence can it come, whither can it go? It hangs on every bush, flutters in every tree, is caught flying by the electric wires, haunts every enclosure, drinks at every pump, cowers at every grating, shudders upon every plot of grass, seeks rest in vain behind the legions of iron rails. In Paris, where nothing is wasted, costly and luxurious city though it be, but where wonderful human ants creep out of holes and pick up every scrap, there is no such thing. There, it blows nothing but dust. There, sharp eyes and sharp stomachs reap even the east wind, and get something out of it.

The wind sawed, and the sawdust whirled. The shrubs wrung their many hands, bemoaning that they had been over-persuaded by the sun to bud; the young leaves pined; the sparrows repented of their early marriages, like men and women; the colours of the rainbow were discernible, not in floral spring, but in the faces of the people whom it nibbled and pinched. And ever the wind sawed, and the sawdust whirled.

When the spring evenings are too long and light to shut out, and such weather is rife, the city which Mr. Podsnap so explanatorily called London, Londres, London, is at its worst. Such a black shrill city, combining the qualities of a smoky house and a scolding wife; such a gritty city; such a hopeless city, with no rent in the leaden canopy of its sky; such a beleaguered city, invested by the great Marsh Forces of Essex and Kent. So the two old schoolfellows felt it to be, as, their dinner done, they turned towards the fire to smoke. Young Blight was gone, the coffee-house waiter was gone, the plates and dishes were gone, the wine was going—but not in the same direction.

"The wind sounds up here," quoth Eugene, stirring the fire, "as if we were keeping a lighthouse. I wish we were."

"Don't you think it would bore us?" Lightwood asked.

"Not more than any other place. And there would be no Circuit to go. But that's a selfish consideration, personal to me."

"And no clients to come," added Lightwood. "Not that that's a selfish consideration at all personal to *me*."

"If we were on an isolated rock in a stormy sea," said Eugene, smoking with his eyes on the fire, "Lady Tippins couldn't put off to visit us, or, better still, might put off and get swamped. People couldn't ask one to wedding breakfasts. There would be no Precedents to hammer at, except the plain-sailing Precedent of keeping the light up. It would be exciting to look out for wrecks."

"But otherwise," suggested Lightwood, "there might be a degree of sameness in the life."

"I have thought of that also," said Eugene, as if he really had been considering the subject in its various bearings with an eye to the business; "but it would be a defined and limited monotony. It would not extend beyond two people. Now, it's a question with me, Mortimer, whether a monotony defined with that precision and limited to that extent might not be more endurable than the unlimited monotony of one's fellow-creatures."

As Lightwood laughed and passed the wine, he remarked, "We shall have an opportunity, in our boating summer, of trying the question."

"An imperfect one," Eugene acquiesced, with a sigh, "but so we shall. I hope we may not prove too much for one another."

"Now, regarding your respected father," said Lightwood, bringing him to a subject they had expressly appointed to discuss: always the most slippery eel of eels of subjects to lay hold of.

"Yes, regarding my respected father," assented Eugene, settling himself in his arm-chair. "I would rather have approached my respected father by candlelight, as a theme requiring a little artificial brilliancy; but we will take him by twilight, enlivened with a glow of Wallsend."

He stirred the fire again as he spoke, and having made it blaze, resumed.

"My respected father has found, down in the parental neighbourhood, a wife for his not-generally-respected son."

"With some money, of course?"

"With some money, of course, or he would not have found her. My respected father—let me shorten the dutiful tautology by substituting in future M. R. F., which sounds military, and rather like the Duke of Wellington."

"What an absurd fellow you are, Eugene!"

"Not at all, I assure you. M. R. F. having always in the clearest manner provided (as he calls it) for his children by pre-arranging from the hour of the birth of each, and sometimes from an earlier period, what the devoted little victim's calling and course in life should be, M. R. F. pre-arranged for myself that I was to be the barrister I am (with the slight addition of an enormous practice, which has not accrued), and also the married man I am not."

"The first you have often told me."

"The first I have often told you. Considering myself sufficiently incongruous on my legal eminence, I have until now suppressed my domestic destiny. You know M. R. F., but not as well as I do. If you knew him as well as I do, he would amuse you."

"Filially spoken, Eugene!"

"Perfectly so, believe me; and with every sentiment of affectionate deference towards M. R. F. But if he amuses me, I can't help it. When my eldest brother was born, of course the rest of us knew (I mean the rest of us would have known, if we had been in existence) that he was heir to the Family Embarrassments—we call it before company the Family Estate. But when my second brother was going to be born by-and-by, 'this,' says M. R. F., 'is a little pillar of the church.' *Was* born, and became a pillar of the church; a very shaky one. My third brother appeared, considerably in advance of his engagement to my mother; but M. R. F., not at all put out by surprise, instantly declared him a Circumnavigator. Was pitchforked into the Navy, but has not circumnavigated. I announced myself, and was disposed of with the highly satisfactory results embodied before you. When my younger brother was half an hour old, it was settled by M. R. F. that he should have a mechanical genius, and so on. Therefore I say that M. R. F. amuses me."

"Touching the lady, Eugene?"

"There M. R. F. ceases to be amusing, because my intentions are opposed to touching the lady."

"Do you know her?"

"Not in the least."

"Hadn't you better see her?"

"My dear Mortimer, you have studied my character. Could I possibly go down there, labelled 'ELIGIBLE. ON VIEW,' and meet the lady, similarly labelled? Anything to carry out M. R. F.'s arrangements, I am sure, with the greatest pleasure—except matrimony. Could I possibly support it? I, so soon bored, so constantly, so fatally?"

"But you are not a consistent fellow, Eugene."

"In susceptibility to boredom," returned that worthy, "I assure you I am the most consistent of mankind."

"Why, it was but now that you were dwelling on the advantages of a monotony of two."

"In a lighthouse. Do me the justice to remember the condition. In a lighthouse."

Mortimer laughed again, and Eugene, having laughed too for the first time, as if he found himself on reflection rather entertaining, relapsed into his usual gloom, and drowsily said, as he enjoyed his cigar, "No, there is no help for it; one of the prophetic deliveries of M. R. F. must for ever remain unfulfilled. With every disposition to oblige him, he must submit to a failure."

It had grown darker as they talked, and the wind was sawing and the sawdust was whirling outside paler windows. The underlying churchyard was already settling into deep dim shade, and the shade was creeping up to the housetops among which they sat. "As if," said Eugene, "as if the churchyard ghosts were rising."

He had walked to the window with his cigar in his mouth, to exalt its flavour by comparing the fireside with the outside, when he stopped midway on his return to his arm-chair, and said:

"Apparently one of the ghosts has lost its way, and dropped in to be directed. Look at this phantom!"

Lightwood, whose back was towards the door, turned his head, and there, in the darkness of the entry, stood a something in the likeness of a man: to whom he addressed the not irrelevant inquiry, "Who the devil are you?"

"I ask your pardons, Governors," replied the ghost, in a hoarse double-barrelled whisper, "but might either on you be Lawyer Lightwood?"

"What do you mean by not knocking at the door?" demanded Mortimer.

"I ask your pardons, Governors," replied the ghost, as before, "but probable you was not aware your door stood open."

"What do you want?"

Hereunto the ghost again hoarsely replied, in its double-barrelled manner, "I ask your pardons, Governors, but might one on you be Lawyer Lightwood?"

"One of us is," said the owner of that name.

"All right, Governors Both," returned the ghost, carefully closing the room door; "'tickler business."

Mortimer lighted the candles. They showed the visitor to be an ill-looking visitor with a squinting leer, who, as he spoke, fumbled at an old sodden fur cap, formless and mangey, that looked like a furry animal, dog or cat, puppy or kitten, drowned and decaying.

"Now," said Mortimer, "what is it?"

"Governors Both," returned the man, in what he meant to be a wheedling tone, "which on you might be Lawyer Lightwood?"

"I am."

"Lawyer Lightwood," ducking at him with a servile air, "I am a man as gets my living, and as seeks to get my living, by the sweat of my brow. Not to risk being done out of the sweat of my brow, by any chances, I should wish afore going further to be swore in."

"I am not a swearer in of people, man."

The visitor, clearly anything but reliant on this assurance, doggedly muttered "Alfred David."

"Is that your name?" asked Lightwood.

"My name?" returned the man. "No; I want to take a Alfred David."

(Which Eugene, smoking and contemplating him, interpreted as meaning Affidavit.)

"I tell you, my good fellow," said Lightwood, with his indolent laugh, "that I have nothing to do with swearing."

"He can swear *at* you," Eugene explained; "and so can I. But we can't do more for you."

Much discomfited by this information, the visitor turned the drowned dog or cat, puppy or kitten, about and about, and looked from one of the Governors Both to the other of the Governors Both, while he deeply considered within himself. At length he decided:

"Then I must be took down."

"Where?" asked Lightwood.

"Here," said the man. "In pen and ink."

"First, let us know what your business is about."

"It's about," said the man, taking a step forward, dropping his hoarse voice, and shading it with his hand, "it's about from five to ten thousand pound reward. That's what it's about. It's about Murder. That's what it's about."

"Come nearer the table. Sit down. Will you have a glass of wine?"

"Yes, I will," said the man; "and I don't deceive you, Governors."

It was given him. Making a stiff arm to the elbow, he poured the wine into his mouth, tilted it into his right cheek, as saying, "What do you think of it?" tilted it into his left cheek, as saying, "What do *you* think of it?" jerked it into his stomach, as saying, "What do *you* think of it?" To conclude, smacked his lips, as if all three replied, "We think well of it."

"Will you have another?"

"Yes, I will," he repeated, "and I don't deceive you, Governors." And also repeated the other proceedings.

"Now," began Lightwood, "what's your name?"

"Why, there you're rather fast, Lawyer Lightwood," he replied, in a remonstrant manner. "Don't you see, Lawyer Lightwood? There you're a little bit fast. I'm going to earn from five to ten thousand pound by the sweat of my brow; and as a poor man doing justice to the sweat of my brow, is it likely I can afford to part with so much as my name without its being took down?"

Deferring to the man's sense of the binding powers of pen and ink and paper, Lightwood nodded acceptance of Eugene's nodded proposal to take those spells in hand. Eugene, bringing them to the table, sat down as clerk or notary.

"Now," said Lightwood, "what's your name?"

But further precaution was still due to the sweat of this honest fellow's brow.

"I should wish, Lawyer Lightwood," he stipulated, "to have that T'other Governor as my witness that what I said I said. Consequent, will the T'other Governor be so good as chuck me his name and where he lives?"

Eugene, cigar in mouth and pen in hand, tossed him his card. After spelling it out slowly, the man made it into a little roll, and tied it up in an end of his neckerchief still more slowly.

"Now," said Lightwood, for the third time, "if you have quite completed your various preparations, my friend, and have fully ascertained that your spirits are cool and not in any way hurried, what's your name?"

"Roger Riderhood."

"Dwelling-place?"

"Lime'us Hole."

"Calling or occupation?"

Not quite so glib with this answer as with the previous two, Mr. Riderhood gave in the definition, "Waterside character."

"Anything against you?" Eugene quietly put in as he wrote.

Rather baulked, Mr. Riderhood evasively remarked, with an innocent air, that he believed the T'other Governor had asked him summa't."

"Ever in trouble?" said Eugene.

"Once." (Might happen to any man, Mr. Riderhood added incidentally.)

"On suspicion of——?"

"Of seaman's pocket," said Mr. Riderhood. "Whereby I was in reality the man's best friend, and tried to take care of him."

"With the sweat of your brow?" asked Eugene.

"Till it poured down like rain," said Roger Riderhood.

Eugene leaned back in his chair, and smoked with his eyes negligently turned on the informer, and his pen ready to reduce him to more writing. Lightwood also smoked, with his eyes negligently turned on the informer.

"Now let me be took down again," said Riderhood, when he had turned the drowned cap over and under, and had brushed it the wrong way (if it had a right way) with his sleeve. "I give information that the man that done the Harmon Murder is Gaffer Hexam, the man that found the body. The hand of Jesse Hexam, commonly called Gaffer on the river and alongshore, is the hand that done that deed. His hand and no other."

The two friends glanced at one another with more serious faces than they had shown yet.

"Tell us on what grounds you make this accusation," said Mortimer Lightwood.

"On the grounds," answered Riderhood, wiping his face with his sleeve, "that I was Gaffer's pardner, and suspected of him many a long day and many a dark night. On the grounds that I knowed his ways. On the grounds that I broke the pardnership because I see the danger; which I warn you his daughter may tell you another story about that, for anythink I can say, but you know what it'll be worth, for she'd tell you lies, the world round and the heavens broad, to save her father. On the grounds that it's well understood along the cause'ays and the stairs that he done it. On the grounds that he's fell off from, because he done it. On the grounds that I will swear he done it. On the grounds that you may take me where you will, and get me sworn to it. *I* don't want to back out of the consequences. I have made up *my* mind. Take me anywheres."

"All this is nothing," said Lightwood.

"Nothing?" repeated Riderhood, indignantly and amazedly.

"Merely nothing. It goes to no more than that you suspect this man of the crime. You may do so with some reason, or you may do so with no reason, but he cannot be convicted on your suspicion."

"Haven't I said—I appeal to the T'other Governor as my witness—haven't I said from the first minute that I opened my mouth in this here world-without-end-everlasting chair" (he evidently used that form of words as next in force to an affidavit), "that I was willing to swear that he done it? Haven't I said, Take me and get me sworn to it? Don't I say so now? You won't deny it, Lawyer Lightwood?"

"Surely not; but you only offer to swear to your suspicion, and I tell you it is not enough to swear to your suspicion."

"Not enough, ain't it, Lawyer Lightwood?" he cautiously demanded.

"Positively not."

"And did I say it *was* enough? Now, I appeal to the T'other Governor. Now, fair! Did I say so?"

"He certainly has not said that he had no more to tell," Eugene observed in a low voice without looking at him, "whatever he seemed to imply."

"Hah!" cried the informer, triumphantly perceiving that the remark was generally in his favour, though apparently not closely understanding it. "Fort'nate for me I had a witness!"

"Go on, then," said Lightwood. "Say out what you have to say. No after-thought."

"Let me be took down then!" cried the informer, eagerly and anxiously. "Let me be took down, for by George and the Draggin I'm a coming to it now! Don't do nothing to keep back from a honest man the fruits of the sweat of his brow! I give information, then, that he told me that he done it. Is *that* enough?"

"Take care what you say, my friend," returned Mortimer.

"Lawyer Lightwood, take care, you, what I say; for I judge you'll be answerable for follering it up!" Then, slowly and emphatically beating it all out with his open right hand on the palm of his left; "I, Roger Riderhood, Lime'us Hole,

Waterside character, tell you, Lawyer Lightwood, that the man Jesse Hexam, commonly called upon the river and alongshore Gaffer, told me that he done the deed. What's more, he told me with his own lips that he done the deed. What's more, he said that he done the deed. And I'll swear it!"

"Where did he tell you so?"

"Outside," replied Riderhood, always beating it out, with his head determinedly set askew, and his eyes watchfully dividing their attention between his two auditors, "outside the door of the Six Jolly Fellowships, towards a quarter arter twelve o'clock at midnight—but I will not in my conscience undertake to swear to so fine a matter as five minutes—on the night when he picked up the body. The Six Jolly Fellowships stands on the spot still. The Six Jolly Fellowships won't run away. If it turns out that he warn't at the Six Jolly Fellowships that night at midnight, I'm a liar."

"What did he say?"

"I'll tell you (take me down, T'other Governor, I ask no better). He come out first; I come out last. I might be a minute arter him; I might be half a minute, I might be a quarter of a minute; I cannot swear to that, and therefore I won't. That's knowing the obligations of a Alfred David, ain't it?"

"Go on."

"I found him a waiting to speak to me. He says to me, 'Rogue Riderhood'—for that's the name I'm mostly called by—not for any meaning in it, for meaning it has none, but because of its being similar to Roger."

"Never mind that."

"'Scuse *me*, Lawyer Lightwood, it's a part of the truth, and as such I do mind it, and I must mind it and I will mind it. 'Rogue Riderhood,' he says, 'words passed betwixt us on the river to-night.' Which they had; ask his daughter! 'I threatened you,' he says, 'to chop you over the fingers with my boat's stretcher, or take a aim at your brains with my boat-hook. I did so on accounts of your looking too hard at what I had in tow, as if you was suspicious, and on accounts of your holding on to the gunwale of my boat.' I says to him, 'Gaffer, I know it.' He says to me, 'Rogue Riderhood, you are a man in a dozen'—I think he said in a score, but of that I am not positive, so take the lowest figure, for precious be the obligations of a Alfred David. 'And,' he says, 'when your fellow-men is up, be it their lives or be it their watches, sharp is ever the word with you. Had you suspicions?' I says, 'Gaffer, I had; and what's more, I have.' He falls a shaking, and he says, 'Of what?' I says, 'Of foul play.' He falls a shaking worse, and he says, 'There *was* foul play then. I done it for his money. Don't betray me!' Those were the words as ever he used."

There was a silence, broken only by the fall of the ashes in the grate. An opportunity which the informer improved by smearing himself all over the head and neck and face with his drowned cap, and not at all improving his own appearance.

"What more?" asked Lightwood.

"Of him, d'ye mean, Lawyer Lightwood?"

"Of anything to the purpose."

"Now, I'm blest if I understand you, Governors Both," said the informer, in a creeping manner: propitiating both, though only one had spoken. "What? Ain't *that* enough?"

"Did you ask him how he did it, where he did it, when he did it?"

"Far be it from me, Lawyer Lightwood! I was so troubled in my mind, that I wouldn't have knowed more, no, not for the sum as I expect to earn from you by the sweat of my brow, twice told! I had put an end to the pardnership. I had cut the connexion. I couldn't undo what was done; and when he begs and prays, 'Old pardner, on my knees, don't split upon me!' I only makes answer

'Never speak another word to Roger Riderhood, nor look him in the face!' and I shuns that man."

Having given these words a swing to make them mount the higher and go the further, Rogue Riderhood poured himself out another glass of wine unbidden, and seemed to chew it, as, with the half-emptied glass in his hand, he stared at the candles.

Mortimer glanced at Eugene, but Eugene sat glowering at his paper, and would give him no responsive glance. Mortimer again turned to the informer, to whom he said:

"You have been troubled in your mind a long time, man?"

Giving his wine a final chew, and swallowing it, the informer answered in a single word:

"Hages!"

"When all that stir was made, when the Government reward was offered, when the police were on the alert, when the whole country rang with the crime!" said Mortimer, impatiently.

"Hah!" Mr. Riderhood very slowly and hoarsely chimed in, with several retrospective nods of his head. "Warn't I troubled in my mind then!"

"When conjecture ran wild, when the most extravagant suspicions were afloat, when half-a-dozen innocent people might have been laid by the heels any hour in the day!" said Mortimer, almost warming.

"Hah!" Mr. Riderhood chimed in, as before. "Warn't I troubled in my mind through it all!"

"But he hadn't," said Eugene, drawing a lady's head upon his writing-paper, and touching it at intervals, "the opportunity then of earning so much money, you see."

"The T'other Governor hits the nail, Lawyer Lightwood! It was that as turned me. I had many times and again struggled to relieve myself of the trouble on my mind, but I couldn't get it off. I had once very nigh got it off to Miss Abbey Potterson which keeps the Six Jolly Fellowships—there is the 'ouse, it won't run away,—there lives the lady, she ain't likely to be struck dead afore you get there—ask her!—but I couldn't do it. At last, out comes the new bill with your own lawful name, Lawyer Lightwood, printed to it, and then I asks the question of my own intellects, Am I to have this trouble on my mind for ever? Am I never to throw it off? Am I always to think more of Gaffer than of my own self? If he's got a daughter, ain't *I* got a daughter?"

"And echo answered—— ?" Eugene suggested.

"'You have,'" said Mr. Riderhood, in a firm tone.

"Incidentally mentioning, at the same time, her age?" inquired Eugene.

"Yes, Governor. Two-and-twenty last October. And then I put it to myself, 'Regarding the money. It is a pot of money.' For it *is* a pot," said Mr. Riderhood, with candour, "and why deny it?"

"Hear!" from Eugene as he touched his drawing.

"'It is a pot of money; but is it a sin for a labouring man that moistens every crust of bread he earns with his tears—or if not with them, with the colds he catches in his head—is it a sin for that man to earn it? Say there is anything again earning it.' This I put to myself strong, as in duty bound; 'how can it be said without blaming Lawyer Lightwood for offering it to be earned?' And was it for *me* to blame Lawyer Lightwood? No."

"No," said Eugene.

"Certainly not, Governor," Mr. Riderhood acquiesced. "So I made up my mind to get my trouble off my mind, and to earn by the sweat of my brow what was held out to me. And what's more," he added, suddenly turning bloodthirsty,

"I mean to have it! And now I tell you, once and away, Lawyer Lightwood, that Jesse Hexam, commonly called Gaffer, his hand and no other, done the deed, on his own confession to me. And I give him up to you, and I want him took. This night!"

After another silence, broken only by the fall of the ashes in the grate, which attracted the informer's attention as if it were the chinking of money, Mortimer Lightwood leaned over his friend, and said in a whisper:

"I suppose I must go with this fellow to our imperturbable friend at the police-station."

"I suppose," said Eugene, "there is no help for it."

"Do you believe him?"

"I believe him to be a thorough rascal. But he may tell the truth, for his own purpose, and for this occasion only."

"It doesn't look like it."

"*He* doesn't," said Eugene. "But neither is his late partner, whom he denounces, a prepossessing person. The firm are cut-throat Shepherds both, in appearance. I should like to ask him one thing."

The subject of this conference sat leering at the ashes, trying with all his might to overhear what was said, but feigning abstraction as the "Governors Both" glanced at him.

"You mentioned (twice, I think) a daughter of this Hexam's," said Eugene, aloud. "You don't mean to imply that she had any guilty knowledge of the crime?"

The honest man, after considering—perhaps considering how his answer might affect the fruits of the sweat of his brow—replied unreservedly, "No, I don't."

"And you implicate no other person?"

"It ain't what I implicate, it's what Gaffer implicated," was the dogged and determined answer. "I don't pretend to know more than that his words to me was, 'I done it.' Those was his words."

"I must see this out, Mortimer," whispered Eugene, rising. "How shall we go?"

"Let us walk," whispered Lightwood, "and give this fellow time to think of it."

Having exchanged the question and answer, they prepared themselves for going out, and Mr. Riderhood rose. While extinguishing the candles, Lightwood, quite as a matter of course, took up the glass from which that honest gentleman had drunk, and coolly tossed it under the grate, where it fell shivering into fragments."

"Now, if you will take the lead," said Lightwood, "Mr. Wrayburn and I will follow. You know where to go, I suppose?"

"I suppose I do, Lawyer Lightwood."

"Take the lead, then."

The waterside character pulled his drowned cap over his ears with both hands, and making himself more round-shouldered than nature had made him, by the sullen and persistent slouch with which he went, went down the stairs, round by the Temple Church, across the Temple into Whitefriars, and so on by the waterside streets.

"Look at his hang-dog air," said Lightwood, following.

"It strikes me rather as a hang-*man* air," returned Eugene "He has undeniable intentions that way."

They said little else as they followed. He went on before them as an ugly Fate might have done, and they kept him in view, and would have been glad enough to lose sight of him. But on he went before them, always at the same distance, and the same rate. Aslant against the hard implacable weather and the rough wind, he was no more to be driven back than hurried forward, but held on like an advancing Destiny. There came, when they were about midway on their journey, a heavy rush of hail, which in a few minutes pelted the streets clear, and whitened them. It made no difference to him. A man's life being to be taken and the price of it got, the hailstones to arrest the purpose must lie larger and deeper than those. He crushed through them, leaving marks in the fast-melting slush that were mere shapeless holes; one might have fancied, following, that the very fashion of humanity had departed from his feet.

The blast went by, and the moon contended with the fast-flying clouds, and the wild disorder reigning up there made the pitiful little tumults in the streets of no account. It was not that the wind swept all the brawlers into places of shelter, as it had swept the hail still lingering in heaps wherever there was refuge for it; but that it seemed as if the streets were absorbed by the sky, and the night were all in the air.

"If he has had time to think of it," said Eugene, "he has not had time to think better of it—or differently of it, if that's better. There is no sign of drawing back in him; and as I recollect this place, we must be close upon the corner where we alighted that night."

In fact, a few abrupt turns brought them to the river side, where they had slipped about among the stones, and where they now slipped more; the wind coming against them in slants and flaws, across the tide and the windings of the river, in a furious way. With that habit of getting under the lee of any shelter which waterside characters acquire, the waterside character at present in question led the way to the lee side of the Six Jolly Fellowship Porters before he spoke.

"Look round here, Lawyer Lightwood, at them red curtains. It's the Fellowships, the 'ouse as I told you wouldn't run away. And has it run away?"

Not showing himself much impressed by this remarkable confirmation of the informer's evidence, Lightwood inquired what other business they had there?

"I wished you to see the Fellowships for yourself, Lawyer Lightwood, that you might judge whether I'm a liar; and now I'll see Gaffer's window for myself, that we may know whether he's at home."

With that, he crept away.

"He'll come back, I suppose?" murmured Lightwood.

"Ay! and go through with it," murmured Eugene.

He came back after a very short interval indeed.

"Gaffer's out, and his boat's out. His daughter's at home, sitting a-looking at the fire. But there's some supper getting ready, so Gaffer's expected. I can find what move he's upon, easy enough, presently."

Then he beckoned and led the way again, and they came to the police-station, still as clean and cool and steady as before, saving that the flame of its lamp—being but a lamp-flame, and only attached to the Force as an outsider—flickered in the wind.

Also, within doors, Mr. Inspector was at his studies as of yore. He recognised the friends the instant they reappeared, but their reappearance had no effect on his composure. Not even the circumstance that Riderhood was their conductor moved him, otherwise than that as he took a dip of ink he seemed, by a settlement of his chin in his stock, to propound to that personage, without looking at him, the question, "What have *you* been up to, last?"

Mortimer Lightwood asked him, would he be so good as look at those notes? Handing him Eugene's.

Having read the first few lines, Mr. Inspector mounted to that (for him) extraordinary pitch of emotion that he said, "Does either of you two gentlemen happen to have a pinch of snuff about him?" Finding that neither had, he did quite as well without it, and read on.

"Have you heard these read?" he then demanded of the honest man.

"No," said Riderhood.

"Then you had better hear them." And so read them aloud, in an official manner.

"Are these notes correct, now, as to the information you bring here and the evidence you mean to give?" he asked, when he had finished reading.

"They are. They are as correct," returned Mr. Riderhood, "as I am. I can't say more than that for 'em."

"I'll take this man myself, sir," said Mr. Inspector to Lightwood. Then to Riderhood, "Is he at home? Where is he? What's he doing? You have made it your business to know all about him, no doubt."

Riderhood said what he did know, and promised to find out in a few minutes what he didn't know.

"Stop," said Mr. Inspector; "not till I tell you. We mustn't look like business. Would you two gentlemen object to making a pretence of taking a glass of something in my company at the Fellowships? Well-conducted house, and highly respectable landlady."

They replied that they would be happy to substitute a reality for the pretence, which, in the main, appeared to be as one with Mr. Inspector's meaning.

"Very good," said he, taking his hat from its peg, and putting a pair of handcuffs in his pocket as if they were his gloves. "Reserve!" Reserve saluted. "You know where to find me?" Reserve again saluted. "Riderhood, when you have found out concerning his coming home, come round to the window of Cosy, tap twice at it, and wait for me. Now, gentlemen."

As the three went out together, and Riderhood slouched off from under the trembling lamp his separate way, Lightwood asked the officer what he thought of this?

Mr. Inspector replied, with due generality and reticence, that it was always more likely that a man had done a bad thing than that he hadn't. That he himself had several times "reckoned up" Gaffer, but had never been able to bring him to a satisfactory criminal total. That if this story was true, it was only in part true. That the two men, very shy characters, would have been jointly and pretty equally "in it;" but that this man had "spotted" the other, to save himself and get the money.

"And I think," added Mr. Inspector, in conclusion, "that if all goes well with him, he's in a tolerable way of getting it. But as this is the Fellowships, gentlemen, where the lights are, I recommend dropping the subject. You can't do better than be interested in some lime works anywhere down about Northfleet, and doubtful whether some of your lime don't get into bad company, as it comes up in barges."

"You hear, Eugene?" said Lightwood, over his shoulder. "You are deeply interested in lime."

"Without lime," returned that unmoved barrister-at-law, "my existence would be unilluminated by a ray of hope."

CHAPTER XIII.

TRACKING THE BIRD OF PREY.

THE two lime merchants, with their escort, entered the dominions of Miss Abbey Potterson, to whom their escort (presenting them and their pretended business over the half-door of the bar, in a confidential way) preferred his figurative request that "a mouthful of fire" might be lighted in Cosy. Always well disposed to assist the constituted authorities, Miss Abbey bade Bob Gliddery attend the gentlemen to that retreat, and promptly enliven it with fire and gaslight. Of this commission the bare-armed Bob, leading the way with a flaming wisp of paper, so speedily acquitted himself, that Cosy seemed to leap out of a dark sleep and embrace them warmly, the moment they passed the lintels of its hospitable door.

"They burn sherry very well here," said Mr. Inspector, as a piece of local intelligence. "Perhaps you gentlemen might like a bottle?"

The answer being By all means, Bob Gliddery received his instructions from Mr. Inspector, and departed in a becoming state of alacrity engendered by reverence for the majesty of the law.

"It's a certain fact," said Mr. Inspector, "that this man we have received our information from," indicating Riderhood with his thumb over his shoulder, "has for some time past given the other man a bad name arising out of your lime barges, and that the other man has been avoided in consequence. I don't say what it means or proves, but it's a certain fact. I had it first from one of the opposite sex of my acquaintance," vaguely indicating Miss Abbey with his thumb over his shoulder, "down away at a distance, over yonder."

Then probably Mr. Inspector was not quite unprepared for their visit that evening? Lightwood hinted.

"Well you see," said Mr. Inspector, "it was a question of making a move. It's of no use moving if you don't know what your move is. You had better by far keep still. In the matter of this lime, I certainly had an idea that it might lie betwixt the two men; I always had that idea. Still I was forced to wait for a start, and I wasn't so lucky as to get a start. This man that we have received our information from, has got a start, and if he don't meet with a check he may make the running and come in first. There may turn out to be something considerable for him that comes in second, and I don't mention who may or who may not try for that place. There's duty to do, and I shall do it, under any circumstances, to the best of my judgment and ability."

"Speaking as a shipper of lime——" began Eugene.

"Which no man has a better right to do than yourself, you know," said Mr. Inspector.

"I hope not," said Eugene; "my father having been a shipper of lime before me, and my grandfather before him—in fact we have been a family immersed to the crowns of our heads in lime during several generations—I beg to observe that if this missing lime could be got hold of without any young female relative of any distinguished gentleman engaged in the lime trade (which I cherish next to my life) being present, I think it might be a more agreeable proceeding to the assisting bystanders, that is to say, lime-burners."

"I also," said Lightwood, pushing his friend aside with a laugh, "should much prefer that."

"It shall be done, gentlemen, if it can be done conveniently," said Mr. Inspector, with coolness. "There is no wish on my part to cause any distress in that quarter. Indeed, I am sorry for that quarter."

"There was a boy in that quarter," remarked Eugene. "He is still there?"

"No," said Mr. Inspector. "He has quitted those works. He is otherwise disposed of."

"Will she be left alone then?" asked Eugene.

"She will be left," said Mr. Inspector, "alone."

Bob's reappearance with a steaming jug broke off the conversation. But although the jug steamed forth a delicious perfume, its contents had not received that last happy touch which the surpassing finish of the Six Jolly Fellowship Porters imparted on such momentous occasions. Bob carried in his left hand one of those iron models of sugar-loaf hats before mentioned, into which he emptied the jug, and the pointed end of which he thrust deep down into the fire, so leaving it for a few moments while he disappeared and reappeared with three bright drinking-glasses. Placing these on the table and bending over the fire, meritoriously sensible of the trying nature of his duty, he watched the wreaths of steam, until at the special instant of projection he caught up the iron vessel and gave it one delicate twirl, causing it to send forth one gentle hiss. Then he restored the contents to the jug; held over the steam of the jug, each of the three bright glasses in succession; finally filled them all, and with a clear conscience awaited the applause of his fellow-creatures.

It was bestowed (Mr. Inspector having proposed as an appropriate sentiment "The lime trade!"), and Bob withdrew to report the commendations of the guests to Miss Abbey in the bar. It may be here in confidence admitted that, the room being close shut in his absence, there had not appeared to be the slightest reason for the elaborate maintenance of this same lime fiction. Only it had been regarded by Mr. Inspector as so uncommonly satisfactory, and so fraught with mysterious virtues, that neither of his clients had presumed to question it.

Two taps were now heard on the outside of the window. Mr. Inspector, hastily fortifying himself with another glass, strolled out with a noiseless foot and an unoccupied countenance. As one might go to survey the weather and the general aspect of the heavenly bodies.

"This is becoming grim, Mortimer," said Eugene in a low voice. "I don't like this."

"Nor I," said Lightwood. "Shall we go?"

"Being here, let us stay. You ought to see it out, and I won't leave you. Besides, that lonely girl with the dark hair runs in my head. It was little more than a glimpse we had of her that last time, and yet I almost see her waiting by the fire to-night. Do you feel like a dark combination of traitor and pickpocket when you think of that girl?"

"Rather," returned Lightwood. "Do you?"

"Very much so."

Their escort strolled back again, and reported. Divested of its various lime-lights and shadows, his report went to the effect that Gaffer was away in his boat, supposed to be on his old look-out; that he had been expected last high-water; that having missed it for some reason or other, he was not, according to his usual habits at night, to be counted on before next high-water, or it might be an hour or so later; that his daughter, surveyed through the window, would seem to be so expecting him, for the supper was not cooking, but set out ready to be cooked; that it would be high-water at about one, and that it was now barely ten; that there was nothing to be done but watch and wait; that the informer was keeping watch at the instant of that present reporting, but that two heads were better than one (especially when the second was Mr. Inspector's); and that the reporter meant to share the watch. And forasmuch as crouching under the lee of a hauled-up boat on a night when it blew cold and strong, and when the weather was varied with blasts of hail at times, might be wearisome to amateurs, the reporter closed with the recommendation that the two gentlemen should remain, for awhile at any rate, in their present quarters, which were weather-tight and warm.

They were not inclined to dispute this recommendation, but they wanted to know where they could join the watchers when so disposed. Rather than trust to a verbal description of the place, which might mislead, Eugene (with a less weighty sense of personal trouble on him than he usually had) would go out with Mr. Inspector, note the spot, and come back.

On the shelving bank of the river, among the slimy stones of a causeway—not the special causeway of the Six Jolly Fellowships, which had a landing-place of its own, but another, a little removed, and very near to the old windmill which was the denounced man's dwelling-place—were a few boats; some, moored and already beginning to float; others, hauled up above the reach of the tide. Under one of these latter Eugene's companion disappeared. And when Eugene had observed its position with reference to the other boats, and had made sure that he could not miss it, he turned his eyes upon the building where, as he had been told, the lonely girl with the dark hair sat by the fire.

He could see the light of the fire shining through the window. Perhaps it drew him on to look in. Perhaps he had come out with the express intention. That part of the bank having rank grass growing on it, there was no difficulty in getting close, without any noise of footsteps: it was but to scramble up a ragged face of pretty hard mud some three or four feet high and come upon the grass and to the window. He came to the window by that means.

She had no other light than the light of the fire. The unkindled lamp stood on the table. She sat on the ground, looking at the brazier, with her face leaning on her hand. There was a kind of film or flicker on her face, which at first he took to be the fitful firelight; but, on a second look, he saw that she was weeping. A sad and solitary spectacle, as shown him by the rising and the falling of the fire.

It was a little window of but four pieces of glass, and was not curtained; he chose it because the larger window near it was. It showed him the room, and the bills upon the wall respecting the drowned people starting out and receding by turns. But he glanced slightly at them, though he looked long and steadily at her. A deep rich piece of colour, with the brown flush of her cheek and the shining lustre of her hair, though sad and solitary, weeping by the rising and the falling of the fire.

She started up. He had been so very still, that he felt sure it was not he who had disturbed her, so merely withdrew from the window and stood near it in the shadow of the wall. She opened the door, and said in an alarmed tone, "Father, was that you calling me?" And again, "Father!" And once again, after listening, "Father! I thought I heard you call me twice before!"

No response. As she re-entered at the door, he dropped over the bank and made his way back, among the ooze and near the hiding-place, to Mortimer Lightwood: to whom he told what he had seen of the girl, and how this was becoming very grim indeed.

"If the real man feels as guilty as I do," said Eugene, "he is remarkably uncomfortable."

"Influence of secrecy," suggested Lightwood.

"I am not at all obliged to it for making me Guy Fawkes in the vault and a Sneak in the area both at once," said Eugene. "Give me some more of that stuff."

Lightwood helped him to some more of that stuff, but it had been cooling, and didn't answer now.

"Pooh," said Eugene, spitting it out among the ashes. "Tastes like the wash of the river."

"Are you so familiar with the flavour of the wash of the river?"

"I seem to be to-night. I feel as if I had been half drowned, and swallowing a gallon of it."

"Influence of locality," suggested Lightwood.

"You are mighty learned to-night, you and your influences," returned Eugene. "How long shall we stay here?"

"How long do you think?"

"If I could choose, I should say a minute," replied Eugene, "for the Jolly Fellowship Porters are not the jolliest dogs I have known. But I suppose we are best here till they turn us out with the other suspicious characters, at midnight."

Thereupon he stirred the fire, and sat down on one side of it. It struck eleven, and he made believe to compose himself patiently. But gradually he took the fidgets in one leg, and then in the other leg, and then in one arm, and then in the other arm, and then in his chin, and then in his back, and then in his forehead, and then in his hair, and then in his nose; and then he stretched himself recumbent on two chairs, and groaned; and then he started up.

"Invisible insects of diabolical activity swarm in this place. I am tickled and twitched all over. Mentally, I have now committed a burglary under the meanest circumstances, and the myrmidons of justice are at my heels."

"I am quite as bad," said Lightwood, sitting up facing him, with a tumbled head, after going through some wonderful evolutions, in which his head had been the lowest part of him. "This restlessness began, with me, long ago. All the time you were out, I felt like Gulliver with the Lilliputians firing upon him."

"It won't do, Mortimer. We must get into the air; we must join our dear friend and brother, Riderhood. And let us tranquillize ourselves by making a compact. Next time (with a view to our peace of mind) we'll commit the crime, instead of taking the criminal. You swear it?"

"Certainly."

"Sworn! Let Tippins look to it. Her life's in danger."

Mortimer rang the bell to pay the score, and Bob appeared to transact that business with him: whom Eugene, in his careless extravagance, asked if he would like a situation in the lime-trade?

"Thankee sir, no sir," said Bob. "I've a good sitiwation here, sir."

"If you change your mind at any time," returned Eugene, "come to me at my works, and you'll always find an opening in the lime-kiln."

"Thankee sir," said Bob.

"This is my partner," said Eugene, "who keeps the books and attends to the wages. A fair day's wages for a fair day's work is ever my partner's motto."

"And a very good 'un it is, gentlemen," said Bob, receiving his fee, and drawing a bow out of his head with his right hand, very much as he would have drawn a pint of beer out of the beer engine.

"Eugene," Mortimer apostrophized him, laughing quite heartily when they were alone again, "how *can* you be so ridiculous?"

"I am in a ridiculous humour," quoth Eugene; "I am a ridiculous fellow. Everything is ridiculous. Come along!"

It passed into Mortimer Lightwood's mind that a change of some sort, best expressed perhaps as an intensification of all that was wildest and most negligent and reckless in his friend, had come upon him in the last half-hour or so. Thoroughly used to him as he was, he found something new and strained in him that was for the moment perplexing. This passed into his mind, and passed out again; but he remembered it afterwards.

"There's where she sits, you see," said Eugene, when they were standing under the bank, roared and riven at by the wind. "There's the light of her fire."

"I'll take a peep through the window," said Mortimer.

"No, don't!" Eugene caught him by the arm. "Best not make a show of her. Come to our honest friend."

He led him to the post of watch, and they both dropped down and crept under the lee of the boat; a better shelter than it had seemed before, being directly contrasted with the blowing wind and the bare night.

"Mr. Inspector at home?" whispered Eugene.

"Here I am, sir."

"And our friend of the perspiring brow is at the far corner there? Good. Anything happened?"

"His daughter has been out, thinking she heard him calling, unless it was a sign to him to keep out of the way. It might have been."

"It might have been Rule Britannia," muttered Eugene, "but it wasn't. Mortimer!"

"Here!" (On the other side of Mr. Inspector.)

"Two burglaries now, and a forgery!"

With this indication of his depressed state of mind, Eugene fell silent.

They were all silent for a long while. As it got to be flood-tide, and the water came nearer to them, noises on the river became more frequent, and they listened more. To the turning of steam-paddles, to the clinking of iron chain, to the creaking of blocks, to the measured working of oars, to the occasional violent barking of some passing dog on ship-board, who seemed to scent them lying in their hiding-place. The night was not so dark but that, besides the lights at bows and mastheads gliding to and fro, they could discern some shadowy bulk attached; and now and then a ghostly lighter with a large dark sail, like a warning arm, would start up very near them, pass on, and vanish. At this time of their watch, the water close to them would be often agitated by some impulsion given it from a distance. Often they believed this beat and plash to be the boat they lay in wait for, running in ashore; and again and again they would have started up, but for the immobility with which the informer, well used to the river, kept quiet in his place.

The wind carried away the striking of the great multitude of city church clocks, for those lay to leeward of them; but there were bells to windward that told them of its being One—Two—Three. Without that aid they would have known how the night wore, by the falling of the tide, recorded in the appearance of an ever-widening black wet strip of shore, and the emergence of the paved causeway from the river, foot by foot.

As the time so passed, this slinking business became a more and more precarious one. It would seem as if the man had had some intimation of what was in hand against him, or had taken fright. His movements might have been planned to gain for him, in getting beyond their reach, twelve hours' advantage. The honest man who had expended the sweat of his brow became uneasy, and began to complain with bitterness of the proneness of mankind to cheat him—him invested with the dignity of Labour!

Their retreat was so chosen that while they could watch the river, they could watch the house. No one had passed in or out, since the daughter thought she heard the father calling. No one could pass in or out without being seen.

"But it will be light at five," said Mr. Inspector, "and then *we* shall be seen."

"Look here," said Riderhood, "what do you say to this? He may have been lurking in and out, and just holding his own betwixt two or three bridges, for hours back."

"What do you make of that?" said Mr. Inspector. Stoical, but contradictory.

"He may be doing so at this present time."

"What do you make of *that?*" said Mr. Inspector.

"My boat's among them boats here at the cause'ay."

"And what do you make of your boat?" said Mr. Inspector.

"What if I put off in her and take a look round? I know his ways, and the likely nooks he favours. I know where he'd be at such a time of the tide, and where he'd be at such another time. Ain't I been his pardner? None of you need show. None of you need stir. I can shove her off without help; and as to me being seen, I'm about at all times."

"You might have given a worse opinion," said Mr. Inspector, after brief consideration. "Try it."

"Stop a bit. Let's work it out. If I want you, I'll drop round under the Fellowships and tip you a whistle."

"If I might so far presume as to offer a suggestion to my honourable and gallant friend, whose knowledge of naval matters far be it from me to impeach," Eugene struck in with great deliberation, "it would be, that to tip a whistle is to advertise mystery and invite speculation. My honourable and gallant friend will, I trust, excuse me, as an independent member, for throwing out a remark which I feel to be due to this house and the country."

"Was that the T'other Governor, or Lawyer Lightwood?" asked Riderhood. For they spoke as they crouched or lay, without seeing one another's faces.

"In reply to the question put by my honourable and gallant friend," said Eugene, who was lying on his back with his hat on his face, as an attitude highly expressive of watchfulness, "I can have no hesitation in replying (it not being inconsistent with the public service) that those accents were the accents of the T'other Governor."

"You've tolerable good eyes, ain't you, Governor? You've all tolerable good eyes, ain't you?" demanded the informer.

All.

"Then if I row up under the Fellowships and lay there, no need to whistle. You'll make out that there's a speck of something or another there, and you'll know it's me, and you'll come down that cause'ay to me. Understood all?"

Understood all.

"Off she goes then!"

In a moment, with the wind cutting keenly at him sideways, he was staggering down to his boat; in a few moments he was clear, and creeping up the river under their own shore.

Eugene had raised himself on his elbow to look into the darkness after him. "I wish the boat of my honourable and gallant friend," he murmured, lying down again and speaking into his hat, "may be endowed with philanthropy enough to turn bottom-upward and extinguish him!—Mortimer."

"My honourable friend."

"Three burglaries, two forgeries, and a midnight assassination."

Yet in spite of having those weights on his conscience, Eugene was somewhat enlivened by the late slight change in the circumstances of affairs. So were his two companions. Its being a change was everything. The suspense seemed to have taken a new lease, and to have begun afresh from a recent date. There was something additional to look for. They were all three more sharply on the alert, and less deadened by the miserable influences of the place and time.

More than an hour had passed, and they were even dozing, when one of the three—each said it was he, and he had *not* dozed—made out Riderhood in his boat at the spot agreed on. They sprang up, came out from their shelter, and went down to him. When he saw them coming, he dropped alongside the causeway; so that they, standing on the causeway, could speak with him in whispers, under the shadowy mass of the Six Jolly Fellowship Porters fast asleep.

"Blest if I can make it out!" said he, staring at them.

"Make what out? Have you seen him?"

"No."

"What *have* you seen?" asked Lightwood. For he was staring at them in the strangest way.

"I've seen his boat."

"Not empty?"

"Yes, empty. And what's more,—adrift. And what's more,—with one scull gone. And what's more,—with t'other scull jammed in the thowels and broke short off. And what's more,—the boat's drove tight by the tide 'atwixt two tiers of barges. And what's more,—he's in luck again, by George if he ain't!"

CHAPTER XIV.

THE BIRD OF PREY BROUGHT DOWN.

COLD on the shore, in the raw cold of that leaden crisis in the four-and-twenty hours when the vital force of all the noblest and prettiest things that live is at its lowest, the three watchers looked each at the blank faces of the other two, and all at the blank face of Riderhood in his boat.

"Gaffer's boat, Gaffer in luck again, and yet no Gaffer!" So spake Riderhood, staring disconsolate.

As if with one accord, they all turned their eyes towards the light of the fire shining through the window. It was fainter and duller. Perhaps fire, like the higher animal and vegetable life it helps to sustain, has its greatest tendency towards death, when the night is dying and the day is not yet born.

"If it was me that had the law of this here job in hand," growled Riderhood with a threatening shake of his head, "blest if I wouldn't lay hold of *her*, at any rate!"

"Ay, but it is not you," said Eugene. With something so suddenly fierce in him that the informer returned submissively; "Well, well, well, T'other Governor, I didn't say it was. A man may speak."

"And vermin may be silent," said Eugene. "Hold your tongue, you water-rat!"

Astonished by his friend's unusual heat, Lightwood stared too, and then said: "What can have become of this man?"

"Can't imagine. Unless he dived overboard." The informer wiped his brow ruefully as he said it, sitting in his boat and always staring disconsolate.

"Did you make his boat fast?"

"She's fast enough till the tide runs back. I couldn't make her faster than she is. Come aboard of mine, and see for your ownselves."

There was a little backwardness in complying, for the freight looked too much for the boat; but on Riderhood's protesting "that he had had half-a-dozen, dead and alive, in her afore now, and she was nothing deep in the water nor down in the stern even then, to speak of," they carefully took their places, and trimmed the crazy thing. While they were doing so, Riderhood still sat staring disconsolate

"All right. Give way!" said Lightwood.

"Give way, by George!" repeated Riderhood, before shoving off. "If he's gone and made off any how, Lawyer Lightwood, it's enough to make me give way in a different manner. But he always *was* a cheat, con-found him! He always was a infernal cheat, was Gaffer. Nothing straightfor'ard, nothing on the square. So mean, so underhanded. Never going through with a thing, nor carrying it out like a man!"

"Hallo! Steady!" cried Eugene (he had recovered immediately on embarking), as they bumped heavily against a pile; and then in a lower voice reversed his late apostrophe by remarking ("I wish the boat of my honourable and gallant friend may be endowed with philanthropy enough *not* to turn bottom-upward and extinguish us!) Steady, steady! Sit close, Mortimer. Here's the hail again. See how it flies, like a troop of wild cats, at Mr. Riderhood's eyes!"

Indeed he had the full benefit of it, and it so mauled him, though he bent his head low and tried to present nothing but the mangy cap to it, that he dropped under the lee of a tier of shipping, and they lay there until it was over. The squall had come up, like a spiteful messenger before the morning; there followed in its wake a ragged tier of light which ripped the dark clouds until they showed a great grey hole of day.

They were all shivering, and everything about them seemed to be shivering; the river itself, craft, rigging, sails, such early smoke as there yet was on the shore. Black with wet, and altered to the eye by white patches of hail and sleet, the huddled buildings looked lower than usual, as if they were cowering, and had shrunk with the cold. Very little life was to be seen on either bank, windows and doors were shut, and the staring black and white letters upon wharves and warehouses "looked," said Eugene to Mortimer, "like inscriptions over the graves of dead businesses."

As they glided slowly on, keeping under the shore, and sneaking in and out among the shipping, by back-alleys of water, in a pilfering way that seemed to be their boatman's normal manner of progression, all the objects among which they crept were so huge in contrast with their wretched boat as to threaten to crush it. Not a ship's hull, with its rusty iron links of cable run out of hawse-holes long discoloured with the iron's rusty tears, but seemed to be there with a fell intention. Not a figure-head but had the menacing look of bursting forward to run them down. Not a sluice gate, or a painted scale upon a post or wall, showing the depth of water, but seemed to hint, like the dreadfully facetious Wolf in bed in Grandmamma's cottage, "That's to drown *you* in, my dears!" Not a lumbering black barge, with its cracked and blistered side impending over them, but seemed to suck at the river with a thirst for sucking them under. And everything so vaunted the spoiling influences of water—discoloured copper, rotten wood, honey-combed stone, green dank deposit—that the after-consequences of being crushed, sucked under, and drawn down, looked as ugly to the imagination as the main event.

Some half-hour of this work, and Riderhood unshipped his sculls, stood holding on to a barge, and hand over hand longwise along the barge's side gradually worked his boat under her head into a secret little nook of scummy water. And driven into that nook, and wedged as he had described, was Gaffer's boat; that boat with the stain still in it, bearing some resemblance to a muffled human form.

"Now tell me I'm a liar!" said the honest man.

("With a morbid expectation," murmured Eugene to Lightwood, "that somebody is always going to tell him the truth.")

"This is Hexam's boat," said Mr. Inspector. "I know her well."

"Look at the broken scull. Look at the t'other scull gone. *Now* tell me I am a liar!" said the honest man.

Mr. Inspector stepped into the boat. Eugene and Mortimer looked on.

"And see now!" added Riderhood, creeping aft, and showing a stretched rope made fast there and towing overboard. "Didn't I tell you he was in luck again?"

"Haul in," said Mr. Inspector.

"Easy to say haul in," answered Riderhood. "Not so easy done. His luck's got fouled under the keels of the barges. I tried to haul in last time, but I couldn't. See how taut the line is!"

"I must have it up," said Mr. Inspector. "I am going to take this boat ashore, and his luck along with it. Try easy now."

He tried easy now; but the luck resisted; wouldn't come.

"I mean to have it, and the boat too," said Mr. Inspector, playing the line.

But still the luck resisted; wouldn't come.

"Take care," said Riderhood. "You'll disfigure. Or pull asunder perhaps."

"I am not going to do either, not even to your Grandmother," said Mr. Inspector; "but I mean to have it. Come!" he added, at once persuasively and with authority to the hidden object in the water, as he played the line again; "it's no good this sort of game, you know. You *must* come up. I mean to have you."

There was so much virtue in this distinctly and decidedly meaning to have it, that it yielded a little, even while the line was played.

"I told you so," quoth Mr. Inspector, pulling off his outer coat, and leaning well over the stern with a will. "Come!"

It was an awful sort of fishing, but it no more disconcerted Mr. Inspector than if he had been fishing in a punt on a summer evening by some soothing weir high up the peaceful river. After certain minutes, and a few directions to the rest to "ease her a little for'ard," and "now ease her a trifle aft," and the like, he said composedly, "All clear!" and the line and the boat came free together.

Accepting Lightwood's proffered hand to help him up, he then put on his coat, and said to Riderhood, "Hand me over those spare sculls of yours, and I'll pull this in to the nearest stairs. Go ahead you, and keep out in pretty open water, that I mayn't get fouled again."

His directions were obeyed, and they pulled ashore directly; two in one boat, two in the other.

"Now," said Mr. Inspector, again to Riderhood, when they were all on the slushy stones; "you have had more practice in this than I have had, and ought to be a better workman at it. Undo the tow-rope, and we'll help you haul in."

Riderhood got into the boat accordingly. It appeared as if he had scarcely had a moment's time to touch the rope or look over the stern, when he came scrambling back, as pale as the morning, and gasped out:

"By the Lord, he's done me!"

"What do you mean?" they all demanded.

He pointed behind him at the boat, and gasped to that degree that he dropped upon the stones to get his breath.

"Gaffer's done me. It's Gaffer!"

They ran to the rope, leaving him gasping there. Soon, the form of the bird of prey, dead some hours, lay stretched upon the shore, with a new blast storming at it and clotting the wet hair with hailstones.

Father, was that you calling me? Father! I thought I heard you call me twice before! Words never to be answered, those, upon the earthside of the grave. The wind sweeps jeeringly over Father, whips him with the frayed ends of his dress and his jagged hair, tries to turn him where he lies stark on his back, and force his face towards the rising sun, that he may be shamed the more. A lull, and the wind is secret and prying with him; lifts and lets fall a rag; hides palpitating under another rag; runs nimbly through his hair and beard. Then, in a rush, it cruelly taunts him. Father, was that you calling me? Was it you, the voiceless and the dead? Was it you, thus buffeted as you lie here in a heap? Was it you, thus baptized unto Death, with these flying impurities now flung upon your face? Why not speak, Father? Soaking into this filthy ground as you lie here, is your own shape. Did you never see such a shape soaked into your boat? Speak, Father. Speak to us, the winds, the only listeners left you!

"Now see," said Mr. Inspector, after mature deliberation: kneeling on one knee beside the body, when they had stood looking down on the drowned man, as he had many a time looked down on many another man: "the way of it was this. Of course you gentlemen hardly failed to observe that he was towing by the neck and arms."

They had helped to release the rope, and of course not.

"And you will have observed before, and you will observe now, that this knot, which was drawn chock-tight round his neck by the strain of his own arms, is a slip-knot:" holding it up for demonstration.

Plain enough.

"Likewise you will have observed how he had run the other end of this rope to his boat."

It had the curves and indentations in it still, where it had been twined and bound.

"Now see," said Mr. Inspector, "see how it works round upon him. It's a wild tempestuous evening when this man that was," stooping to wipe some hailstones out of his hair with an end of his own drowned jacket, "—there; Now he's more like himself, though he's badly bruised,—when this man that was, rows out upon the river on his usual lay. He carries with him this coil of rope. He always carries with him this coil of rope. It's as well known to me as he was himself. Sometimes it lay in the bottom of his boat. Sometimes he hung it loose round his neck. He was a light-dresser was this man;—you see?" lifting the loose neckerchief over his breast, and taking the opportunity of wiping the dead lips with it—"and when it was wet, or freezing, or blew cold, he would hang this coil of line round his neck. Last evening he does this. Worse for him! He dodges about in his boat, does this man, till he gets chilled. His hands," taking up one of them, which dropped like a leaden weight, "get numbed. He sees some object that's in his way of business, floating. He makes ready to secure that object. He unwinds the end of his coil that he wants to take some turns on in his boat, and he takes turns enough on it to secure that it shan't run out. He makes it too secure, as it happens. He is a little longer about this than usual, his hands being numbed. His object drifts up, before he is quite ready for it. He catches at it, thinks he'll make sure of the contents of the pockets anyhow, in case he should be parted from it, bends right over the stern, and in one of these heavy squalls, or in the cross-swell of two steamers, or in not being quite prepared, or through all or most or some, gets a lurch, overbalances, and goes head-foremost overboard. Now see! He can swim, can this man, and instantly he strikes out. But in such striking-out he tangles his arms, pulls strong on the slip-knot, and it runs home. The object he had expected to take in tow, floats by, and his own boat tows him dead, to where we found him, all entangled in his own line. You'll ask me how I make out about the pockets? First, I'll tell you more; there was silver in 'em. How do I make that out? Simple and satisfactory. Because he's got it here." The lecturer held up the tightly clenched right hand.

"What is to be done with the remains?" asked Lightwood.

"If you wouldn't object to standing by him half a minute, sir," was the reply,

"I'll find the nearest of our men to come and take charge of him;—I still call it *him*, you see," said Mr. Inspector, looking back as he went, with a philosophical smile upon the force of habit.

"Eugene," said Lightwood—and was about to add "we may wait at a little distance," when turning his head he found that no Eugene was there.

He raised his voice and called "Eugene! Holloa!" But no Eugene replied.

It was broad daylight now, and he looked about. But no Eugene was in all the view.

Mr. Inspector speedily returning down the wooden stairs, with a police constable, Lightwood asked him if he had seen his friend leave them? Mr. Inspector could not exactly say that he had seen him go, but had noticed that he was restless.

"Singular and entertaining combination, sir, your friend."

"I wish it had not been a part of his singular and entertaining combination to give me the slip under these dreary circumstances at this time of the morning," said Lightwood. "Can we get anything hot to drink?"

We could, and we did. In a public-house kitchen with a large fire. We got hot brandy and water, and it revived us wonderfully. Mr. Inspector having to Mr. Riderhood announced his official intention of "keeping his eye upon him," stood him in a corner of the fire-place, like a wet umbrella, and took no further outward and visible notice of that honest man, except ordering a separate service of brandy and water for him: apparently out of the public funds.

As Mortimer Lightwood sat before the blazing fire, conscious of drinking brandy and water then and there in his sleep, and yet at one and the same time drinking burnt sherry at the Six Jolly Fellowships, and lying under the boat on the river shore, and sitting in the boat that Riderhood rowed, and listening to the lecture recently concluded, and having to dine in the Temple with an unknown man who described himself as M. R. F. Eugene Gaffer Harmon, and said he lived at Hailstorm,—as he passed through these curious vicissitudes of fatigue and slumber, arranged upon the scale of a dozen hours to the second, he became aware of answering aloud a communication of pressing importance that had never been made to him, and then turned it into a cough on beholding Mr. Inspector. For he felt, with some natural indignation, that that functionary might otherwise suspect him of having closed his eyes, or wandered in his attention.

"Here, just before us, you see," said Mr. Inspector.

"*I* see," said Lightwood, with dignity.

"And had hot brandy and water too, you see," said Mr. Inspector, "and then cut off at a great rate."

"Who?" said Lightwood.

"Your friend, you know."

"*I* know," he replied, again with dignity.

After hearing, in a mist through which Mr. Inspector loomed vague and large, that the officer took upon himself to prepare the dead man's daughter for what had befallen in the night, and generally that he took everything upon himself, Mortimer Lightwood stumbled in his sleep to a cab-stand, called a cab, and had entered the army and committed a capital military offence and been tried by court-martial and found guilty and had arranged his affairs and been marched out to be shot, before the door banged.

Hard work rowing the cab through the City to the Temple, for a cup of from five to ten thousand pounds value, given by Mr. Boffin; and hard work holding forth at that immeasurable length to Eugene (when he had been rescued with a rope from the running pavement) for making off in that extraordinary manner! But he offered such ample apologies, and was so very penitent, that when Lightwood got out of the cab, he gave the driver a particular charge to be careful of him. Which the driver (knowing there was no other fare left inside) stared at prodigiously.

In short, the night's work had so exhausted and worn out this actor in it, that he had become a mere somnambulist. He was too tired to rest in his sleep, until he was even tired out of being too tired, and dropped into oblivion. Late in the afternoon he awoke, and in some anxiety sent round to Eugene's lodging hard by, to inquire if he were up yet?

Oh yes, he was up. In fact, he had not been to bed. He had just come home. And here he was, close following on the heels of the message.

"Why, what bloodshot, draggled, dishevelled spectacle is this!" cried Mortimer.

"Are my feathers so very much rumpled?" said Eugene, coolly going up to the looking-glass. "They *are* rather out of sorts. But consider. Such a night for plumage!"

"Such a night?" repeated Mortimer. "What became of you in the morning?"

"My dear fellow," said Eugene, sitting on his bed, "I felt that we had bored one another so long, that an unbroken continuance of those relations must inevitably terminate in our flying to opposite points of the earth. I also felt that I had committed every crime in the Newgate Calendar So, for mingled considerations of friendship and felony, I took a walk."

CHAPTER XV.

TWO NEW SERVANTS.

MR. and Mrs. Boffin sat after breakfast, in the Bower, a prey to prosperity. Mr. Boffin's face denoted Care and Complication. Many disordered papers were before him, and he looked at them about as hopefully as an innocent civilian might look at a crowd of troops whom he was required at five minutes' notice to manœuvre and review. He had been engaged in some attempts to make notes of these papers; but being troubled (as men of his stamp often are) with an exceedingly distrustful and corrective thumb, that busy member had so often interposed to smear his notes, that they were little more legible than the various impressions of itself, which blurred his nose and forehead. It is curious to consider, in such a case as Mr. Boffin's, what a cheap article ink is, and how far it may be made to go. As a grain of musk will scent a drawer for many years, and still lose nothing appreciable of its original weight, so a halfpenny-worth of ink would blot Mr. Boffin to the roots of his hair and the calves of his legs, without inscribing a line on the paper before him, or appearing to diminish in the inkstand.

Mr. Boffin was in such severe literary difficulties that his eyes were prominent and fixed, and his breathing was stertorous, when, to the great relief of Mrs. Boffin, who observed these symptoms with alarm, the yard bell rang.

"Who's that, I wonder?" said Mrs. Boffin.

Mr. Boffin drew a long breath, laid down his pen, looked at his notes as doubting whether he had the pleasure of their acquaintance, and appeared, on a second perusal of their countenances, to be confirmed in his impression that he had not, when there was announced by the hammer-headed young man:

"Mr. Rokesmith."

"Oh!" said Mr. Boffin. "Oh indeed! Our and the Wilfers' Mutual Friend, my dear. Yes. Ask him to come in."

Mr. Rokesmith appeared.

"Sit down, sir," said Mr. Boffin, shaking hands with him. "Mrs. Boffin you're already acquainted with. Well, sir, I am rather unprepared to see you, for, to tell you the truth, I've been so busy with one thing and another, that I've not had time to turn your offer over."

"That's apology for both of us; for Mr. Boffin, and for me as well," said the smiling Mrs. Boffin. "But Lor! we can talk it over now; can't us?"

Mr. Rokesmith bowed, thanked her, and said he hoped so.

"Let me see then," resumed Mr. Boffin, with his hand to his chin. "It was Secretary that you named: wasn't it?"

"I said Secretary," assented Mr. Rokesmith.

"It rather puzzled me at the time," said Mr. Boffin, "and it rather puzzled me and Mrs. Boffin when we spoke of it afterwards, because (not to make a mystery of our belief) we have always believed a Secretary to be a piece of furniture, mostly of mahogany, lined with green baize or leather, with a lot of little drawers in it. Now, you won't think I take a liberty when I mention that you certainly ain't *that*."

Certainly not, said Mr. Rokesmith. But he had used the word in the sense of Steward.

"Why, as to Steward, you see," returned Mr. Boffin, with his hand still to his chin, "the odds are that Mrs. Boffin and me may never go upon the water. Being both bad sailors, we should want a Steward if we did; but there's generally one provided."

Mr. Rokesmith again explained; defining the duties he sought to undertake, as those of general superintendent, or manager, or overlooker, or man of business.

"Now, for instance—come!" said Mr. Boffin, in his pouncing way. "If you entered my employment, what would you do?"

"I would keep exact accounts of all the expenditure you sanctioned, Mr. Boffin. I would write your letters, under your direction. I would transact your business with people in your pay or employment. I would," with a glance and a half-smile at the table, "arrange your papers——"

Mr. Boffin rubbed his inky ear, and looked at his wife.

"—And so arrange them as to have them always in order for immediate reference, with a note of the contents of each outside it."

"I tell you what," said Mr. Boffin, slowly crumpling his own blotted note in his hand; "if you'll turn to at these present papers, and see what you can make of 'em, I shall know better what I can make of you."

No sooner said than done. Relinquishing his hat and gloves, Mr. Rokesmith sat down quietly at the table, arranged the open papers into an orderly heap, cast his eyes over each in succession, folded it, docketed it on the outside, laid it in a second heap, and, when that second heap was complete and the first gone, took from his pocket a piece of string and tied it together with a remarkably dexterous hand at a running curve and a loop.

"Good!" said Mr. Boffin. "Very good. Now let us hear what they're all about; will you be so good?"

John Rokesmith read his abstracts aloud. They were all about the new house. Decorator's estimate, so much. Furniture estimate, so much. Estimate for furniture of offices, so much. Coach-maker's estimate, so much. Horse-dealer's estimate, so much. Harness-maker's estimate, so much. Goldsmith's estimate, so much. Total, so very much. Then came correspondence. Acceptance of Mr. Boffin's offer of such a date, and to such an effect. Rejection of Mr. Boffin's proposal of such a date and to such an effect. Concerning Mr. Boffin's scheme of such another date to such another effect. All compact and methodical

"Apple-pie order!" said Mr. Boffin, after checking off each inscription with his hand, like a man beating time. "And whatever you do with your ink, *I* can't think, for you're as clean as a whistle after it. Now, as to a letter. Let's," said Mr. Boffin, rubbing his hands in his pleasantly childish admiration, "let's try a letter next."

"To whom shall it be addressed, Mr. Boffin?"

"Any one. Yourself."

Mr. Rokesmith quickly wrote, and then read aloud:

"'Mr. Boffin presents his compliments to Mr. John Rokesmith, and begs to say that he has decided on giving Mr. John Rokesmith a trial in the capacity he desires to fill. Mr. Boffin takes Mr. John Rokesmith at his word, in postponing to some indefinite period the consideration of salary. It is quite understood that Mr. Boffin is in no way committed on that point. Mr. Boffin has merely to add, that he relies on Mr. John Rokesmith's assurance that he will be faithful and serviceable. Mr. John Rokesmith will please enter on his duties immediately.'"

"Well! Now, Noddy!" cried Mrs. Boffin, clapping her hands, "that *is* a good one!"

Mr. Boffin was no less delighted; indeed, in his own bosom, he regarded both the composition itself and the device that had given birth to it, as a very remarkable monument of human ingenuity.

"And I tell you, my deary," said Mrs. Boffin, "that if you don't close with Mr. Rokesmith now at once, and if you ever go a muddling yourself again with things never meant nor made for you, you'll have an apoplexy—besides iron-moulding your linen—and you'll break my heart."

Mr. Boffin embraced his spouse for these words of wisdom, and then, congratulating John Rokesmith on the brilliancy of his achievements, gave him his hand in pledge of their new relations. So did Mrs. Boffin.

"Now," said Mr. Boffin, who, in his frankness, felt that it did not become him to have a gentleman in his employment five minutes, without reposing some confidence in him, "you must be let a little more into our affairs, Rokesmith. I mentioned to you, when I made your acquaintance, or I might better say when you made mine, that Mrs. Boffin's inclinations was setting in the way of Fashion, but that I didn't know how fashionable we might or might not grow. Well! Mrs. Boffin has carried the day, and we're going in neck and crop for Fashion."

"I rather inferred that, sir," replied John Rokesmith, "from the scale on which your new establishment is to be maintained."

"Yes," said Mr. Boffin, "it's to be a Spanker. The fact is, my literary man named to me that a house with which he is, as I may say, connected—in which he has an interest——"

"As property?" inquired John Rokesmith.

"Why no," said Mr. Boffin, "not exactly that; a sort of a family tie."

"Association?" the Secretary suggested.

"Ah!" said Mr. Boffin. "Perhaps. Anyhow, he named to me that the house had a board up, 'This Eminently Aristocratic Mansion to be let or sold.' Me and Mrs. Boffin when to look at it, and finding it beyond a doubt Eminently Aristocratic (though a trifle high and dull, which after all may be part of the same thing) took it. My literary man was so friendly as to drop into a charming piece of poetry on that occasion, in which he complimented Mrs. Boffin on coming into possession of—how did it go, my dear?"

Mrs. Boffin replied:

"'The gay, the gay and festive scene,
The halls, the halls of dazzling light.'"

"That's it. And it was made neater by there really being two halls in the house, a front 'un and a back 'un, besides the servants'. He likewise dropped into a very pretty piece of poetry to be sure, respecting the extent to which he would be willing to put himself out of the way to bring Mrs. Boffin round, in case she should ever get low in her spirits in the house. Mrs. Boffin has a wonderful memory. Will you repeat it, my dear?"

Mrs. Boffin complied, by reciting the verses in which this obliging offer had been made, exactly as she had received them.

"'I'll tell thee how the maiden wept, Mrs. Boffin,
"When her true love was slain, ma'am,
"And how her broken spirit slept, Mrs. Boffin,
"And never woke again, ma'am.
"I'll tell thee (if agreeable to Mr. Boffin) how the steed drew nigh,
"And left his lord afar;
"And if my tale (which I hope Mr. Boffin might excuse) should make you sigh,
"I'll strike the light guitar.'"

"Correct to the letter!" said Mr. Boffin. "And I consider that the poetry brings us both in, in a beautiful manner."

The effect of the poem on the Secretary being evidently to astonish him, Mr. Boffin was confirmed in his high opinion of it, and was greatly pleased.

"Now, you see, Rokesmith," he went on, "a literary man—*with* a wooden leg—is liable to jealousy. I shall therefore cast about for comfortable ways and means of not calling up Wegg's jealousy, but of keeping you in your department, and keeping him in his."

"Lor!" cried Mrs. Boffin. "What I say is, the world's wide enough for all of us!"

"So it is, my dear," said Mr. Boffin, "when not literary. But when so, not so. And I am bound to bear in mind that I took Wegg on, at a time when I had no thought of being fashionable or of leaving the Bower. To let him feel himself anyways slighted now, would be to be guilty of a meanness, and to act like having one's head turned by the halls of dazzling light. Which Lord forbid! Rokesmith, what shall we say about your living in the house?"

"In this house?"

"No, no. I have got other plans for this house. In the new house?"

"That will be as you please, Mr. Boffin. I hold myself quite at your disposal. You know where I live at present."

"Well!" said Mr. Boffin, after considering the point; "suppose you keep as you are for the present, and we'll decide by-and-by. You'll begin to take charge at once, of all that's going on in the new house, will you?"

"Most willingly. I will begin this very day. Will you give me the address?"

Mr. Boffin repeated it, and the Secretary wrote it down in his pocket-book. Mrs. Boffin took the opportunity of his being so engaged, to get a better observation of his face than she had yet taken. It impressed her in his favour, for she nodded aside to Mr. Boffin, "I like him."

"I will see directly that everything is in train, Mr. Boffin."

"Thank'ee. Being here, would you care at all to look round the Bower?"

"I should greatly like it. I have heard so much of its story."

"Come!" said Mr. Boffin. And he and Mrs. Boffin led the way.

A gloomy house the Bower, with sordid signs on it of having been, through its long existence as Harmony Jail, in miserly holding. Bare of paint, bare of paper on the walls, bare of furniture, bare of experience of human life. Whatever is built by man for man's occupation, must, like natural creations, fulfil the intention of its existence, or soon perish. This old house had wasted more from desuetude than it would have wasted from use, twenty years for one.

A certain leanness falls upon houses not sufficiently imbued with life (as if they were nourished upon it), which was very noticeable here. The staircase, balustrades, and rails, had a spare look—an air of being denuded to the bone—which the panels of the walls and the jambs of the doors and windows also bore. The scanty moveables partook of it; save for the cleanliness of the place, the dust into which they were all resolving would have lain thick on the floors; and those, both in colour and in grain, were worn like old faces that had kept much alone.

The bedroom where the clutching old man had lost his grip on life, was left as he had left it. There was the old grisly four-post bedstead, without hangings, and with a jail-like upper rim of iron and spikes; and there was the old patch-work counterpane. There was the tight-clenched old bureau, receding atop like a bad and secret forehead; there was the cumbersome old table with twisted legs, at the bedside; and there was the box upon it, in which the will had lain. A few old chairs with patch-work covers, under which the more precious stuff to be preserved had slowly lost its quality of colour without imparting pleasure to any eye, stood against the wall. A hard family likeness was on all these things.

"The room was kept like this, Rokesmith," said Mr. Boffin, "against the son's return. In short, everything in the house was kept exactly as it came to us, for him to see and approve. Even now, nothing is changed but our own room below-stairs that you have just left. When the son came home for the last time in his life, and for the last time in his life saw his father, it was most likely in this room that they met."

As the Secretary looked all round it, his eye rested on a side door in a corner.

"Another staircase," said Mr. Boffin, unlocking the door, "leading down into the yard. We'll go down this way, as you may like to see the yard, and it's all in the road. When the son was a little child, it was up and down these stairs that he mostly came and went to his father. He was very timid of his father. I've seen him sit on these stairs, in his shy way, poor child, many a time. Me and Mrs. Boffin have comforted him, sitting with his little book on these stairs often."

"Ah! And his poor sister too," said Mrs. Boffin. "And here's the sunny place on the white wall where they one day measured one another. Their own little hands wrote up their names here, only with a pencil; but the names are here still, and the poor dears gone for ever."

"We must take care of the names, old lady," said Mr. Boffin. "We must take care of the names. They shan't be rubbed out in our time, nor yet, if we can help it, in the time after us. Poor little children!"

"Ah! Poor little children!" said Mrs. Boffin.

They had opened the door at the bottom of the staircase giving on the yard, and they stood in the sunlight, looking at the scrawl of the two unsteady childish hands two or three steps up the staircase. There was something in this simple memento of a blighted childhood, and in the tenderness of Mrs. Boffin, that touched the Secretary.

Mr. Boffin then showed his new man of business the Mounds, and his own particular Mound which had been left him as his legacy under the will before he acquired the whole estate.

"It would have been enough for us," said Mr. Boffin, "in case it had pleased God to spare the last of those two young lives and sorrowful deaths. We didn't want the rest."

At the treasures of the yard, and at the outside of the house, and at the detached building which Mr. Boffin pointed out as the residence of himself and his wife during the many years of their service, the Secretary looked with interest. It was not until Mr. Boffin had shown him every wonder of the Bower twice over, that he remembered his having duties to discharge elsewhere.

"You have no instructions to give me, Mr. Boffin, in reference to this place?"

"Not any, Rokesmith. No."

"Might I ask, without seeming impertinent, whether you have any intention of selling it?"

"Certainly not. In remembrance of our old master, our old master's children, and our old service, me and Mrs. Boffin mean to keep it up as it stands."

The Secretary's eyes glanced with so much meaning in them at the Mounds, that Mr. Boffin said, as if in answer to a remark:

"Ay, ay, that's another thing. I may sell *them*, though I should be sorry to see the neighbourhood deprived of 'em too. It'll look but a poor dead flat without the Mounds. Still I don't say that I'm going to keep 'em always there, for the sake of the beauty of the landscape. There's no hurry about it; that's all I say at present. I ain't a scholar in much, Rokesmith, but I'm a pretty fair scholar in dust. I can price the Mounds to a fraction, and I know how they can be best disposed of, and likewise that they take no harm by standing where they do. You'll look in to-morrow, will you be so kind?"

"Every day. And the sooner I can get you into your new house, complete, the better you will be pleased, sir?"

"Well, it ain't that I'm in a mortal hurry," said Mr. Boffin, "only when you *do* pay people for looking alive, it's as well to know that they *are* looking alive. Ain't that your opinion?"

"Quite!" replied the Secretary; and so withdrew.

"Now," said Mr. Boffin to himself, subsiding into his regular series of turns in the yard, "if I can make it comfortable with Wegg, my affairs will be going smooth."

The man of low cunning had, of course, acquired a mastery over the man of high simplicity. The mean man had, of course, got the better of the generous man. How long such conquests last, is another matter; that they are achieved, is every day experience, not even to be flourished away by Podsnappery itself. The undesigning Boffin had become so far immeshed by the wily Wegg that his mind misgave him he was a very designing man indeed in purposing to do more for Wegg. It seemed to him (so skilful was Wegg) that he was plotting darkly, when he was contriving to do the very thing that Wegg was plotting to get him to do. And thus, while he was mentally turning the kindest of kind faces on Wegg this morning, he was not absolutely sure but that he might somehow deserve the charge of turning his back on him.

For these reasons Mr. Boffin passed but anxious hours until evening came, and with it Mr. Wegg, stumping leisurely to the Roman Empire. At about this period Mr. Boffin had become profoundly interested in the fortunes of a great military leader known to him as Bully Sawyers, but perhaps better known to fame and easier of identification by the classical student, under the less Britannic name of Belisarius. Even this general's career paled in interest for Mr. Boffin before the clearing of his conscience with Wegg; and hence, when that literary gentleman had according to custom eaten and drunk until he was all a-glow, and when he took up his book with the usual chirping introduction, "And now, Mr. Boffin, sir, we'll decline and we'll fall!" Mr. Boffin stopped him.

"You remember, Wegg, when I first told you that I wanted to make a sort of offer to you?"

"Let me get on my considering cap, sir," replied that gentleman, turning the open book face downward. "When you first told me that you wanted to make a sort of offer to me? Now let me think" (as if there were the least necessity).

"Yes, to be sure I do, Mr. Boffin. It was at my corner. To be sure it was! You had first asked me whether I liked your name, and Candour had compelled a reply in the negative case. I little thought then, sir, how familiar that name would come to be!"

"I hope it will be more familiar still, Wegg."

"Do you, Mr. Boffin? Much obliged to you, I'm sure. Is it your pleasure, sir, that we decline and we fall?" with a feint of taking up the book.

"Not just yet awhile, Wegg. In fact, I have got another offer to make you."

Mr. Wegg (who had had nothing else in his mind for several nights) took off his spectacles with an air of bland surprise.

"And I hope you'll like it, Wegg."

"Thank you, sir," returned that reticent individual. "I hope it may prove so. On all accounts, I am sure." (This, as a philanthropic aspiration.)

"What do you think," said Mr. Boffin, "of not keeping a stall, Wegg?"

"I think, sir," replied Wegg, "that I should like to be shown the gentleman prepared to make it worth my while!"

"Here he is," said Mr. Boffin.

Mr. Wegg was going to say, My Benefactor, and had said My Bene, when a grandiloquent change came over him.

"No, Mr. Boffin, not you, sir. Anybody but you. Do not fear, Mr. Boffin, that I shall contaminate the premises which your gold has bought, with *my* lowly pursuits. I am aware, sir, that it would not become me to carry on my little traffic under the windows of your mansion. I have already thought of that, and taken my measures. No need to be bought out, sir. Would Stepney Fields be considered intrusive? If not remote enough, I can go remoter. In the words of the poet's song, which I do not quite remember:

Thrown on the wide world, doom'd to wander and roam,
Bereft of my parents, bereft of a home,
A stranger to something and what's his name joy,
Behold little Edmund the poor Peasant boy.

—And equally," said Mr. Wegg, repairing the want of direct application in the last line, "behold myself on a similar footing!"

"Now, Wegg, Wegg, Wegg," remonstrated the excellent Boffin. "You are too sensitive."

"I know I am, sir," returned Wegg, with obstinate magnanimity. "I am acquainted with my faults. I always was, from a child, too sensitive."

"But listen," pursued the Golden Dustman; "hear me out, Wegg. You have taken it into your head that I mean to pension you off."

"True, sir," returned Wegg, still with an obstinate magnanimity. "I am acquainted with my faults. Far be it from me to deny them. I *have* taken it into my head."

"But I *don't* mean it."

The assurance seemed hardly as comforting to Mr. Wegg, as Mr. Boffin intended it to be. Indeed, an appreciable elongation of his visage might have been observed as he replied:

"Don't you, indeed, sir?"

"No," pursued Mr. Boffin; "because that would express, as I understand it, that you were not going to do anything to deserve your money. But you are; you are."

"That, sir," replied Mr. Wegg, cheering up bravely, "is quite another pair of shoes. Now, my independence as a man is again elevated. Now, I no longer

> Weep for the hour,
> When to Boffins's Bower,
> The Lord of the valley with offers came;
> Nei her does the moon hide her light
> From the heavens to-night,
> And weep behind her clouds o'er any individual in the present
> Company's shame.

—Please to proceed, Mr. Boffin."

"Thank'ee, Wegg, both for your confidence in me and for your frequent dropping into poetry; both of which is friendly. Well, then; my idea is, that you should give up your stall, and that I should put you into the Bower here, to keep it for us. It's a pleasant spot; and a man with coals and candles and a pound a week might be in clover here."

"Hem! Would that man, sir—we will say that man, for the purposes of argueyment;" Mr. Wegg made a smiling demonstration of great perspicuity here; "would that man, sir, be expected to throw any other capacity in, or would any other capacity be considered extra? Now let us (for the purposes of argueyment) suppose that man to be engaged as a reader: say (for the purposes of argueyment) in the evening. Would that man's pay as a reader in the evening, be added to the other amount, which, adopting your language, we will call clover; or would it merge into that amount, or clover?"

"Well," said Mr. Boffin, "I suppose it would be added."

"I suppose it would, sir. You are right, sir. Exactly my own views, Mr. Boffin." Here Wegg rose, and balancing himself on his wooden leg, fluttered over his prey with extended hand. "Mr. Boffin, consider it done. Say no more, sir, not a word more. My stall and I are for ever parted. The collection of ballads will in future be reserved for private study, with the object of making poetry tributary"—Wegg was so proud of having found this word, that he said it again, with a capital letter—"Tributary to friendship. Mr. Boffin, don't allow yourself to be made uncomfortable by the pang it gives me to part from my stock and stall. Similar emotion was undergone by my own father when promoted for his merits from his occupation as a waterman to a situation under Government. His Christian name was Thomas. His words at the time (I was then an infant, but so deep was their impression on me, that I committed them to memory) were:

> Then farewell, my trim-built wherry,
> Oars and coat and badge farewell!
> Never more at Chelsea Ferry
> Shall your Thomas take a spell!

—My father got over it, Mr. Boffin, and so shall I."

While delivering these valedictory observations, Wegg continually disappointed Mr. Boffin of his hand by flourishing it in the air. He now darted it at his patron, who took it, and felt his mind relieved of a great weight: observing that as they had arranged their joint affairs so satisfactorily, he would now be glad to look into those of Bully Sawyers. Which, indeed, had been left overnight in a very unpromising posture, and for whose impending expedition against the Persians the weather had been by no means favourable all day.

Mr. Wegg resumed his spectacles therefore. But Sawyers was not to be of the party that night; for, before Wegg had found his place, Mrs. Boffin's tread was heard upon the stairs, so unusually heavy and hurried, that Mr. Boffin would have started up at the sound, anticipating some occurrence much out of the common course, even though she had not also called to him in an agitated tone.

Mr. Boffin hurried out, and found her on the dark staircase, panting, with a lighted candle in her hand.

"What's the matter, my dear?"

"I don't know; I don't know; but I wish you'd come up-stairs."

Much surprised, Mr. Boffin went up-stairs and accompanied Mrs. Boffin into their own room: a second large room on the same floor as the room in which the late proprietor had died. Mr. Boffin looked all round him, and saw nothing more unusual than various articles of folded linen on a large chest, which Mrs. Boffin had been sorting.

"What is it, my dear? Why, you're frightened! *You* frightened?"

"I am not one of that sort certainly," said Mrs. Boffin, as she sat down in a chair to recover herself, and took her husband's arm; "but it's very strange!"

"What is, my dear?"

"Noddy, the faces of the old man and the two children are all over the house to-night."

"My dear?" exclaimed Mr. Boffin. But not without a certain uncomfortable sensation gliding down his back.

"I know it must sound foolish, and yet it is so."

"Where did you think you saw them?"

"I don't know that I think I saw them anywhere. I felt them."

"Touched them?"

"No. Felt them in the air. I was sorting those things on the chest, and not thinking of the old man or the children, but singing to myself, when all in a moment I felt there was a face growing out of the dark."

"What face?" asked her husband, looking about him.

"For a moment it was the old man's, and then it got younger. For a moment it was both the children's, and then it got older. For a moment it was a strange face, and then it was all the faces."

"And then it was gone?"

"Yes; and then it was gone."

"Where were you then, old lady?"

"Here, at the chest. Well, I got the better of it, and went on sorting, and went on singing to myself. 'Lor!' I says, 'I'll think of something else—something comfortable—and put it out of my head.' So I thought of the new house and Miss Bella Wilfer, and was thinking at a great rate with that sheet there in my hand, when, all of a sudden, the faces seemed to be hidden in among the folds of it, and I let it drop."

As it still lay on the floor where it had fallen, Mr. Boffin picked it up and laid it on the chest.

"And then you ran down-stairs?"

"No. I thought I'd try another room, and shake it off. I says to myself, 'I'll go and walk slowly up and down the old man's room three times, from end to end, and then I shall have conquered it.' I went in with the candle in my hand, but the moment I came near the bed, the air got thick with them."

"With the faces?"

"Yes, and I even felt they were in the dark behind the side-door, and on the little staircase, floating away into the yard. Then, I called you."

Mr. Boffin, lost in amazement, looked at Mrs. Boffin. Mrs. Boffin, lost in her own fluttered inability to make this out, looked at Mr. Boffin.

"I think, my dear," said the Golden Dustman, "I'll at once get rid of Wegg for the night, because he's coming to inhabit the Bower, and it might be put into his head or somebody else's, if he heard this and it got about, that the house is haunted. Whereas we know better. Don't we?"

"I never had the feeling in the house before," said Mrs. Boffin; "and I have been about it alone at all hours of the night. I have been in the house when

Death was in it, and I have been in the house when Murder was a new part of its adventures, and I never had a fright in it yet."

"And won't again, my dear," said Mr. Boffin. "Depend upon it, it comes of thinking and dwelling on that dark spot."

"Yes; but why didn't it come before?" asked Mrs. Boffin.

This draft on Mr. Boffin's philosophy could only be met by that gentleman with the remark that everything that is at all, must begin at some time. Then, tucking his wife's arm under his own, that she might not be left by herself to be troubled again, he descended to release Wegg. Who, being something drowsy after his plentiful repast, and constitutionally of a shirking temperament, was well enough pleased to stump away, without doing what he had come to do, and was paid for doing.

Mr. Boffin then put on his hat, and Mrs. Boffin her shawl; and the pair, further provided with a bunch of keys and a lighted lantern, went all over the dismal house—dismal everywhere, but in their own two rooms—from cellar to cock-loft. Not resting satisfied with giving that much chase to Mrs. Boffin's fancies, they pursued them into the yard and outbuildings, and under the Mounds. And setting the lantern, when all was done, at the foot of one of the Mounds, they comfortably trotted to and fro for an evening walk, to the end that the murky cobwebs in Mrs. Boffin's brain might be blown away.

"There, my dear!" said Mr. Boffin when they came in to supper. "That was the treatment, you see. Completely worked round, haven't you?"

"Yes, deary," said Mrs. Boffin, laying aside her shawl. "I'm not nervous any more. I'm not a bit troubled now. I'd go anywhere about the house the same as ever. But——"

"Eh!" said Mr. Boffin.

"But I've only to shut my eyes."

"And what then?"

"Why then," said Mrs. Boffin, speaking with her eyes closed, and her left hand thoughtfully touching her brow, "then, there they are! The old man's face, and it gets younger. The two children's faces, and they get older. A face that I don't know. And then all the faces!"

Opening her eyes again, and seeing her husband's face across the table, she leaned forward to give it a pat on the cheek, and sat down to supper, declaring it to be the best face in the world.

CHAPTER XVI.

MINDERS AND REMINDERS.

THE Secretary lost no time in getting to work, and his vigilance and method soon set their mark on the Golden Dustman's affairs. His earnestness in determining to understand the length and breadth and depth of every piece of work submitted to him by his employer, was as special as his despatch in transacting it. He accepted no information or explanation at second hand, but made himself the master of everything confided to him.

One part of the Secretary's conduct, underlying all the rest, might have been mistrusted by a man with a better knowledge of men than the Golden Dustman had. The Secretary was as far from being inquisitive or intrusive as Secretary could be, but nothing less than a complete understanding of the whole of the affairs would content him. It soon became apparent (from the knowledge with which he set out) that he must have been to the office where the Harmon will was registered, and must have read the will. He anticipated Mr. Boffin's consideration whether he should be advised with on this or that topic, by showing that he already knew of it and understood it. He did this with no attempt at concealment, seeming to be satisfied that it was part of his duty to have prepared himself at all attainable points for its utmost discharge.

This might—let it be repeated—have awakened some little vague mistrust in a man more worldly-wise than the Golden Dustman. On the other hand, the Secretary was discerning, discreet, and silent, though as zealous as if the affairs had been his own. He showed no love of patronage or the command of money, but distinctly preferred resigning both to Mr. Boffin. If, in his limited sphere, he sought power, it was the power of knowledge; the power derivable from a perfect comprehension of his business.

As on the Secretary's face there was a nameless cloud, so on his manner there was a shadow equally indefinable. It was not that he was embarrassed, as on that first night with the Wilfer family; he was habitually unembarrassed now, and yet the something remained. It was not that his manner was bad, as on that occasion; it was now very good, as being modest, gracious, and ready. Yet the something never left it. It has been written of men who have undergone a cruel captivity, or who have passed through a terrible strait, or who in self-preservation have killed a defenceless fellow-creature, that the record thereof has never faded from their countenances until they died. Was there any such record here?

He established a temporary office for himself in the new house, and all went well under his hand, with one singular exception. He manifestly objected to communicate with Mr. Boffin's solicitor. Two or three times, when there was some slight occasion for his doing so, he transferred the task to Mr. Boffin; and his evasion of it soon became so curiously apparent, that Mr. Boffin spoke to him on the subject of his reluctance.

"It is so," the Secretary admitted. "I would rather not."

Had he any personal objection to Mr. Lightwood?

"I don't know him."

Had he suffered from law-suits?

"Not more than other men," was his short answer.

Was he prejudiced against the race of lawyers?

"No. But while I am in your employment, sir, I would rather be excused from going between the lawyer and the client. Of course if you press it, Mr. Boffin, I am ready to comply. But I should take it as a great favour if you would not press it without urgent occasion."

Now, it could not be said that there *was* urgent occasion, for Lightwood retained no other affairs in his hands than such as still lingered and languished about the undiscovered criminal, and such as arose out of the purchase of the house. Many other matters that might have travelled to him, now stopped short at the Secretary, under whose administration they were far more expeditiously and satisfactorily disposed of than they would have been if they had got into Young Blight's domain. This the Golden Dustman quite understood. Even the matter immediately in hand was of very little moment as requiring personal appearance on the Secretary's part, for it amounted to no more than this:—The death of Hexam rendering the sweat of the honest man's brow unprofitable, the honest man had shufflingly declined to moisten his brow for nothing, with that severe exertion which is known in legal circles as swearing your way through a stone wall. Consequently, that new light had gone sputtering out. But, the airing of the old facts had led some one concerned to suggest that it would be well before they were reconsigned to their gloomy shelf—now probably for ever—to induce or compel that Mr. Julius Handford to reappear and be questioned. And all traces of Mr. Julius Handford being lost, Lightwood now referred to his client for authority to seek him through public advertisement.

"Does your objection go to writing to Lightwood, Rokesmith?"

"Not in the least, sir."

"Then perhaps you'll write him a line, and say he is free to do what he likes. I don't think it promises."

"*I* don't think it promises," said the Secretary.

"Still, he may do what he likes."

"I will write immediately. Let me thank you for so considerately yielding to my disinclination. It may seem less unreasonable, if I avow to you that although I don't know Mr. Lightwood, I have a disagreeable association connected with him. It is not his fault; he is not at all to blame for it, and does not even know my name."

Mr. Boffin dismissed the matter with a nod or two. The letter was written, and next day Mr. Julius Handford was advertised for. He was requested to place himself in communication with Mr. Mortimer Lightwood, as a possible means of furthering the ends of justice, and a reward was offered to any one acquainted with his whereabout who would communicate the same to the said Mr. Mortimer Lightwood at his office in the Temple. Every day for six weeks this advertisement appeared at the head of all the newspapers, and every day for six weeks the Secretary, when he saw it, said to himself, in the tone in which he had said to his employer,—"*I* don't think it promises!"

Among his first occupations the pursuit of that orphan wanted by Mrs. Boffin held a conspicuous place. From the earliest moment of his engagement he showed a particular desire to please her, and knowing her to have this object at heart, he followed it up with unwearying alacrity and interest.

Mr. and Mrs. Milvey had found their search a difficult one. Either an eligible orphan was of the wrong sex (which almost always happened) or was too old, or too young, or too sickly, or too dirty, or too much accustomed to the streets, or too likely to run away; or, it was found impossible to complete the philanthropic transaction without buying the orphan. For, the instant it became known that anybody wanted the orphan, up started some affectionate relative of the orphan who put a price upon the orphan's head. The suddenness of an orphan's rise in the market was not to be paralleled by the maddest records of the Stock Exchange. He would be at five thousand per cent. discount out at nurse making a mud pie at nine in the morning, and (being inquired for) would go up to five thousand per cent. premium before noon. The market was "rigged," in various artful ways. Counterfeit stock got into circulation. Parents boldly represented themselves as dead, and brought their orphans with them. Genuine orphan-stock was surreptitiously withdrawn from the market. It being announced, by emissaries posted for the purpose, that Mr. and Mrs. Milvey were coming down the court, orphan scrip would be instantly concealed, and production refused, save on a condition usually stated by the brokers as a "gallon of beer." Likewise, fluctuations of a wild and South-Sea nature were occasioned by orphan-holders keeping back, and then rushing into the market a dozen together. But, the uniform principle at the root of all these various operations was bargain and sale; and that principle could not be recognised by Mr. and Mrs. Milvey.

At length tidings were received by the Reverend Frank of a charming orphan to be found at Brentford. One of the deceased parents (late his parishioners) had a poor widowed grandmother in that agreeable town, and she, Mrs. Betty Higden, had carried off the orphan with maternal care, but could not afford to keep him.

The Secretary proposed to Mrs. Boffin, either to go down himself and take a preliminary survey of this orphan, or to drive her down, that she might at once form her own opinion. Mrs. Boffin preferring the latter course, they set off one morning in a hired phaeton, conveying the hammer-headed young man behind them.

The abode of Mrs. Betty Higden was not easy to find, lying in such complicated back settlements of muddy Brentford that they left their equipage at the sign of the Three Magpies, and went in search of it on foot. After many inquiries and defeats, there was pointed out to them in a lane, a very small cottage residence, with a board across the open doorway, hooked on to which board by the armpits was a young gentleman of tender years, angling for mud with a headless wooden horse and line. In this young sportsman, distinguished by a crisply curling auburn head and a bluff countenance, the Secretary descried the orphan.

It unfortunately happened as they quickened their pace, that the orphan, lost to considerations of personal safety in the ardour of the moment, overbalanced himself and toppled into the street. Being an orphan of a chubby conformation, he then took to rolling, and had rolled into the gutter before they could come up. From the gutter he was rescued by John Rokesmith, and thus the first meeting with Mrs. Higden was inaugurated by the awkward circumstance of their being in possession—one would say at first sight unlawful possession—of the orphan upside down and purple in the countenance. The board across the doorway too, acting as a trap equally for the feet of Mrs. Higden coming out, and the feet of Mrs. Boffin and John Rokesmith going in, greatly increased the difficulty of the situation: to which the cries of the orphan imparted a lugubrious and inhuman character.

At first, it was impossible to explain, on account of the orphan's "holding his breath:" a most terrific proceeding, superinducing, in the orphan, lead-colour rigidity and a deadly silence, compared with which his cries were music yielding the height of enjoyment. But as he gradually recovered, Mrs. Boffin gradually introduced herself, and smiling peace was gradually wooed back to Mrs. Betty Higden's home.

It was then perceived to be a small home with a large mangle in it, at the handle of which machine stood a very long boy, with a very little head, and an open mouth of disproportionate capacity that seemed to assist his eyes in staring at the visitors. In a corner below the mangle, on a couple of stools, sat two very little children: a boy and a girl; and when the very long boy, in an interval of staring, took a turn at the mangle, it was alarming to see how it lunged itself at these two innocents, like a catapult designed for their destruction, harmlessly retiring when within an inch of their heads. The room was clean and neat. It had a brick floor, and a window of diamond panes, and a flounce hanging below the chimney-piece, and strings nailed from bottom to top outside the window on which scarlet-beans were to grow in the coming season if the Fates were propitious. However propitious they might have been in the seasons that were gone, to Betty Higden in the matter of beans, they had not been very favourable in the matter of coins; for it was easy to see that she was poor.

She was one of those old women, was Mrs. Betty Higden, who by dint of an indomitable purpose and a strong constitution fight out many years, though each year has come with its new knock-down blows fresh to the fight against her, wearied by it; an active old woman, with a bright dark eye and a resolute face, yet quite a tender creature too; not a logically-reasoning woman, but God is good, and hearts may count in Heaven as high as heads.

"Yes sure!" said she, when the business was opened, "Mrs. Milvey had the kindness to write to me, ma'am, and I got Sloppy to read it. It was a pretty letter. But she's an affable lady."

The visitors glanced at the long boy, who seemed to indicate by a broader stare of his mouth and eyes that in him Sloppy stood confessed.

"For I ain't, you must know," said Betty, "much of a hand at reading writing-hand, though I can read my Bible and most print. And I do love a newspaper. You mightn't think it, but Sloppy is a beautiful reader of a newspaper. He do the Police in different voices."

The visitors again considered it a point of politeness to look at Sloppy, who, looking at them, suddenly threw back his head, extended his mouth to its utmost width, and laughed loud and long. At this the two innocents, with their brains in that apparent danger, laughed, and Mrs. Higden laughed, and the orphan laughed, and then the visitors laughed. Which was more cheerful than intelligible.

Then Sloppy seeming to be seized with an industrious mania or fury, turned to at the mangle, and impelled it at the heads af the innocents with such a creaking and rumbling, that Mrs. Higden stopped him.

"The gentlefolks can't hear themselves speak, Sloppy. Bide a bit, bide a bit!"

"Is that the dear child in your lap?" said Mrs. Boffin.

"Yes, ma'am, this is Johnny."

"Johnny, too!" cried Mrs. Boffin, turning to the Secretary; "already Johnny! Only one of the two names left to give him! He's a pretty boy."

With his chin tucked down in his shy, childish manner, he was looking furtively at Mrs. Boffin out of his blue eyes, and reaching his fat dimpled hand up to the lips of the old woman, who was kissing it by times.

"Yes, ma'am, he's a pretty boy, he's a dear darling boy, he's the child of my own last left daughter's daughter. But she's gone the way of all the rest."

"Those are not his brother and sister?" said Mrs. Boffin.

"Oh, dear no, ma'am. Those are Minders."

"Minders?" the Secretary repeated.

"Left to be Minded, sir. I keep a Minding-School. I can take only three, on account of the mangle. But I love children, and Four-pence a week is Four-pence. Come here, Toddles and Poddles."

Toddles was the pet name of the boy; Poddles of the girl. At their little unsteady pace, they came across the floor, hand-in-hand, as if they were traversing an extremely difficult road intersected by brooks, and, when they had had their heads patted by Mrs. Betty Higden, made lunges at the orphan, dramatically representing an attempt to bear him, crowing, into captivity and slavery. All the three children enjoyed this to a delightful extent, and the sympathetic Sloppy again laughed long and loud. When it was discreet to stop the play, Betty Higden said, "Go to your seats, Toddles and Poddles," and they returned hand-in-hand across country, seeming to find the brooks rather swollen by late rains.

"And Master—or Mister—Sloppy?" said the Secretary, in doubt whether he was man, boy, or what.

"A love-child," returned Betty Higden, dropping her voice; "parents never known; found in the street. He was brought up in the——" with a shiver of repugnance, "——the House."

"The Poor-house?" said the Secretary.

Mrs. Higden set that resolute old face of hers, and darkly nodded yes.

"You dislike the mention of it."

"Dislike the mention of it?" answered the old woman. "Kill me sooner than take me there. Throw this pretty child under cart-horses' feet and a loaded waggon, sooner than take him there. Come to us and find us all a-dying, and set a light to us all where we lie, and let us all blaze away with the house into a heap of cinders, sooner than move a corpse of us there!"

A surprising spirit in this lonely woman after so many years of hard working and hard living, my Lords and Gentlemen and Honourable Boards! What is it that we call it in our grandiose speeches? British independence, rather perverted? Is that, or something like it, the ring of the cant?

"Do I never read in the newspapers," said the dame, fondling the child—"God help me and the like of me!—how the worn-out people that do come down to that, get driven from post to pillar and pillar to post, a-purpose to tire them out! Do I never read how they are put off, put off, put off—how they are grudged, grudged, grudged the shelter, or the doctor, or the drop of physic, or the bit of bread? Do I never read how they grow heartsick of it and give it up, after having let themselves drop so low, and how they after all die out for want of help? Then I say, I hope I can die as well as another, and I'll die without that disgrace."

Absolutely impossible, my Lords and Gentlemen and Honourable Boards, by any stretch of legislative wisdom to set these perverse people right in their logic?

"Johnny, my pretty," continued old Betty, caressing the child, and rather mourning over it than speaking to it, "your old Granny Betty is nigher fourscore year than threescore and ten. She never begged nor had a penny of the Union money in all her life. She paid scot and she paid lot when she had money to pay; she worked when she could, and she starved when she must. You pray that your Granny may have strength enough left her at the last (she's strong for an old one, Johnny), to get up from her bed and run and hide herself, and swown to death in a hole, sooner than fall into the hands of those Cruel Jacks we read of, that dodge and drive, and worry and weary, and scorn and shame, the decent poor."

A brilliant success, my Lords and Gentlemen and Honourable Boards, to have brought it to this in the minds of the best of the poor! Under submission, might it be worth thinking of, at any odd time?

The fright and abhorrence that Mrs. Betty Higden smoothed out of her strong face as she ended this diversion, showed how seriously she had meant it.

"And does he work for you?" asked the Secretary, gently bringing the discourse back to Master or Mister Sloppy.

"Yes," said Betty with a good-humoured smile and nod of the head. "And well too."

"Does he live here?"

"He lives more here than anywhere. He was thought to be no better than a Natural, and first come to me as a Minder. I made interest with Mr. Blogg the Beadle to have him as a Minder, seeing him by chance up at church, and thinking I might do something with him. For he was a weak rickety creetur then."

"Is he called by his right name?"

"Why, you see, speaking quite correctly, he has no right name. I always understood he took his name from being found on a Sloppy night."

"He seems an amiable fellow."

"Bless you, sir, there's not a bit of him," returned Betty, "that's not amiable. So you may judge how amiable he is, by running your eye along his heighth."

Of an ungainly make was Sloppy. Too much of him longwise, too little of him broadwise, and too many sharp angles of him angle-wise. One of those shambling male human creatures born to be indiscreetly candid in the revelation of buttons; every button he had about him glaring at the public to a quite preternatural extent. A considerable capital of knee and elbow and wrist and ankle, had Sloppy, and he didn't know how to dispose of it to the best advantage, but was always investing it in wrong securities, and so getting himself into embarrassed circumstances. Full-Private Number One in the Awkward Squad of the rank and file of life, was Sloppy, and yet had his glimmering notions of standing true to the Colours.

"And now," said Mrs. Boffin, "concerning Johnny."

As Johnny, with his chin tucked in and his lips pouting, reclined in Betty's lap, concentrating his blue eyes on the visitors and shading them from observation with a dimpled arm, old Betty took one of his fresh fat hands in her withered right, and fell to gently beating it on her withered left.

"Yes, ma'am. Concerning Johnny."

"If you trust the dear child to me," said Mrs. Boffin, with a face inviting trust, "he shall have the best of homes, the best of care, the best of education, the best of friends. Please God I will be a true good mother to him!"

"I am thankful to you, ma'am, and the dear child would be thankful if he was old enough to understand." Still lightly beating the little hand upon her own. "I wouldn't stand in the dear child's light, not if I had all my life before me, instead of a very little of it. But I hope you won't take it ill that I cleave to the child closer than words can tell, for he's the last living thing left me."

"Take it ill, my dear soul? Is it likely? And you so tender of him as to bring him home here!"

"I have seen," said Betty, still with that light beat upon her hard rough hand, "so many of them on my lap. And they are all gone but this one! I am ashamed to seem so selfish, but I don't really mean it. It'll be the making of his fortune, and he'll be a gentleman when I am dead. I—I—don't know what comes over me. I—try against it. Don't notice me!" The light beat stopped, the resolute mouth gave way, and the fine strong old face broke up into weakness and tears.

Now, greatly to the relief of the visitors, the emotional Sloppy no sooner beheld his patroness in this condition, than, throwing back his head and throwing open his mouth, he lifted up his voice and bellowed. This alarming note of something wrong instantly terrified Toddles and Poddles, who were no sooner heard to roar surprisingly, than Johnny, curving himself the wrong way and striking out at Mrs. Boffin with a pair of indifferent shoes, became a prey to despair. The absurdity of the situation put its pathos to the rout. Mrs. Betty Higden was herself in a moment, and brought them all to order with that speed, that Sloppy, stopping short in a polysyllabic bellow, transferred his energy to the mangle, and had taken several penitential turns before he could be stopped.

"There, there, there!" said Mrs. Boffin, almost regarding her kind self as the most ruthless of women. "Nothing is going to be done. Nobody need be frightened. We're all comfortable; ain't we, Mrs. Higden?"

"Sure and certain we are," returned Betty.

"And there really is no hurry, you know," said Mrs. Boffin, in a lower voice. "Take time to think of it, my good creature!"

"Don't you fear *me* no more, ma'am," said Betty; "I thought of it for good yesterday. I don't know what come over me just now, but it'll never come again."

"Well, then, Johnny shall have more time to think of it," returned Mrs. Boffin; "the pretty child shall have time to get used to it. And you'll get him more used to it, if you think well of it; won't you?"

Betty undertook that, cheerfully and readily.

"Lor," cried Mrs. Boffin, looking radiantly about her, "we want to make everybody happy, not dismal!—And perhaps you wouldn't mind letting me know how used to it you begin to get, and how it all goes on?"

"I'll send Sloppy," said Mrs. Higden.

"And this gentleman who has come with me will pay him for his trouble," said Mrs. Boffin. "And Mr. Sloppy, whenever you come to my house, be sure you never go away without having had a good dinner of meat, beer, vegetables, and pudding."

This still further brightened the face of affairs; for, the highly sympathetic Sloppy, first broadly staring and grinning, and then roaring with laughter, Toddles and Poddles followed suit, and Johnny trumped the trick. T and P considering these favourable circumstances for the resumption of that dramatic descent upon Johnny, again came across-country hand-in-hand upon a buccaneering expedition; and this having been fought out in the chimney corner behind Mrs. Higden's chair, with great valour on both sides, those desperate pirates returned hand-in-hand to their stools, across the dry bed of a mountain torrent.

"You must tell me what I can do for you, Betty my friend," said Mrs. Boffin confidentially, "if not to-day, next time."

"Thank you all the same, ma'am, but I want nothing for myself. I can work. I'm strong. I can walk twenty mile if I'm put to it." Old Betty was proud, and said it with a sparkle in her bright eyes.

"Yes, but there are some little comforts that you wouldn't be the worse for," returned Mrs. Boffin. "Bless ye, I wasn't born a lady any more than you."

"It seems to me," said Betty, smiling, "that you were born a lady, and a true one, or there never was a lady born. But I couldn't take anything from you, my dear. I never did take anything from any one. It ain't that I'm not grateful, but I love to earn it better."

"Well, well!" returned Mrs. Boffin. "I only spoke of little things, or I wouldn't have taken the liberty."

Betty put her visitor's hand to her lips, in acknowledgment of the delicate answer. Wonderfully upright her figure was, and wonderfully self-reliant her look, as, standing facing her visitor, she explained herself further.

"If I could have kept the dear child, without the dread that's always upon me of his coming to that fate I have spoken of, I could never have parted with him, even to you. For I love him, I love him, I love him! I love my husband long dead and gone, in him; I love my children dead and gone, in him; I love my young and hopeful days dead and gone, in him. I couldn't sell that love, and look you in your bright kind face. It's a free gift. I am in want of nothing. When my strength fails me, if I can but die out quick and quiet, I shall be quite content. I have stood between my dead and that shame I have spoken of, and it has been kept off from every one of them. Sewed into my gown," with her hand upon her breast, "is just enough to lay me in the grave. Only see that it's rightly spent, so as I may rest free to the last from that cruelty and disgrace, and you'll have done much more than a little thing for me, and all that in this present world my heart is set upon."

Mrs. Betty Higden's visitor pressed her hand. There was no more breaking up of the strong old face into weakness. My Lords and Gentlemen and Honourable Boards, it really was as composed as our own faces, and almost as dignified.

And now, Johnny was to be inveigled into occupying a temporary position on Mrs. Boffin's lap. It was not until he had been piqued into competition with the two diminutive Minders, by seeing them successively raised to that post and retire from it without injury, that he could be by any means induced to leave Mrs. Betty Higden's skirts; towards which he exhibited, even when in Mrs. Boffin's embrace, strong yearnings, spiritual and bodily; the former expressed in a very gloomy visage, the latter in extended arms. However, a general description of the toy-wonders lurking in Mrs. Boffin's house, so far conciliated this worldly-minded orphan as to induce him to stare at her frowningly, with a fist in his mouth, and even at length to chuckle when a richly-caparisoned horse on wheels, with a miraculous gift of cantering to cake-shops, was mentioned. This sound being taken up by the Minders, swelled into a rapturous trio which gave general satisfaction.

So, the interview was considered very successful, and Mrs. Boffin was pleased, and all were satisfied. Not least of all, Sloppy, who undertook to conduct the visitors back by the best way to the Three Magpies, and whom the hammer-headed young man much despised.

This piece of business thus put in train, the Secretary drove Mrs. Boffin back to the Bower, and found employment for himself at the new house until evening. Whether, when evening came, he took a way to his lodgings that led through fields, with any design of finding Miss Bella Wilfer in those fields, is not so certain as that she regularly walked there at that hour.

And, moreover, it is certain that there she was.

No longer in mourning, Miss Bella was dressed in as pretty colours as she could muster. There is no denying that she was as pretty as they, and that she and the colours went very prettily together. She was reading as she walked, and of course it is to be inferred, from her showing no knowledge of Mr. Rokesmith's approach, that she did not know he was approaching.

"Eh?" said Miss Bella, raising her eyes from her book, when he stopped before her. "Oh! it's you."

"Only I. A fine evening!"

"Is it?" said Bella, looking coldly round. "I suppose it is, now you mention it. I have not been thinking of the evening."

"So intent upon your book?"

"Ye-e-es," replied Bella, with a drawl of indifference.

"A love story, Miss Wilfer?"

"Oh dear no, or I shouldn't be reading it. It's more about money than anything else."

"And does it say that money is better than anything?"

"Upon my word," returned Bella, "I forget what it says, but you can find out for yourself, if you like, Mr. Rokesmith. I don't want it any more."

The Secretary took the book—she had fluttered the leaves as if it were a fan—and walked beside her.

"I am charged with a message for you, Miss Wilfer."

"Impossible, I think!" said Bella, with another drawl.

"From Mrs. Boffin. She desired me to assure you of the pleasure she has in finding that she will be ready to receive you in another week or two at furthest."

Bella turned her head towards him, with her prettily-insolent eyebrows raised, and her eyelids drooping. As much as to say, "How did *you* come by the message, pray?"

"I have been waiting for an opportunity of telling you that I am Mr. Boffin's Secretary."

"I am as wise as ever," said Miss Bella, loftily, "for I don't know what a Secretary is. Not that it signifies."

"Not at all."

A covert glance at her face, as he walked beside her, showed him that she had not expected his ready assent to that proposition.

"Then are you going to be always there, Mr. Rokesmith?" she inquired, as if that would be a drawback.

"Always? No. Very much there? Yes."

"Dear me!" drawled Bella in a tone of mortification.

"But my position there as Secretary, will be very different from yours as guest. You will know little or nothing about me. I shall transact the business; you will transact the pleasure. I shall have my salary to earn; you will have nothing to do but to enjoy and attract."

"Attract, sir?" said Bella, again with her eyebrows raised, and her eyelids drooping. "I don't understand you."

Without replying on this point, Mr. Rokesmith went on.

"Excuse me; when I first saw you in your black dress——"

("There!" was Miss Bella's mental exclamation. "What did I say to them at home? Everybody noticed that ridiculous mourning!")

"When I first saw you in your black dress, I was at a loss to account for that distinction between yourself and your family. I hope it was not impertinent to speculate upon it?"

"I hope not, I am sure," said Miss Bella, haughtily. "But you ought to know best how you speculated upon it."

Mr. Rokesmith inclined his head in a deprecatory manner, and went on.

"Since I have been entrusted with Mr. Boffin's affairs, I have necessarily come to understand the little mystery. I venture to remark that I feel persuaded that much of your loss may be repaired. I speak, of course, merely of wealth, Miss Wilfer. The loss of a perfect stranger, whose worth, or worthlessness, I cannot estimate—nor you either—is beside the question. But this excellent gentleman and lady are so full of simplicity, so full of generosity, so inclined towards you, and so desirous to—how shall I express it?—to make amends for their good fortune, that you have only to respond."

As he watched her with another covert look, he saw a certain ambitious triumph in her face which no assumed coldness could conceal.

"As we have been brought under one roof by an accidental combination of circumstances, which oddly extends itself to the new relations before us, I have taken the liberty of saying these few words. You don't consider them intrusive, I hope?" said the Secretary with deference.

"Really, Mr. Rokesmith, I can't say what I consider them," returned the young lady. "They are perfectly new to me, and may be founded altogether on your own imagination."

"You will see."

These same fields were opposite the Wilfer premises. The discreet Mrs. Wilfer now looking out of window and beholding her daughter in conference with her lodger, instantly tied up her head and came out for a casual walk.

"I have been telling Miss Wilfer," said John Rokesmith, as the majestic lady came stalking up, "that I have become, by a curious chance, Mr. Boffin's Secretary or man of business."

"I have not," returned Mrs. Wilfer, waving her gloves in her chronic state of dignity, and vague ill-usage, "the honour of any intimate acquaintance with Mr. Boffin, and it is not for me to congratulate that gentleman on the acquisition he has made."

"A poor one enough," said Rokesmith.

"Pardon me," returned Mrs. Wilfer, "the merits of Mr. Boffin may be highly distinguished—may be more distinguished than the countenance of Mrs. Boffin would imply—but it were the insanity of humility to deem him worthy of a better assistant."

"You are very good. I have also been telling Miss Wilfer that she is expected very shortly at the new residence in town."

"Having tacitly consented," said Mrs. Wilfer, with a grand shrug of her shoulders, and another wave of her gloves, "to my child's acceptance of the proffered attentions of Mrs. Boffin, I interpose no objection."

Here Miss Bella offered the remonstrance: "Don't talk nonsense, ma, please."

"Peace!" said Mrs. Wilfer.

"No, ma, I am not going to be made so absurd. Interposing objections!"

"I say," repeated Mrs. Wilfer, with a vast access of grandeur, "that I am *not* going to interpose objections. If Mrs. Boffin (to whose countenance no disciple of Lavater could possibly for a single moment subscribe)," with a shiver, "seeks to illuminate her new residence in town with the attractions of a child of mine, I am content that she should be favoured by the company of a child of mine."

"You use the word, ma'am, I have myself used," said Rokesmith, with a glance at Bella, "when you speak of Miss Wilfer's attractions there."

"Pardon me," returned Mrs. Wilfer, with dreadful solemnity, "but I had not finished."

"Pray excuse me."

"I was about to say," pursued Mrs. Wilfer, who clearly had not had the faintest idea of saying anything more: "that when I use the term attractions, I do so with the qualification that I do not mean it in any way whatever."

The excellent lady delivered this luminous elucidation of her views with an air of greatly obliging her hearers, and greatly distinguishing herself. Whereat Miss Bella laughed a scornful little laugh and said:

"Quite enough about this, I am sure, on all sides. Have the goodness, Mr. Rokesmith, to give my love to Mrs. Boffin——"

"Pardon me!" cried Mrs. Wilfer. "Compliments."

"Love!" repeated Bella, with a little stamp of her foot.

"No!" said Mrs. Wilfer, monotonously. "Compliments."

("Say Miss Wilfer's love, and Mrs. Wilfer's compliments," the Secretary proposed, as a compromise.)

"And I shall be very glad to come when she is ready for me. The sooner, the better."

"One last word, Bella," said Mrs. Wilfer, "before descending to the family apartment. I trust that as a child of mine you will ever be sensible that it will be graceful in you, when associating with Mr. and Mrs. Boffin upon equal terms, to remember that the Secretary, Mr. Rokesmith, as your father's lodger, has a claim on your good word."

The condescension with which Mrs. Wilfer delivered this proclamation of patronage, was as wonderful as the swiftness with which the lodger had lost caste in the Secretary. He smiled as the mother retired down-stairs; but his face fell, as the daughter followed.

"So insolent, so trivial, so capricious, so mercenary, so careless, so hard to touch, so hard to turn!" he said, bitterly.

And added as he went up-stairs. "And yet so pretty, so pretty!"

And added presently, as he walked to and fro in his room. "And if she knew!"

She knew that he was shaking the house by his walking to and fro; and she declared it another of the miseries of being poor, that you couldn't get rid of a haunting Secretary, stump—stump—stumping overhead in the dark, like a Ghost.

CHAPTER XVII.

A DISMAL SWAMP.

AND now, in the blooming summer days, behold Mr. and Mrs. Boffin established in the eminently aristocratic family mansion, and behold all manner of crawling, creeping, fluttering, and buzzing creatures, attracted by the gold dust of the Golden Dustman!

Foremost among those leaving cards at the eminently aristocratic door before it is quite painted, are the Veneerings: out of breath, one might imagine, from the impetuosity of their rush to the eminently aristocratic steps. One copper-plate Mrs. Veneering, two copper-plate Mr. Veneerings, and a connubial copper-plate Mr. and Mrs. Veneering, requesting the honour of Mr. and Mrs. Boffin's company at dinner with the utmost Analytical solemnities. The enchanting Lady Tippins leaves a card. Twemlow leaves cards. A tall custard-coloured phaeton tooling up in a solemn manner leaves four cards, to wit, a couple of Mr. Podsnaps, a Mrs. Podsnap, and a Miss Podsnap. All the world and his wife and daughter leave cards. Sometimes the world's wife has so many daughters, that her card reads rather like a Miscellaneous Lot at an Auction; comprising Mrs. Tapkins, Miss Tapkins, Miss Frederica Tapkins, Miss Antonina Tapkins, Miss Malvina Tapkins, and Miss Euphemia Tapkins; at the same time, the same lady leaves the card of Mrs. Henry George Alfred Swoshle, *née* Tapkins; also, a card, Mrs. Tapkins at Home, Wednesdays, Music, Portland Place.

Miss Bella Wilfer becomes an inmate, for an indefinite period, of the eminently aristocratic dwelling. Mrs. Boffin bears Miss Bella away to her Milliner's and Dressmaker's, and she gets beautifully dressed. The Veneerings find with swift remorse that they have omitted to invite Miss Bella Wilfer. One Mrs. Veneering and one Mr. and Mrs. Veneering requesting that additional honour, instantly do penance in white cardboard on the hall table. Mrs. Tapkins likewise discovers her omission, and with promptitude repairs it; for herself, for Miss Tapkins, for Miss Frederica Tapkins, for Miss Antonina Tapkins, for Miss Malvina Tapkins, and for Miss Euphemia Tapkins. Likewise, for Mrs. Henry George Alfred Swoshle, *née* Tapkins. Likewise, for Mrs. Tapkins at Home, Wednesdays, Music, Portland Place.

Tradesmen's books hunger, and tradesmen's mouths water, for the gold dust of the Golden Dustman. As Mrs. Boffin and Miss Wilfer drive out, or as Mr. Boffin walks out at his jog-trot pace, the fishmonger pulls off his hat with an air of reverence founded on conviction. His men cleanse their fingers on their woollen aprons before presuming to touch their foreheads to Mr. Boffin or Lady. The gaping salmon and the golden mullet lying on the slab seem to turn up their eyes sideways, as they would turn up their hands if they had any, in worshipping admiration. The butcher, though a portly and a prosperous man, doesn't know what to do with himself, so anxious is he to express humility when discovered by the passing Boffins taking the air in a mutton grove. Presents are made to the Boffin servants, and bland strangers with business-cards meeting said servants in the street, offer hypothetical corruption. As, "Supposing I was to be favoured with an order from Mr. Boffin, my dear friend, it would be worth my while"—to do a certain thing that I hope might not prove wholly disagreeable to your feelings.

But no one knows so well as the Secretary, who opens and reads the letters, what a set is made at the man marked by a stroke of notoriety. Oh the varieties of dust for ocular use, offered in exchange for the gold dust of the Golden Dustman! Fifty-seven churches to be erected with half-crowns, forty-two parsonage houses to be repaired with shillings, seven-and-twenty organs to be built with halfpence, twelve hundred children to be brought up on postage stamps. Not that a half-crown, shilling, halfpenny, or postage stamp, would be particularly acceptable from Mr. Boffin, but that it is so obvious he is the man to make up the deficiency. And then the charities, my Christian brother! And mostly in difficulties, yet mostly lavish, too, in the expensive articles of print and paper. Large fat private double letter, sealed with ducal coronet. "Nicodemus Boffin, Esquire. My Dear Sir,—Having consented to preside at the forthcoming Annual Dinner of the Family Party Fund, and feeling deeply impressed with the immense usefulness of that noble Institution and the great importance of its being supported by a List of Stewards that shall prove to the public the interest taken in it by popular and distinguished men, I have undertaken to ask you to become a Steward on that occasion. Soliciting your favourable reply before the 14th instant, I am, My Dear Sir, Your faithful servant, LINSEED. P.S. The Steward's fee is limited to three Guineas." Friendly this, on the part of the Duke of Linseed (and thoughtful in the postscript), only lithographed by the hundred and presenting but a pale individuality of address to Nicodemus Boffin, Esquire, in quite another hand. It takes two noble Earls and a Viscount, combined, to inform Nicodemus Boffin, Esquire, in an equally flattering manner, that an estimable lady in the West of England has offered to present a purse containing twenty pounds, to the Society for Granting Annuities to Unassuming Members of the Middle Classes, if twenty individuals will previously present purses of one hundred pounds each. And those benevolent noblemen very kindly point out that if Nicodemus Boffin, Esquire, should wish to present two or more purses, it will not be inconsistent with the design of the estimable lady in the West of England, provided each purse be coupled with the name of some member of his honoured and respected family.

These are the corporate beggars. But there are, besides, the individual beggars; and how does the heart of the Secretary fail him when he has to cope with *them!* And they must be coped with to some extent, because they all enclose documents (they call their scraps documents; but they are, as to papers deserving the name, what minced veal is to a calf), the non-return of which would be their ruin. That is to say, they are utterly ruined now, but they would be more utterly ruined then. Among these correspondents are several daughters of general officers, long accustomed to every luxury of life (except spelling), who little thought, when their gallant fathers waged war in the Peninsula, that they would ever have to appeal to those whom Providence, in its inscrutable wisdom, has blessed with untold gold, and from among whom they select the name of Nicodemus Boffin, Esquire, for a maiden effort in this wise, understanding that he has such a heart as never was. The Secretary learns, too, that confidence between man and wife would seem to obtain but rarely when virtue is in distress, so numerous are the wives who take up their pens to ask Mr. Boffin for money without the knowledge of their devoted husbands, who would never permit it; while, on the other hand, so numerous are the husbands who take up their pens to ask Mr. Boffin for money without the knowledge of their devoted wives, who would instantly go out of their senses if they had the least suspicion of the circumstance. There are the inspired beggars, too. These were sitting, only yesterday evening, musing over a fragment of candle which must soon go out and leave them in the dark for the rest of their nights, when surely some angel whispered the name of Nicodemus Boffin, Esquire, to their souls, imparting rays of hope, nay confidence, to which they had long been strangers! Akin to these are the suggestively-befriended beggars. They were partaking of a cold potato and water by the flickering and gloomy light of a lucifer match, in their lodgings (rent considerably in arrear, and heartless landlady threatening expulsion "like a dog" into the streets), when a gifted friend happening to look in, said, "Write immediately to Nicodemus Boffin, Esquire," and would take no denial. There are the nobly independent beggars, too. These, in the days of their abundance, ever regarded gold as dross, and have not yet got over that only impediment in the way of their amassing wealth, but they want no dross from Nicodemus Boffin, Esquire: No, Mr. Boffin; the world may term it pride, paltry pride if you will, but they wouldn't take it if you offered it; a loan, sir—for fourteen weeks to the day, interest calculated at the rate of five per cent. per annum, to be bestowed upon any charitable institution you may name—is all they want of you, and if you have the meanness to refuse it, count on being despised by these great spirits. There are the beggars of punctual business-habits too. These will make an end of themselves at a quarter to one P.M. on Tuesday, if no Post-office order is in the interim received from Nicodemus Boffin, Esquire; arriving after a quarter to one P.M. on Tuesday, it need not be sent, as they will then (having made an exact memorandum of the heartless circumstances) be "cold in death." There are the beggars on horse-back too, in another sense from the sense of the proverb. These are mounted and ready to start on the highway to affluence. The goal is before them, the road is in the best condition, their spurs are on, the steed is willing, but, at the last moment, for want of some special thing—a clock, a violin, an astronomical tele-scope, an electrifying machine—they must dismount for ever, unless they receive its equivalent in money from Nicodemus Boffin, Esquire. Less given to detail are the beggars who make sporting ventures. These, usually to be addressed in reply under initials at a country post-office, inquire in feminine hands, Dare one who cannot disclose herself to Nicodemus Boffin, Esquire, but whose name might startle him were it revealed, solicit the immediate advance of two hundred pounds from unexpected riches exercising their noblest privilege in the trust of a common humanity?

In such a Dismal Swamp does the new house stand, and through it does the Secretary daily struggle breast-high. Not to mention all the people alive who have made inventions that won't act, and all the jobbers who job in all the job-beries jobbed; though these may be regarded as the Alligators of the Dismal Swamp, and are always lying by to drag the Golden Dustman under.

But the old house. There are no designs against the Golden Dustman there? There are no fish of the shark tribe in the Bower waters? Perhaps not. Still, Wegg is established there, and would seem, judged by his secret proceedings, to cherish a notion of making a discovery. For, when a man with a wooden leg lies prone on his stomach to peep under bedsteads; and hops up ladders, like some extinct bird, to survey the tops of presses and cupboards; and provides himself an iron rod which he is always poking and prodding into dust-mounds; the probability is that he expects to find something.

BOOK THE SECOND.

BIRDS OF A FEATHER.

CHAPTER I

OF AN EDUCATIONAL CHARACTER.

THE school at which young Charley Hexam had first learned from a book—the streets being, for pupils of his degree, the great Preparatory Establishment in which very much that is never unlearned is learned without and before book—was a miserable loft in an unsavoury yard. Its atmosphere was oppressive and disagreeable; it was crowded, noisy, and confusing; half the pupils dropped asleep, or fell into a state of waking stupefaction; the other half kept them in either condition by maintaining a monotonous droning noise, as if they were performing, out of time and tune, on a ruder sort of bagpipe. The teachers, animated solely by good intentions, had no idea of execution, and a lamentable jumble was the upshot of their kind endeavours.

It was a school for all ages, and for both sexes. The latter were kept apart, and the former were partitioned off into square assortments. But, all the place was pervaded by a grimly ludicrous pretence that every pupil was childish and innocent. This pretence, much favoured by the lady-visitors, led to the ghastliest absurdities. Young women old in the vices of the commonest and worst life, were expected to profess themselves enthralled by the good child's book, the Adventures of Little Margery, who resided in the village cottage by the mill; severely reproved and morally squashed the miller, when she was five and he was fifty; divided her porridge with singing birds; denied herself a new nankeen bonnet, on the ground that the turnips did not wear nankeen bonnets, neither did the sheep who ate them; who plaited straw and delivered the dreariest orations to all comers, at all sorts of unseasonable times. So, unwieldy young dredgers and hulking mudlarks were referred to the experiences of Thomas Twopence, who, having resolved not to rob (under circumstances of uncommon atrocity) his particular friend and benefactor, of eighteenpence, presently came into supernatural possession of three and sixpence, and lived a shining light ever afterwards. (Note, that the benefactor came to no good.) Several swaggering sinners had written their own biographies in the same strain; it always appearing from the lessons of those very boastful persons, that you were to do good, not because it *was* good, but because you were to make a good thing of it. Contrariwise, the adult pupils were taught to read (if they could learn) out of the New Testament; and by dint of stumbling over the syllables and keeping their bewildered eyes on the particular syllables coming round to their turn, were as absolutely ignorant of the sublime history, as if they had never seen or heard of it. An exceedingly and

www.ingramcontent.com/pod-product-compliance
Lightning Source LLC
LaVergne TN
LVHW021411110826
845150LV00007B/1871

* 9 7 8 1 4 2 5 5 1 1 4 0 1 *